Dance Education

Dance Education

A Redefinition

Susan R. Koff

methuen | drama
LONDON • NEW YORK • OXFORD • NEW DELHI • SYDNEY

METHUEN DRAMA
Bloomsbury Publishing Plc
50 Bedford Square, London, WC1B 3DP, UK
1385 Broadway, New York, NY 10018, USA

BLOOMSBURY, METHUEN DRAMA and the Methuen Drama logo are trademarks of
Bloomsbury Publishing Plc

First published in Great Britain 2021

Copyright © Susan R. Koff and contributors, 2021

Susan R. Koff has asserted her right under the Copyright, Designs and Patents Act,
1988, to be identified as author of this work.

For legal purposes the Acknowledgments on p. xi constitute an extension
of this copyright page.

Cover design and illustration by Charlotte Daniels

All rights reserved. No part of this publication may be reproduced or transmitted
in any form or by any means, electronic or mechanical, including photocopying,
recording, or any information storage or retrieval system, without prior
permission in writing from the publishers.

Bloomsbury Publishing Plc does not have any control over, or responsibility for, any third-party websites referred to or in this book. All internet addresses given in this book were correct at the time of going to press. The author and publisher regret any inconvenience caused if addresses have changed or sites have ceased to exist, but can accept no responsibility for any such changes.

A catalogue record for this book is available from the British Library.

A catalog record for this book is available from the Library of Congress.

ISBN: HB: 978-1-3500-8801-6
PB: 978-1-3500-9035-4
ePDF: 978-1-3500-8802-3
eBook: 978-1-3500-8803-0

Typeset by Deanta Global Publishing Services, Chennai, India

To find out more about our authors and books visit www.bloomsbury.com
and sign up for our newsletters.

To my guiding light, Richard A. Magill.

CONTENTS

Preface ix
Acknowledgments xi

Section I Dance Education: A Definition of Our Lives 1

Introduction 2

1 Essential Questions: Viewing Dance, Understanding Dance, and Reflecting upon Dance 3

2 History of Dance Education (Formal Educational Settings) 16

3 Defining Dance Education: Whose Definition? 32

4 Pedagogy and Philosophy of Pedagogy 47

Section II Dance in Educational and Life Settings 61

Introduction 62

5 Global Dance Education: A Research Summary *Ann Kipling Brown* 63

6 Formal Dance Education 77

7 Non-Formal Dance Education: Dance in Studios and Other Settings 89

8 Informal Dance Education 101

9 The Formation of a Dancer *John-Mario Sevilla* 109

Section III Dance in Our Lives 119

Introduction 120

10 Ethnorelativism in Dance Education *Alfdaniels Mabingo and Susan Koff* 121

11 Giving Thanks to the Land: Indigenous Pedagogies within US Dance Education *William S. Huntington* 133

12 Dance as an Aspect of Everyday Living 148

Glossary 157
Notes 159
Bibliography 182
Index 195

PREFACE

I am standing in my university library in the dance book section. It is like a candy store, and it is impossible to find what I am seeking without a call number. Yes, the Library of Congress system dictates the categorization, and it seems to be done by naming. One book is on dance history, and other books about dance history are together, but when I seek the history of a specific sub-set, it is in a completely different location.

Naming is both fascinating and frustrating. As soon as we name something, it has meaning to all who hear that name. Dance education is a concept I have been naming for most of my career, and still no one is sure what it means. I have published, presented, and discussed dance education in multiple contexts, in many different countries. Now I am collecting these ideas in one place, this book. In order to clarify a name, dance education, I have to draw from all those subcategories that I find in the library organization. This sets up a vicious circle as I try to demystify and name by digging into the mysterious names that exist. Sometimes I wonder, is there a way out of this circle? As soon as this is published, will it already be dated and need to be revised? The end of this book is where I make peace with that concept and recognize that there is never a definitive name, as there is never a definitive definition. There is, rather, only a chance to dive in and explore how this confusion arose.

In the process of this investigation there are some overriding concepts that are repeated or are consciously avoided throughout this text and throughout all three sections with varying emphasis:

- Colonialism: "Colonialism is a practice of domination, which involves the subjugation of one people to another."[1]
- Reflection through philosophical concepts: Many different philosophical concepts are presented and provide important avenues through which to consider concepts that are not absolute. Self-reflection and "ethnorelativism" (emphasized in Chapter 10) become an outgrowth of this process.
- This text aims to avoid "othering," "*a set of dynamics, processes, and structures that engender marginality and persistent inequality across any of the full range of human differences based on group identities.*"[2]

This text is written to embrace, open, and celebrate differences and people without furthering mistakes recognized from the past and without intentionally creating new problems as we move into an uncertain future.

Each section will be introduced with the salient points of the individual chapters. However, the entire volume leads to the final chapter, which is centered on the ideas of Maxine Greene, an educational philosopher. Through eleven chapters, this book will cover educational history, educational philosophy, and education in multiple contexts. There is never a sense of definitive explication but rather that "there is always, always more."[3]

ACKNOWLEDGMENTS

This book has been a compilation of many years of academic thinking, working with colleagues and students. I gratefully appreciate all those colleagues and students, past and future, for their guidance for helping me by challenging my ideas and helping me frame my thoughts. I am especially indebted to those colleagues I have met internationally who have provided the support and community that enables this work to continue. So many of you are cited here.

I appreciate the support from the Center for the Humanities at New York University, and the wonderful editorial eye of Danielle Staropoli. To John Wilson, thank you for formative feedback. All the contributors to this book assisted its vision, and it became our collective vision.

Thank you for the guiding spirits at Methuen, especially Anna Brewer and Meredith Benson who assisted with warmth and good humor.

Finally, I am still inspired by the work of my father, Theodore H. Koff. Long gone, his inspiration burns bright and has created the image of the academic I always strive to be.

SECTION I

Dance Education

A Definition of Our Lives

Introduction

To set the stage, Chapter 1 begins with a fresh perspective that tries to move beyond the very names that restrict or categorize. This is all meant to be inclusive without being specific. A redefinition can make sense only when contextualized in the way dance education has come to be a discipline and has been discussed in all the years that dancing has existed.

This is followed by an academic and mostly historical process. It is impossible to define, let alone redefine, dance education without first beginning in history and uncovering how this discipline was originally considered. This look through history is mostly Western in focus because of the types of records that have been kept, but it acknowledges a much larger world, painted in broad strokes, without becoming specific. Each country, and each culture, has its own way of recording the history of what it considers important and worthy of many texts. The history presented here is not meant to be exhaustive, but rather to lay a foundation to articulate the concepts that have led to confusion. The history presentation moves in and out of pedagogical and educational history, acknowledging that these concepts are also largely Western but have been adopted in many non-Western locations. Also woven through these chapters are philosophical ideas and how they drive or undergird the discussions and concepts.

The summary of this first section is all the background information necessary to move forward in the definition of dance education. Definitions are proposed, but only after careful consideration of contexts, history, pedagogy, and the many perspectives that have been brought together in these introductory chapters. Definitions that are brought forth are open-ended and are reconsidered throughout the balance of this book.

1

Essential Questions

Viewing Dance, Understanding Dance, and Reflecting upon Dance

Introduction

There are those who say that dance, as a nonverbal form of expression, is a perfect meeting place for people of diverse backgrounds and languages. It is a romantic notion. In reality, the systems that perpetuate Western versions of dance tend to create a hierarchy with Western forms above forms with non-Western lineages.[1] This is evident within formal education institutions of dance when those who specialize in a non-Western form of dance are told they are deficient in the "technique" that they need to be successful. Technique becomes code for Western forms of dance in which the ballet aesthetic and capabilities are emphasized.

In instances when **pedagogy** in dance is a meeting point between cultures, there also needs to be acknowledgment that dance knowledge, skills, worldviews, and civilizations from non-Western cultures are not the same as those from Western cultures.[2] In fact, there is nothing universal between one dance form and another, regardless of the cultures that they represent.[3] Classes in formal dance settings (to be discussed in Chapter 6) should be reconsidered in order to be an open space for pedagogies of all cultures, offering an authentic platform for sharing and exchanging information. Furthermore, there is nothing universal about dance technique when looked at across the world of dance. As Susan Foster mused, "what if implicit in the notion of technique itself are different attitudes toward the body and its relationship to subjectivity? Can technique be separated from spirit? from pleasure? or from moveability?"[4]

Dance encompasses all academic disciplines as well as popular culture and realms without academic discussion. Dance itself is a "human cultural phenomenon" and can be viewed as a way to learn cultural cues through the context of movement, which is called enculturation.[5] One way of approaching this is through cross-cultural dance studies. The critical quality of culture as seen in dance, is that it is dynamic and, therefore, continually changing and reforming. This chapter attempts to clarify these many disciplines; however, the many disciplines in dance can be a limiting factor when dance is discussed. This will be addressed in Chapter 3.

Rather than analyzing all the possible types of dance in the world, all possible types of dancers, or all possible settings, this discussion turns to essential questions about dance. These questions were created to cut across cultural boundaries and provide a way to view dance, regardless of the culture of origin. This chapter will touch upon a pedagogical perspective on these essential questions and discuss how these questions will arise during the text as the different areas are covered. The focus on these questions will emphasize the horizontal rather than hierarchical relationships of dance forms from multiple cultural backgrounds. An avoidance of lists of what is present, what is named, or what is included also supports the horizontal relationships between dance forms. This chapter will introduce **colonialism** in dance and how it has created those vertical relationships between techniques. Colonialism is a frequently recurring theme in this volume.

These essential questions are also created to examine the difference between **emic** and **etic** perspectives.[6] The terms emic and etic arise from yet another discipline, anthropology, and clarify that, in order to experience another culture, one must have a cultural informant or someone native to a particular culture. Otherwise, that culture is analyzed from perspectives that are not culturally congruent. These terms arose through observation and analysis of nonverbal behavior, making the application especially accessible for the study of dance. These terms and the concepts they embody again dispute any notion of universality in dance.[7] Ultimately, many themes that are present in the book will be introduced here to lay the groundwork for further detailed discussions about dance education, how it is situated, perceived, defined, and, finally, experienced.

The essential questions to be examined are:

- What is dance? What defines dance as an art form?
- How do people talk about dance?
- How is dance made, and for what purpose? How is dance performed, and for what purpose?
- How do dance works convey meanings, messages, or feelings (symbols)?

- How do social contexts shape the making and interpretation of dance?
- How is dance passed from one generation to the next? How does it change?[8] (Note: These questions were devised by Jessica Sand Blonde when co-writing the syllabus, Dance as an Art Form, for the New York University Dance Education Program.)

What Is Dance? What Defines Dance as an Art Form?

There is no single definition of dance. The "myth" is that dance, like other art forms, is considered universal or a universal language.[9] Dance is as varied as spoken language: there are many forms.[10] In moving away from the hierarchical alignment of dance forms, the discussion also needs to move away from an elitist perspective, where some forms are considered art and others are seen as utilitarian or having other purposes. Whether or not dance is created with art as its focus, dance can only be analyzed for its real values, from the inside. When one analyzes or views dance from outside of one's own culture, the focus should not be on a viewer/performer distinction, but rather on the experience. Dance has to be discussed more in a specific cultural context, instead of a broad definition being relied upon. This leads to a discussion of "authenticity," and a dance can only be seen as authentic or not from within its own culture.[11] Rather than a succinct, universal definition of dance being given, which is impossible, several definitions will be offered for consideration. "Dancing is moving, but not all moving is dancing" is a nice entry into definitions that are worth pondering.[12] Some "see dance as a rich and interesting expressive form through which to view cultural perceptions about the human body."[13] Continuing from an anthropologist's perspective, dance "is an expression of heightened experience of kinesthetic responses to external and internal stimuli."[14] This definition still leaves space for many possibilities. Other definitions tend to be limiting, such as "rhythmic movement with music," because dance is so much more. Rather than proposing narrow definitions, "It is sufficient to say that whatever is labelled 'dance,' and accepted as such by those who do it and watch it, is regarded as 'dance.'"[15] It has also been stated that dance is "nonverbal behaviour composed of movements that convey a heightened, aesthetic sense of body, rhythm, and space."[16] Through all these definitions, art is not prominently at the forefront.

In search of a definition, one can discuss how dance is viewed, seen, or used, such as in devotion, as a political tool, for entertainment, as a guardian of culture, in fertility festivals, in burial ceremonies, for healing, worship, expression, resistance, or spirituality.[17] Dance has also been used for propaganda and political oppression. Though all these uses and contexts were not originally created as art, viewing dance from an expressive, performative, and entertainment perspective prompts or encourages the focus to be on the artistry involved. Sacred or transcendent practices in dance mentioned here (for example, in religious practice) might consider art to be of only secondary importance to the initial purpose.

Definitions of dance as an art form depend on who is creating the definition. Dance has been viewed, discussed, and practiced by religious participants, community members, political dignitaries, educators, audience members (when an audience is present), and scholars in every possible discipline including art, anthropology, history, philosophy, etc. There is not a single community or perspective that has not discussed dance.

In early dance history writings, dance was discussed as "the mother of the arts," because it is "The creator and the thing created, the artist and the work are still one and the same thing."[18] "Dance, the art of the stone age, the art of primitive[19] life par excellence, holds a hegemony over all art materials."[20] Curt Sachs goes on to say, "let us consider as dance all rhythmical motion not related to the work motif."[21] Currently, dance continues to be expressed as an evolutionary process of "a basic ability to participate consciously in the rhythms of their own bodily becoming."[22] So, the definition of rhythm is used, far beyond any formal music. In defining "bodily becoming," philosopher LaMothe states:

> Dancing, in this sense, is not a question of learning steps or mastering technique or performing on stage; it is a question of discovering and disciplining ourselves to our own capacity to move. It is a question of learning how to participate as consciously as possible in the rhythms of bodily becoming so that we can align our actions with creating a world in which we want to live—and being born into it.[23]

"Dance is movement, but all movement is not yet dance."[24] Likewise Maxine Sheets-Johnstone continues this conversation by explaining:

> When we listen and attend in this way, when we read descriptions of infant behaviors and interactions, when we observe infants, when we reflect back upon our own fundamental knowledge of ourselves and the world, we realize that our most basic human concepts are foundationally corporeal concepts; they derive from our own dynamic bodily lives.[25]

The conclusion of this discussion is that there is no single definition, either correct or incorrect, of dance. When many different possible definitions are considered and unpacked, the clearest way to approach this topic is to be open to more definitions and more possibilities of what dance can and does encompass.

How Do People Talk about Dance?

Talking about dance is as complex as defining dance. It would seem at first that talking about dance is talking about the body, but it is so much more. The complexity lies in the multifaceted realm of dance. It is expressive and something just as inward as it is outward. So, it cannot all be measured or empirically perceived. As an art form, there are interpretation and subjective perception.

In talking about dance, it is also important to move beyond the Cartesian mind/body split and acknowledge the holistic person.[26] Though Antonio Damasio enters into this discussion from a neurology perspective, dance embraces this conversation because it reveals the total involvement with and about dance that is not solely about the bodily movements that are created and perceived.

Movement is primary to the being, but all movement is not dance.[27] However, as dance is movement, the extrapolation of that idea is that dance is primary to the being. Talking about dance becomes complex and belongs in different disciplines, such as philosophy, history, anthropology, and psychology. Each discipline then takes a slightly different perspective when talking about dance, making the subject of dance that much more complex in both practice and discussion about the practice.

How Is Dance Made, and for What Purpose? How Is Dance Performed, and for What Purpose?

For as many purposes that exist for living, thinking, and evolving human beings, there is dance. Most commonly, these purposes fall under the larger headings of religion and life cycles. Curt Sachs's list of purposes includes medicine, fertility, initiation, marriage, and funerals.[28] There are also dances for war, peace, seduction, and play. Most of these purposes are part of the life cycle, which is an important aspect of many religions.

Dance can also be about the perpetuation of social customs, status, and relationships. Contrarily, it can be a political statement and subversion. It can also be about expression, entertainment, and socialization. For as many reasons as people have to gather and be together, there can be dance. It can be "an emblem of cultural identity," "an expression of religious worship," "an expression of social order and power," "an expression of social mores," "a medium of cultural fusion," or individual artistic expression.[29]

The manner in which dance is made depends on the purpose. Dance can be spontaneous, or created with a specific intention, or an established and replicated form. It can be passed on to others in exactness or in a frame of possibility. There is no single way that dance is made and no single purpose to create dance. For as many reasons as there is dance, there is a different kind of audience (or no audience) and a different setting. For as many locations as there are in the world, there can be a dance. For as many different kinds of people there are in the world, there can be a dance. For these reasons, dance can mistakenly be considered universal; yet it is not, because dance is context-specific and cannot be universally performed, appreciated, or experienced. There is not one type, form, or setting of and for dance.

How Do Dance Works Convey Meanings, Messages, or Feelings?

How Do Social Contexts Shape the Making and Interpretation of Dance?

Meanings, messages, and feelings of dance are context-specific. Without being a reductionist, the contexts can be discussed as ritual and religion, social, and theatrical.[30] One must be part of the culture in which dance is performed to fully perceive what the dance is conveying. Otherwise, a cultural interpreter is necessary and helpful. Therefore, the social context of a dance is totally intertwined with the delivery of the meanings, messages, or feelings of a dance.

> From a perspective of bodily becoming, then, dancing is not only the medium in which human culture persists, it is also the means by which given shapes of culture appear. Culture—its tools, roles, and modes of communication—are what humans create as they mobilize the sensory awareness of themselves as movement that the practice of ritual dancing brings to life. Dancing exercises the capacity that is required to use any tool, word, or power in a human manner.[31]

Most of this interpretation or conveyance of meanings, messages, or feelings is done through symbols that are culturally specific and culturally interpreted. Dance has been discussed as "a language or symbol system," but one that is neither universally interpreted nor universally understood.[32] A gesture that is specific and meaningful in one culture may be purely abstract and unclear in another culture. This is why a dance that one views or participates in from a culture other than one's own should be framed in the context and values of the very culture that it represents.

From an educational perspective, simply teaching dance steps is an injustice to any form of dance. All dance teaching, regardless of the setting, should include the cultural context in which the dance was originally created and its meaning. Often, the setting in which the dance or dance form is taught is not the intended setting. So, the cultural information and context should be presented to the students in order for them to be aware of what the dance or dance form is representing.

How Is Dance Passed from One Generation to the Next? How Does It Change?

A recurrent theme in this chapter is that all dance is contextually specific. Therefore, it is not passed to others in a single codified way, but rather it is passed to others in as many ways as there are dances and dance forms. The single focus of this text is to reengage with or reimagine definitions and broaden expectations, including the discussion of passing on dance forms. Passing on dance forms ultimately is a culturally situated, context-specific teaching process. It can be anything from a traditional Western group class to the master–apprentice model or to an informal setting where learners are watching people practice a dance form and then joining in.

As stated earlier, this text is not about listing every possible dance form or every possible context, but about broadening perceptions while sensing that there is not a universal answer to any of these questions. These questions, therefore, are meant to assist the viewer or participant in engaging with differences, possibilities, and focus so that dance is neither viewed nor practiced with a universal lens.

The passing on of dance forms and practices is closely tied to teaching, in its myriad forms. Chapter 4 discusses pedagogy from a mostly Western perspective. Though all dance forms are passed on to the next generation through culturally specific practices, it is most often called pedagogy specifically when practiced in a Western context. An issue arises when, as discussed in Chapter 4, a non-Western dance practice is taught in a Western context. Philosophically, one could ask whether it is the actual dance practice that is being taught if the context is not congruent with the form. Further chapters that include a definition of pedagogies as formal, non-formal, and informal will present pedagogies by the interactions and not by the dance forms.

Cultural repressiveness, or colonialism, may be an unintended consequence when a dance form that is normally practiced as a religious event or a rite of passage is taught in a Westernized dance studio. It can also be termed "tokenism" and even "racism," because, in the Westernized context, the form itself has no context.[33] To some participants it may be viewed as a multicultural event, but multiculturalism itself can be called into question as tokenism.[34] However, to others it may seem inappropriate. Even the best intentions of being transparent and open may end up having a negative connotation. In the final analysis, not every dance form is available to be learned and passed on indiscriminately throughout the world.

It is possible to experience and share aspects of a dance form outside its original context. The burden is on the instructor or teacher to reveal as much information as possible about the form and the essence that is being presented in that unnatural setting, while not intending to make experts out of the participants. Ultimately, then, the passing on of any dance form happens according to the context in which it is practiced. The participation may be open or it may be restricted. The teaching may be one-on-one or it may be to a group. There may be no discernible instruction—it may rely on the participant or participants simply paying attention and trying all that others are doing.

> Here, movement patterns that characterize a culture's distinctive orientation in nature accumulate in number, concentrate along certain trajectories of human possibility, stratify in hierarchies of specialized skill and ability, and are increasingly abstracted from the natural world. At some extreme the tension between culture and nature collapses, and the process begins again.[35]

Additional Questions

There are two questions not directly addressed in the questions guiding this chapter:

Why do people dance?
Who dances or who can dance?

The first question is discussed indirectly and in different approaches throughout this chapter. There are many reasons why people dance, including for living, for moving, and for being alive. To summarize all that has been discussed previously, people can dance for aspects of the life cycle, healing, religious devotion, expression, and entertainment. Reasons can also be summarized as for peace and social change, empowerment, quality of life, well-being, freedom, and relationship to society.[36]

The second question, who dances or who can dance, has been sidestepped throughout this discussion as it is much more complex and constantly changing. To make a list of who dances, who can dance, and who is able to dance would be exhausting, as it would need to include every possible form of dance and all cultures that have dance, meaning all cultures. Instead, this discussion will focus on embracing all who live. That is, all who dance, who can dance, and who are able to dance. Everyone wants to live and have a full life, in whatever manner has meaning to them. One of the many aspects of embracing a full life is freedom of expression. Everyone is entitled to freedom of expression. Chapter 3, in defining dance education, broadens the definition to emphasize expression. This current chapter explores the many reasons for expression as proposed by the basic questions outlined earlier.

Freedom of expression can be a political as well as a social discussion; however, political and social issues will not be explored here. As the world rapidly changes and becomes more globally aware, these questions of expression, lifestyle, and ability to make choices become more prominent and are discussed and addressed in many arenas throughout the world. Along the way, participation in dance has broadened to become more inclusive, ranging from technically capable to having no perceived capabilities; from the very young to the very old; from very rich to very poor; from the able-bodied to persons with a range of disabilities; and this list continues. There are no limitations of characteristics including identity, capability, and socioeconomic means. The only limitation is access, which is the social and political question that will not be addressed.

More recently, advocates have worked to broaden access to include those who are disabled or have special needs (emotionally or physically), those who are marginalized because of identity or otherwise, and those from underrepresented groups within a society. Dance education programs and initiatives for students with special needs have been created in many locations to be inclusive and to reach populations such as the disabled, the elderly, or those with a specific illness such as Parkinson's disease. The development of these programs is in response to a history of limited access.

Questions of Language or Naming

Naming leads to many actions and reactions toward dance and all the questions addressed in this chapter. Some of the language constantly used in conversation regarding the development of dance includes diversity, cultural diversity, pluralism, and multiculturalism. These are complex words and mean different things to different groups of people. The concept of seeing the world as complex is rooted in the many social and political movements experienced throughout the world. These are efforts to acknowledge the history of colonialism, when one group is suppressed by another. Since the inception of colonialism in many parts of the world, suppressed groups have worked to reclaim their identity, and one way to do that is through the cultural expressions of dance, though in some instances the actual cultural representation of dance was also suppressed.

Listing the forms that have re-emerged with recognized value, as a reaction to colonialism, will result in exclusion, because it is simply not possible to create such a list. But some examples are influenced by political decisions to place value on these dance forms, such as the recognition of the numerous forms of Aboriginal dance in Australia or the emerging visibility of Maori dance in New Zealand society.

In the United States, slavery and its lasting remnants have placed some dance forms with African lineage in many different locations in society. This is still an issue that emerges, as do attempts to rectify the issues, which are centered in continuing racism. As the United States includes so many other cultures, many of the dance forms from cultures other than African American are marginalized or emerging from **marginalization**, and all are facing some similar and some dissimilar issues.

The language issues or issues of naming are deep-seated and express many issues in dance education and pedagogy. First, both dance education and pedagogy, as discussed in Chapter 4, are Western in focus and not easily applied to non-Western contexts of dance. The purpose of this current chapter has been to move away from the categorization that leads to the very issue of nomenclature. Naming non-Western ideas with Western terms can be a return to imperialism, colonialism, or "othering." At one time, dance from non-Western contexts was called "primitive dance." As Keali'inohomoku stated, "There is not and never has been a dance genre that could rightly be called 'Primitive Dance.'"[37] When something is made the "other," then a hierarchy is created in which one is better than or higher than the other. This leads to a more complex problem; for example, in Western contexts, the bending of the knees in African dance forms is inadvertently called a "plié," which is Western language forced upon a non-Western dance form. Savigliano states that "The primitive, as a placeholder of difference on the scale of progress and civilization, served as a justification for conquest and for the ensuing studies." In other words, primitive is a return to colonialism. "Race figures prominently as an organizational tool in these collections and its biological, psychological, and social moorings often slip into one another by way of 'culture' and observations on 'cultural difference.'"[38] Nomenclature continues colonialization and exacerbates issues.

Why do "dance" and "dance education" most commonly refer to Westernized forms of ballet and modern dance, whereas "cultural dance," "world dance," and "ethnic dance" mean really everything else, in some instances even including jazz and hip-hop, forms that actually originated in the West? This confused use of language permeates discussion of dance history, pedagogy, and meaning. Though groundbreaking at its time, Keali'inohomoku's calling "ballet a form of ethnic dance" has been widely disseminated, and yet the concept still seems novel.[39] Perhaps all dance should be called ethnic or the name of the form, rather than a separation into one form and then "otherness." Colonialization led to the spread of ballet throughout many parts of the world.[40] It also led to the hierarchy of ballet over what were indigenous forms, leading to the issues being confronted here.[41]

Simply, the categorization of dance forms is problematic. As stated earlier, the categories of "world dance," "ethnic dance," or "cultural dance" create a hierarchical othering, and so retiring those terms is a step in the right direction. Some scholars refuse categorization, as it eventually leads to hierarchical relationships.[42] As Vissicaro stated, "global dance or world dance does not exist, nor can it happen since cultural knowledge is and always will be context specific."[43] Many terms denote political divisions and cultural politics. But, then, what terms to use? Western and non-Western seemed reasonable, until the identification of hip-hop and jazz as Western, which is confusing in itself. Both forms began in the West, and yet the evolution of each form has a non-Western origin. Some scholars, when dealing with the United States, use the terms White dance and Black dance, but this is solely US-centric, and so it does not solve the larger issue.[44] The US-centric discussion of Black dance and White dance is also applied to dance pedagogy and dance history.[45] Addressing racism in the United States is an important step forward, but it sometimes ignores the issues of so many other marginalized populations throughout the world for the very reason that it is focused in the United States. While attempting to remove the supremacy of Western concert forms, the focus of this White dance and Black dance discussion remains permanently in the United States, and the choice of words does not encompass the rest of the world of dance.

Returning to terms, some scholars use the term "Eurocentric" and "non-Eurocentric." These terms seem to come closest to something that can be applied in many contexts; however, just the fact that there are binaries in all these terms is still problematic. An entire edited text deals with this issue of naming, in response to a US university dance department that also changed its name responding to nomenclature (University of California Los Angeles World Arts and Cultures).[46] The text, *Worlding Dance*, makes clear that this issue cannot be easily resolved, because something will always have new implications, and someone or something will be omitted or marginalized. Choosing the term "world dance" still has issues according to Savigliano: "Although World Dance is loosely defined in opposition to Western or Westernized dance forms, World Dances, in themselves, denote fusion and the challenges of articulating the aesthetics and pedagogies of other dance practices with those already established in the world of (Western or Westernized) Dance."[47] Foster stated that moving from "ethnic" as a label to "world" as a label would create a more neutral focus on dance, "Yet through this relabeling, the colonial history that produced the ethnic continues to operate."[48]

Ultimately these many systems of naming and categorization can be considered analogous to the organization in a museum. Something will always be misplaced or miscategorized, depending on the perspectives of both viewers and participants. Without offering any new terms, Savigliano presents a new approach to world dance:

> Rather than a form of classification and an emergent discipline, World Dance would thus participate in the making of an untotalizing alternative to globalism, based on decisions (not on observations or accommodations to prescriptions) to expose our movements to the world. These ethico-political decisions would entail dismantling otherness and differences as sources of identity and belonging, risking explorations into dissolution

and betting on chosen, eventful reconstitutions. World dancers affiliated as neighbors, neighboring as we move each other into dancing, outside rubrics, disciplines, traditions. Beyond difference, otherness and marginality, dancing as moving the outside.[49]

Multiculturalism, Diversity, or Pluralism?

In order to remove some dance forms from a marginalized position, there are many organized approaches toward multiculturalism, diversity, or pluralism. This is another layer where language and intent intrude on the discussion. Even the discussion of multiculturalism is situated in the discipline of humanities, which leads to the discussion of smaller disciplines within one larger discipline that will be presented in Chapter 3.[50] Though beginning in the humanities, the discussion of multiculturalism takes on new meanings in each discipline. The intent of multiculturalism arises from cultural and/or political perspectives. There are cultural or political movements in societies attempting to rectify past transgressions. What is meant by these words, and are they interchangeable? Multiculturalism usually means representing many different cultures. Though noble in its intent, multiculturalism has been approached superficially in application by having selected aspects of a culture presented, often through dance, music, clothing, and/or food. Usually, only one view of the represented culture is presented. However, each culture is very diverse within itself, meaning that there is no single representation of each and every culture.[51] So, multiculturalism eventually fails, because it is not demonstrating the complexity of each culture and is usually only a superficial display.

This leads to the concept of "boutique multiculturalism," as defined by Stanley Fish.[52] The concept of superficially honoring another culture through any type of cultural representation is "boutique multiculturalism." It allows one to "check off a box," so to speak, thus achieving inclusion. Its mistake is that, though the intention has come from a well-meaning and inclusive perspective, no cultural values, representation, or depth have been studied, learned, experienced, or included. All have remained on the surface. Many locations of dance education have fallen into this same mistake, and there is not yet a clear way to embrace a culture other than one's own.

Summary

The questions addressed in this chapter are an attempt to counter boutique multiculturalism, so that cultures other than one's own are embraced with a level of inside, or emic, perspective.[53] This chapter is also focused on a global perspective, so that it is not a list of countries or dance forms. It is important to be clear about one's perspective, knowing that, when seeing something from the inside, one has an emic perspective. When seeing something from the outside, one has an etic perspective. Emic views are intrinsic, and etic views are extrinsic. Mistakes of boutique multiculturalism occur when one tries to experience a culture from an etic, or outside, perspective which is not specific. This is why the experience remains superficial. Moving away from a listing of cultures, the guiding questions in this chapter are meant to sidestep that level of categorization.

The questions guiding this chapter also address the issue that sometimes a cultural dance expression is not open to those from outside the culture. This must be respected, along with respect for the culture, introducing the pedagogical discussions of culturally responsive pedagogy. When a dance form is taught outside of its cultural setting, then cultural context needs to be given to help convey what the form is intended to represent. Otherwise, there are just movements, and not cultural representation. Symbolic meaning is not universal, just as dance as expression is not universal.

Overall, this chapter has been structured to go beyond the typical categorization of dance forms and organization by country; instead, it aims to look at dance through the perspectives presented by these questions. The overall intent of both this chapter and the entire book is to remove the hierarchical thinking that often comes with categorization. It is also intended to remove the concept of universal application of ideas, as well as looking at dance as if it is universal. Through this, many concepts and issues have been introduced that will be revisited throughout this book.

Colonialism can be neither ignored nor erased. The dance world is in the place it is today as a result of colonialism, globalism, and many other forces. Even with this analysis or new way of looking, it should be clear that dance forms change because there is no codified recording of the form. It is an oral and embodied tradition that evolves naturally as it is literally passed on from one participant to another. As some dance forms are dependent upon invention and change, change can also be a value of that form, even if the changes came about because of responses to outside forces.

2

History of Dance Education (Formal Educational Settings)

Discussing dance education means first discussing the context, or where it takes place, and how it is treated in that context. The term dance education comes from the very formal, graded contexts of structured schooling which include other subjects. The establishment of dance as a separate discipline within formal school structures, alongside other subjects, was introduced in the United States within higher education. It already existed in some form in the primary and secondary educational structure as "physical education," and so the discussion will begin there. This historical discussion is from a Western perspective, because the Western model was then emulated in other areas, specifically the East, including Singapore, Hong Kong, Indonesia, and Korea.[1] Developed as a historical overview, this chapter will follow through to the current day and delineate how this history has evolved. It will also include the ways in which this model has been emulated in higher education in other countries. This entire discussion emanates not just from a Western perspective, but from a decidedly US-centric perspective. It is impossible to include every perspective in a single text. Therefore, this is not meant to be an exhaustive history, but rather an overview to provide a clear context. Going back even further in a contextual frame necessitates the definition of education, which is "not to be confused with training or learning."[2] John Dewey, who is cited throughout this chapter, is actually a source for the Wikipedia article.

The physical education model for dance in higher education was influenced by the model of dance in public education, specifically in New York City, which was, and is, a major urban city in the United States with a large population, as well as being at the forefront of the development of concert dance. The physical education system of the public schools became the location in which to implement new ideas influencing the large immigrant populations, particularly in the late 1800s and early 1900s. Additionally, the dance that was introduced into higher education initially ignored dance education that was concurrently taking place in non-Western communities. So, a Western focus also begins the story of inclusion and exclusion.

Historical Context: Nineteenth-Century Attitude

Physical education was introduced into public education in the United States originally for purposes of health and hygiene. There were two reasons. First, a large immigrant population arrived in the United States with many different customs relating to health and hygiene. The school system was considered one of the locations that could influence local customs that had been brought to the United States. Second, following the Industrial Revolution, which resulted in more leisure time, there was now a need to have structured activity to achieve good health. Physicians were more likely to be the physical educational leaders of the time and they promoted movement systems, which later became dance, as a way to maintain health.[3] The movement systems they favored were forms of gymnastics, based on practices from ancient Greece. There were vestiges of puritanical thought that prohibited dancing (ideas that were brought to the United States by earlier immigrants), but the later part of the nineteenth century saw a shift away from those attitudes.

Influential Physical Education Leaders (Early 1900s)

Within the United States, three physical education leaders emerged who had a strong influence on the development of dance education in the early 1900s: Luther Gulick, Thomas Wood, and Clark Hetherington. Luther Gulick, a medical doctor, developed the idea of holistic education for the YMCA (Young Men's Christian Association, an organization developed mostly in the West to influence healthy "body, mind and spirit"[4]) and promoted these practices in his work throughout the northeastern region of the United States. He encouraged the acceptance of both play and dance in physical education.[5] Gulick, along with Thomas Wood (also a medical doctor), supported John Dewey's ideas of educating the whole child, leading to more natural forms of movement within physical education.[6] Wood's work was primarily at Teachers College at Columbia University (New York) and was directly influenced by Dewey's work.[7] Clark Hetherington worked in California for some time before coming to New York in the 1930s. He had worked with Wood briefly in California and also advocated for natural movement and play. The groundbreaking work of these three physical educators within the United States created the possibility for dance education to grow through the emphasis on natural movement and play, especially because the focus on natural dance was considered to provide creative activity, which none of the other movement forms provided.[8] Their work was considered significant because of the new ideas they accepted, the way in which they advanced physical education and made space for these new ideas, and the respect that they each received in their own careers and in the institutions that supported them. Though Wood, Gulick, and Hetherington paved the way for dance education in the United States, their legacies are carried forward through physical education and are largely ignored in dance education.

Natural Dance and Structured Activity

The gymnastics forms in schools were initially formal and rigid. New educational ideas allowed educators to soften the forms to more natural gymnastics. When these movement forms were influenced by ballet, they were renamed aesthetic dancing. But, as aesthetic dance also had a sense of formalism, there was an additional shift to a form called natural dancing, which probably also reflected the influence of Isadora Duncan as well as the physical education leaders mentioned earlier. Within these shifts in physical education, there started to be a separation of the types of movement based on gender, with the more rigid gymnastics being taught to male students, and the natural dance being taught to female students.

Folk dance was also popular during this time. It was a significant aspect of the physical education curriculum and will be discussed later. It is one of the dance forms that remained in the physical education curriculum, even when dance became its own curricular area. This development was seen prominently in the large New York City public-school system in the early parts of the 1900s, and the dances represented were mostly from Europe, also reflecting the large European immigrant population of the time.[9]

Though it is not the definitive description, Mabel Lee offers a good summary of the development of different forms of dance within physical education: "The 'dance exercises' of the 1850s and 1860s gave way to the 'fancy steps' of the 1870s and 1880s. They in turn gave way to the esthetic dancing of the 1890s, which gave way to such other forms of artistic expression as modified ballet and natural dancing, and then 'modern dance.'"[10] During these years, information was carried and transmitted in letters, printed academic publications, and infrequent scholarly gatherings, as well as formal tertiary physical education. The development and transmission of new ideas were not linear and depended on the ability of practitioners to access these forms of information.

European and American Contrasts (German and Swedish Approaches Contrasted to US)

In England, the development of the types of activities in physical education was similar to that in the United States in that, first, the Industrial Revolution created the need for more formal exercise programs within schools. The initial programs that were introduced into public education were also from the Swedish and German gymnastics systems. As Germany was a European country that was directly affected by both the First World War and the Second World War, it was not desirable to follow the militaristic nature of its gymnastics in other countries, and so different systems were sought. Rudolf von Laban's move from Germany to England before the Second World War encouraged the formation of England's own dance-based movement system in public education, modern educational dance.

The actual development of dance education in Germany, and in other parts of Eastern Europe, was truncated by the Second World War and the subsequent political alignments of Eastern European countries. However, up to that time, the aesthetic developed in Germany had become more aligned with the political leanings of pre-war Germany.[11] This in itself is a complicated history and one which still has signs of influence in European dance education.

Additionally, physical education in the United States was trying to move away from the European ideals that were represented in gymnastics systems.[12] However, attitudes were conflicted, as people in the United States were not completely ready to deem those systems no longer useful.[13] Whether the Swedish and German gymnastics systems were discarded or molded, they had a strong influence on the development of both dance education within physical education and physical education itself. (There are many resources that offer a complete look at the Swedish and German gymnastics systems.)[14]

Two people whose ideas greatly influenced the development of physical education and dance in both the United States and Europe will be discussed next. John Dewey (mentioned earlier) was not a dancer or a physical educator, but rather a philosopher whose ideas were adopted in many forms of education. Rudolf von Laban (mentioned earlier) had a movement/dance background and greatly influenced first movement education in England (modern educational dance, as it was named, owing to Laban's influence) and then dance education in the United States. The influence of both men is still felt today, not only in the United States and England, but throughout the world.

John Dewey

John Dewey was an educational philosopher active from the latter years of the 1800s to the first part of the 1900s. His influence can be seen in the progressive education movement in all forms of education, including physical education and dance education.[15] Progressive education, as defined by Dewey, is child-centered and merges thinking and doing in the educational process.[16] He first worked in Chicago and then New York City at Teachers College, where his ideas were included in new practices being tried in the very large and culturally diverse public-school system. At Teachers College, his influences could be seen in the natural dancing promoted by Gertrude Colby.[17] He also influenced education in England and other countries and even outside the West, including in China.

Rudolf von Laban

The educational philosophies developed by John Dewey influenced Dartington Hall, a progressive education boarding school that existed from 1926 to 1987 in Devon, England. From Dartington Hall, progressive education moved to public education in England as a prevailing philosophy. This became the perfect location for Rudolf von Laban, a German dancer and choreographer, who was exiled from Germany during the Third Reich and spent the rest of his life in England; "by the late 1950s modern educational dance and educational gymnastics were well established in many teacher-training colleges and schools [in England]."[18] Though the start of dance in schools was similar to that in the United States (through physical education), Laban's influence resulted in a slightly different direction taken in England than in the United States, but the difference is only in the form that was presented.

The form difference was the introduction of modern educational dance in England, rather than the creative exploration ideas found in the United States. In England, modern educational dance (in this instance) was also seen as a contrast to rigid training systems, but was also overtaken by the popularity of scientific sports and physical education systems. For these reasons, modern educational dance became less and less popular in schools. Dance with an arts focus then entered public schools much later and, by 1965, was much more focused as an art form.[19]

English Approach before and after Laban

In England, the development of dance education was similar in that, first, the Industrial Revolution created the need for more formal exercise programs within schools. The initial programs that were introduced in public education were also from the Swedish and German gymnastics systems. As in other Western European countries, the desire was to move away from the German gymnastic model. Rhythmic work became part of physical education before the First World War through the eurythmics of Émile Jaques-Dalcroze, and exploration for young children was inspired by the Montessori method.

Both of these (rhythmic work and exploration) were mostly for females and children.[20]

Though modern dance exploration was active during the early part of the twentieth century in both the United States and Central Europe, the Central European influences were stronger in England, and the United States was developing its own aesthetic. The development in England was eventually called modern educational dance rather than modern dance.[21]

Laban's Legacy Today

Laban's work has a legacy not only in dance education, but also in dance studies; these two subdisciplines will be discussed in the next chapter. However, there is a complete disconnect between what dance studies has acknowledged about the background and perspective of the man and the uncritical pathway that dance education established having absorbed Laban's work without criticism or evaluation. Examination of Laban's original work shows that he embraced and was embraced by the Nazi regime and was engaged to create pageants that generated a public perception of the Nazi perspective. Though he left Germany because of his interest in cults, which were not "purely Aryan," he never came out publicly against the Nazi regime and was seen as entirely sympathetic in his actions and attitude.[22] In England, because of the complete transformation of Laban's work into modern educational dance, the prevalent view in dance education is that he completely separated himself from his previous work in Germany. However, closer examination of his scales of movement, as his exercises are called, demonstrates a continuation of Nazi formality along with its adherence to conformity.

In addition, some historians will question the actual morality of Laban's past work, and whether it is appropriate to accept his work in light of his past activities:

> The history of dance has not concerned itself enough with the questions about the interaction of morality and ethical responsibility. However the question may be posed, it must first be faced fully and consciously: Can artistic productivity abolish moral responsibility? Anybody who says "yes" and thinks that art has nothing to do with morality should at least not try to justify as moral the flagrant violations of human rights as Mary Wigman tried to do . . . equally false is the attempt to make the work of Rudolf von Laban great by turning him into a hero.[23]

In addition to questioning Laban's morality and whether it should be considered when using his concepts, there is also the question of the application of the Laban lens and methodology of modern educational dance. There are many in the dance education community who apply Laban movement analysis universally, regardless of the context. Yes, there are useful tools within the Laban structure for evaluating as well as generating movement. However, within its application, the Laban framework should first be culturally and historically situated and then applied with skepticism. From a positive perspective, the implementation of modern educational dance in England took the professional focus away from dance in schools. From a critical perspective, teachers should be aware that adhering to this framework might be replacing one ideology (professionalism) with another. Is this a form of curricular hegemony?[24]

Further embedded in this discussion is the issue that, now, two distinct branches of dance, dance studies and dance education, each operate in a vacuum without considering that they share the world of dance, with its theoretical structures, histories, and backgrounds. It is as if these are two different disciplines that do not speak to each other or understand each other. The lack of communication is not beneficial to the discipline of dance. Demystification and deconstruction of dance education will hopefully bring the bridging of gaps within the discipline of dance a step closer. This discussion will continue in the following chapter.

Historic Context Summary: First Half of the Twentieth Century

At the beginning of the 1900s, there were five types of systems included in physical education in the United States: German gymnastics, Swedish gymnastics, games and sports (influenced by the English), athletics, and dance.[25] In Europe, two people outside physical education worked to alleviate the rigid systems so that these systems became more like dance. François Delsarte was a French music and drama teacher. Some of his followers incorporated his ideas into more rigid exercise systems, leading to aesthetic dance. The work of Émile Jaques-Dalcroze, a Swiss music teacher and composer, became popular with early professional dancers and emphasized a rhythmic system.[26] Some of this emphasis on rhythmic activity moved into schools. The influence of these two people extended to the United States.

Males and females were separated for physical education throughout the first half of the twentieth century. The dance developed through the many influences discussed in this chapter remained primarily for females throughout this period of time. This is clearly documented and expanded in some sample history texts identified here.[27]

Second Half of the Twentieth Century

The dialogue about dance as exercise and dance as art was ongoing and similar in both England and the United States throughout the first half of the twentieth century. Dance became a separate discipline in public education in both countries much later (the 1980s). In the earlier part of the 1900s, the discussion was led by academics in the field of physical education expressing their concern about the new developments in professional dance and its influence on physical education. Over the years, the discussion was led more and more by dance educators, subsequently leading to dance educators aligning with other arts educators (art, music, and theatre) by the 1980s in the United States.

An additional event that led to the rapid growth of dance in the United States was Title IX (a US Education Act) in 1972, which ultimately resulted in the combination of men's and women's physical education at all levels: elementary, secondary, and tertiary. This event gave rise to dance units separating from physical education and aligning with the arts.[28] It also created a more inclusive environment for men and women in dance, regardless of the level of education.

The alignment of dance with the arts in public education in the United States developed more rapidly in the 1980s. Dance was already becoming aligned with the arts in higher education, but this developed much later in the public (elementary and secondary) education sector. Though dance was a strong component of physical education requirements in public education, it could not stand on its own. The combined arts education advocacy led to dance teacher certification and dance standards throughout the United States, in conjunction with other arts standards.[29] This advocacy was strengthened through the combined forces of four art forms (dance, art, music, and theatre), leading not only to dance teacher certification in many states, but also to the combined National Standards for the Arts (1994), which were led by the Music Educators National Conference (MENC). Most recently, a revision added a fifth form, media arts, leading to the National Core Arts Standards.[30] Through the strength of the arts that were more established in education (music and visual art), dance teacher certification began in different states, and the number of states has continued to grow, with California adding dance teacher certification as recently as 2016. Consequently, this growth in the arts direction and definition resulted in dance's complete split from its alignment with physical education throughout the United States.

This shift has also been seen around the world, but at varying times, according to local contexts and attitudes.[31] In some places, dance is actually set in different curricular contexts according to the age and grade of students. For example, in elementary education, it can be taught by generalist teachers so that it is neither art nor physical education, but its own subject.

Combined arts education advocacy gave dance a voice within a larger educational policy arena in the US government, which continues today. This is also evident in many other countries. However, the split from physical education weakened the strength of research, especially concerning deepening knowledge of the body and its optimal functioning. It also resulted in a split of dance forms, as Western concert dance moved into alignment with the arts, but folk and social dance (and sometimes ballroom dance) remained in their traditional home, physical education. The fear of this split was already evident in the 1950s, when physical education was laying its claim to dance as both art and activity.[32]

The Beginning of Dance in American Higher Education

Dance courses had long existed in physical education in higher or tertiary education, as individual or clusters of courses, but not as a degree. The many shifts of emphasis that were discussed previously also affected the type and focus of dance in higher education. Beginning with the program at the University of Wisconsin in 1926, dance started as a degree subject within physical education, first as its own discipline in higher education (in the United States) with just a single academic focus (or single word, dance) rather than a multidimensional course of study including many of the subsets that exist today, such as choreography, performance, dance history, and dance education. This model of dance in higher education has been emulated by countries around the world. As stated previously, dance courses had already been an aspect of physical education, but this was the first time a dance major was established.

At its inception as a degree, dance remained within physical education at Wisconsin because Margaret H'Doubler's idea (as the proposer of the major) was to develop a "sound and scientifically based approach to learning in human movement."[33] Not many years later (1930), Martha Hill became an instructor of dance in the Physical Education Department at New York University (NYU), but the "major overriding concept that Hill would bring to NYU was the idea of dance as a performing art."[34] This began the tension between dance as art and dance as activity in higher education. Interestingly, however, Hill originally wrote about the value of dance, during the Second World War, as being good for both physical fitness as well as morale.[35]

The burgeoning professional modern dance field led to the expansion and exploration of dance in higher education. Previously, there had been resistance to the professionalism of ballet entering higher education. However, in the professional world, beginning with the explorations of Isadora Duncan and Denishawn (Ruth St. Denis and Ted Shawn) and followed by Martha Graham, Doris Humphrey, Charles Weidman, Hanya Holm, and Mary Wigman, there was an interest in expanding this field of new modern dance in higher education. For many years following this inception, dance degree programs began both within physical education programs and in liberal arts colleges. The complete separation from physical education started early on, but still continues today in some areas.

Margaret H'Doubler

Margaret H'Doubler had a physical education background and traveled to New York City from the University of Wisconsin to earn credentials for a promotion at Wisconsin in physical education (an MA degree from Teachers College) in 1916. Though she was originally interested in basketball, her supervisor gave her an assignment to explore dance in order to bring it back to Wisconsin.[36] This supervisor was responding to the new types of dance taking hold in New York City at the time. With supportive and forward-thinking academic leaders in physical education, as well as the development of dance in New York, the environment was established to bring newer forms of dance to the University of Wisconsin. Janice Ross, John Wilson, Mary Brennan, and Thomas Hagood have written extensively about the climate and all the elements that created these changes and led to this development, and they remain some of the foremost historians of H'Doubler's work.[37]

John Dewey, as mentioned earlier, was also an influential philosopher of education at Teachers College in the early part of the 1900s. H'Doubler expressed interest in continuing her studies in philosophy and she was active in a student philosophy organization while at Teachers College.[38] Progressive education and student-centered learning are part of the lasting legacy of John Dewey, and these elements are clearly hallmarks of creative movement.[39] Also, both Gertrude Colby (at Teachers College) and Bird Larson (at Barnard College) were exploring some similar concepts to H'Doubler in the early part of the twentieth century, developing actual courses in those institutions. It is possible that historians attribute the development of dance in higher education to H'Doubler because of her indelible writings, as well as the actual degree area that she founded, while acknowledging the influences of Dewey, Colby, and Larson. However, there is no documentation that H'Doubler studied with Dewey while at Teachers College or that she interacted with Colby and Larson.[40]

H'Doubler was interested in amateurism in sport and she continued to value it in her exploration of dance in New York. Rather than seek professional performances and training, she searched for dance that was consistent with the educational philosophy of mind-body connection that she had already developed.[41] She also thought Dewey's definition of "experience" aligned with her focus as well as the progressive education focus of the Wisconsin Idea.[42] Most of the dance studios she explored in New York offered rigid instruction, whether it was ballet or some of the newer forms of dance. Not until she discovered a music educator who had an integrated movement model resembling creative movement was she satisfied that she could develop a model of dance that she thought would work at Wisconsin. According to Ross, H'Doubler created dance education "to focus on the qualitative immediacy of experience in dance. Instead of emphasizing preparation for a performance, or the methodological acquisition of rote skills, H'Doubler followed Dewey's lead and made broad, openly structured explorations in dance the priority of her classroom."[43]

In 1926, the dance major (for dance teachers) proposed by H'Doubler was approved by the Department of Physical Education at Wisconsin. Besides actual dance courses, there was a balance between science and humanities courses, so that the curriculum was reflective of her integrated philosophy of education.[44] Interestingly, when the history of the first dance degree is taught today, many students hear that the first dance major was created in 1926. It is rarely mentioned as the first dance education major or a major focused on teaching.

An element buried in this history is H'Doubler's view as stated by Marion Van Tuyl: "Folk dance, ethnic dance, tap dance, she considered lesser forms always holding her vision of the ideal dance."[45] These dance forms were already in the physical education curriculum. One could speculate that, if this was H'Doubler's prevailing vision, it could lead to the discussion of the separation of dance forms within the university, so that folk and "ethnic" forms remained in physical education as dance became its own discipline (a traditional format that is consistently up for discussion, even today). This could also be seen as the initiation of dance within the university having a decidedly Western focus, based on and developed from dance explorations that were occurring in the United States in the early part of the twentieth century.

H'Doubler's legacy today is also the "complex tale of the acceptance of middle-class white women, their intellects and their bodies, into American higher education."[46] So, within this huge step forward for women, moving out of Victorian concepts of the body, also came the stereotypical Western focus of dance in higher education that is still being addressed today. It should not be forgotten that physical education was segregated by gender at the time, and so the earlier dance degrees were designed for women.

Martha Hill

Chronologically, the next focus on dance within higher education is the work of Martha Hill. She was hired by the Physical Education department of NYU specifically to teach dance, which coincided with the flourishing development of American modern dance in New York City.[47] Hill was at NYU until 1951 but for many of those years she shared her time with Bennington College in Vermont, where dance developed within the context of the liberal arts, not physical education. Bennington developed the first Bachelor of Arts (BA) dance major in the country (Wisconsin's was a Bachelor of Science, BS), and the students were encouraged to study in New York City to supplement their study at Bennington. At Bennington, Hill first created a summer school of dance, followed by the degree program. The summer school ended in 1942, and the degree program ended later.

Besides the Bennington students' exposure to the professional dance studios in New York City, Hill also brought professional modern dancers from New York to Bennington to teach, creating a model very different from that at Wisconsin. The Bennington version was a model infused with professionalism. This development was integrated into both the Bennington summer program in dance and the curricular degree. Hill went on to become the first director of dance at Juilliard in 1951, bringing the collaboration of professional dance with higher education back to New York City and introducing the conservatory model to higher education.

Tension between Dance as Art or Dance as Activity

The contrasting visions of Margaret H'Doubler and Martha Hill for dance in higher education played out in the subsequent development of dance departments and dance majors across the country. This separation can be viewed as "the growing friction between physical education and art-dance as they sought to share common ground, common space, and common resources in education."[48] Once Bennington had introduced dance into higher education, even before a conservatory model appeared, there was much debate about the purpose of dance in higher education. These debates began shortly after Wisconsin established its dance major. The participants in this debate included people from the academic dance world, the professional dance world, and physical education.[49] The irony is that this debate continues today, though the physical educators are no longer involved. However, Hagood thinks that H'Doubler's perspective was much more inclusive as it "supports a need for education *between* activity influenced physical education and professionally influenced art-dance. The philosopher-scientist-artist must instill in students a life-long interest in the creative expressive body."[50] H'Doubler had a strong interest in all these areas (science, philosophy, and art) and actually envisioned a more expansive form of dance in higher education rather than a strong split between physical education and art. But finally, maintaining a more inclusive stance for dance in higher education led to a de facto choice because she no longer had a say in what occurred in dance in higher education. "H'Doubler rejected notions of educational dance as a professionally focused 'art-dance,' for the more liberal idea of dance as the 'creative side of movement.' By intellectualizing dance, and by not donning the robe of 'artist,' H'Doubler effectively cut herself out of the future of dance in the academy."[51]

Certainly, H'Doubler and Hill knew each other and engaged with each other on some level. H'Doubler attended the Bennington summer program to observe, and at times her students attended as well. Some of the schism could emanate from teaching methods that were prevalent in the contrasting models that they each created in higher education. The model of teaching a movement class at Wisconsin was very student centered and emulated the progressive and experiential concepts of Dewey,[52] though H'Doubler would not acknowledge that she was influenced by Dewey.[53] The students had a "voice" within the class, and there was time for them to reflect. Contrarily, the professional model was very teacher directed, with "authoritarian styles and specialized goals."[54]

Some consider that, as the professional model became more popular in higher education, H'Doubler's legacy was diminished.[55]

After initially teaching dance within physical education (at NYU), Martha Hill subsequently taught dance in the liberal arts context (Bennington) and then within a conservatory (Juilliard), leading to the subtext of "who can teach?" Within the conservatory, those who teach are qualified by virtue of their professional career. The discussion of who is qualified to teach began first in physical education departments as some professional dancers were initially hired. Those with academic degrees and careers in physical education and the liberal arts were in conflict with those whose professional credentials became their qualification. Even a professional dance critic, John Martin, questioned this in his 1939 publication *Introduction to the Dance*. Hagood paraphrases Martin to say that he "suggests that the relationship between the professional dancers and the educator be reversed; that the professional come to the educator to learn to teach."[56]

Tensions in the Second Half of the Twentieth Century

Prior to and following dance becoming its own discipline within higher education, its close alignment with physical education was clear to observe in professional organizations, specifically the American Alliance for Health and Physical Education (its inception in a prior form dates back to 1885), which over the years became the American Alliance for Health, Physical Education, Recreation, and Dance. The addition of the "D" was a great accomplishment for the dance educators who were members and used both the conferences and publications to discuss, debate, and consider the future of dance, both in higher education and public education.[57] From an organizational perspective, dance education broke from this association with physical education beginning in 1999 with the founding of the National Dance Education Organization. The development of dance organizations and what it implies about the location of dance in higher education will be more thoroughly discussed in Chapter 3.

Alma Hawkins, who became chair of the dance program in physical education at University of California at Los Angeles (UCLA) in 1953, attempted to move dance forward within higher education, responding to the changing field.[58] She merged dance as an art form with the liberal arts perspective while trying to diffuse the overt professionalism of the conservatory model.⁵⁹ Her merged perspective, elaborated in her book *Modern Dance in Higher Education*, presented a way for dance to exist within the university as a discipline because she clearly articulated the mission of the modern university and how dance contributed to it as a full discipline.⁶⁰ However, her articulation of the place of dance as a discipline was challenged when Eugene Loring (a professional dancer and choreographer) was hired as the first Dance Department head at the University of California at Irvine in 1966.⁶¹ The creation of this new University of California campus emphasized professionalism in higher education. The blurring of education and professionalism was now complete. In many places this model continues today, and in some instances is still controversial. One of the controversies for Hawkins was that professionals in higher education lacked teaching qualifications.⁶²

By the 1950s there were many different dance degrees within both physical education and dance or other arts in the United States, including Adelphi University, Mills College, UCLA, Smith College, and Sarah Lawrence College.⁶³ Those who had a dance background but were in physical education demonstrated some defensiveness against the many different types of programs that were developing and their implications for the place of dance in public schooling.⁶⁴

The tension concerning the place of dance within higher education manifested itself in many different ways, including the curriculum, degrees offered, faculty qualifications, teaching methods, and goals for graduates. The tension within the curriculum was not, in the earlier part of the twentieth century, about which dance forms were included, in terms of culture of origin. That discussion was left for the end of the twentieth century and the early part of the twenty-first century. As different models of dance degree programs spread from the United States to other countries, the models emulated were varied and based on all that were present in the United States—educational, liberal arts, and conservatory models. Regardless of which part of the world these models traveled to, they still resembled those in the United States, dominated by Western concert forms, even if that form is not representative of the culture in which it is situated. This is illustrated by many examples in which ballet is privileged over other dance forms.

The contrasting physical education model and liberal arts model were initially developed in this fashion:

Wisconsin Curriculum⁶⁵

Kinesiology

Technique (in the H'Doubler method of fundamental movement skills)

Dance history

Composition

Rhythmic analysis

Teaching methods
Dance philosophy

Bennington Curriculum[66]
Techniques of the "big four": Graham, Humphrey, Weidman, and Holm
Dance composition
History
Criticism
Music for dance
Dance production
Ballet (after the innovations by Lincoln Kirstein)

The contrast between the two is that established techniques were the focus in liberal arts programs, but not the physical education model. The other stark contrast is that, at its inception, only the physical education model retained ties to the movement sciences. This contrast is still seen today. Finally, only the physical education model included philosophy and teaching methods.

In the later part of the twentieth century, the contrast came to be between the conservatory model, as exemplified by Julliard and the many professional models being developed, and the model advocated by Alma Hawkins and then developed in two conferences that will be mentioned in Chapter 3.[67] In Hawkins's model, she emphasized teacher education for tertiary education and she strongly supported dance within tertiary education being integrated into the values of that setting, which did not include professionalism. She summed it up by stating that "the purpose of education and of professional dance are different."[68]

Summary

Dance entered formal elementary, secondary, and tertiary education through physical education in both the United States and Europe. There were many different forms of dance, some long-standing, such as folk, and others that evolved through various movement and artistic concepts of the time. Evolving attitudes to the body were also influential. Elementary and secondary education dance remained aligned with physical education for many years more than in tertiary education. In some locations around the world, dance remains aligned with physical education.

The development of dance in tertiary education had the same beginnings as in elementary and secondary education, but began rapidly changing, first in the United States and then spreading to other parts of the world. Between 1926, with the creation of the first tertiary dance major, and now, dance has either become established separately from physical education, or has been split from physical education as the discipline has evolved. From its inception, a topic of continual discussion is the purpose of the dance degree: Is it for the holistic development of the student or about professionalism? This discussion has not yet been resolved and does have implications for the balance of the discussions in this book. It will be approached in light of the definition of dance education, which begins in the next chapter.

3

Defining Dance Education

Whose Definition?

Introduction

Dance education is a misunderstood term that is often defined as dance training alone, rather than a much more comprehensive education. When seen or presented as dance training within a formal educational setting, dance is considered a frill or expendable pleasantry rather than an essential part of the curriculum. However, the definition proposed here includes dance education as part of the foundation of a well-rounded education for all, be it as a public-school course, as a general education course that completes the undergraduate student's broad education in expressive capacities, or as a lifelong activity connected to one's community. Adhering to this definition includes dance education forms from non-Western cultures, creating a more horizontal rather than vertical alignment of multiple areas of dance content within formal educational settings. Simply put, dance education is about teaching a mode of expression, not a set of skills.

Teaching dance has been around for a very long time and in many parts of the world. Wherever there is dance, there is teaching or passing down traditions and movement ideas. When one looks at the global history of dance, of which there is no single definitive source, those who were dancing were learning to dance within a multitude of settings, each one embodying different characteristics that were appropriate to the setting. Dance education became a recognized term when dance entered formal academic settings, be they elementary, secondary, or tertiary. In this sense, dance education as a term is entirely from the Western world. Before this term was imposed, dance education existed; however, it was never named.

Non-formal Settings

In Chapter 2, the history of dance education was discussed within formal (or graded) settings. Formal settings will be discussed more thoroughly in Chapter 6. However, long before dance entered formal educational institutions, dance existed within many formal non-educational institutions, or non-formal, as this definition will be used. These settings will be discussed more thoroughly in Chapter 7. Dance in non-formal settings is typically a school or program that trains in a specific form, such as the Paris Opera Ballet School, the Martha Graham School, or a hālau hula.

Dance education was never a term used in these types of schools, which today have expanded to include every proprietary studio and training program in the United States and all over the world. The purpose of these programs has always been the actual training in specified forms of dance. Depending on the school, the goal could be professionalism, as in the case of the Paris Opera Ballet School, the Martha Graham School, and many others. Or it could be community and cultural exploration, as in a hālau hula. These are the locations where the terms "dance education" and "dance training" have become confused with one another, because these locations began long before the differentiation of those terms.

Dance in Formal Settings Scholarship: Organizations and Publications

As presented in Chapter 2, dance entered formal educational settings for many different reasons and through many different pathways. In order to establish itself as an academic discipline, dance needed scholarship, which led to the establishment of professional organizations and journals that both advocated for and supported dance as an academic discipline.[1] Alma Hawkins, mentioned in Chapter 2, emphasized research as an important component for dance as a fully-fledged discipline within the university.[2] Besides the contribution of scholarship, these organizations and publications contributed to the naming that is at the heart of this discussion. As this history is traced, it is important to note that, while there were developments all over the world, most of the detail presented here is in North America, reflecting the expertise of the author. Some of the history will include international organizations and some will include organizations that may have been founded in North America but have been replicated in other parts of the world.

At the beginning of dance in formal settings, the organization already in place for physical education, the American Alliance for Health and Physical Education and Recreation (AHPER), began to include dance in both its organization (National Section on Dancing, leading to Dance Division) and publication (*Journal of Health, Physical Education and Recreation*). *Impulse*, a journal devoted exclusively to dance, existed from 1950 to 1970.[3] Looking at the 20-year history of *Impulse*, it is clear that it includes dancers from the performance sector as well as academia, and there was no division of areas within academia, as the journal did not participate in naming or labeling. *Impulse* charts the development both of the increase in organizations in dance and the increase in publications following the cessation of its own publication.[4]

Before *Impulse*, when all dance scholarship, meetings, and discussions took place in one organization, the previously mentioned National Section on Dancing, there was a common place for all to discuss the new field of dance in academia, higher education. As it was totally inclusive, dance for children was also a topic. The critical element is that all who were involved in dance education in any formal setting, from elementary to secondary to tertiary education, were meeting and discussing together. There were disagreements, but discussions in the same place allowed for some common understandings to emerge.

A critical contribution from *Impulse* was the introduction to the development of new organizations in dance and a significant report on the Developmental Conference on Dance, held in 1967.[5] This unique gathering, organized by Alma Hawkins of UCLA, followed the Dance as Discipline Conference, organized by the Dance Division of AHPER, which was perhaps the last time that tertiary dance educators across the United States gathered to discuss the future of the discipline in higher education, the purpose of dance in higher education, and important elements within a curriculum in higher education. There are subsequent organizations in which those in higher education gather, but never with the magnitude of this significant gathering.

During a relatively similar time period to that of the *Impulse* publication (1956–1978), six national organizations devoted to dance within the United States were formed:

- American Dance Guild (ADG)
- Congress on Research in Dance (CORD)
- American Dance Therapy Association (ADTA)
- American College Dance Festival Association (ACDFA)
- Dance Critics Association
- Society of Dance History Scholars (SDHS).[6]

Now organizations were separated by focus. Organizations with dance education specifically as the focus are the National Dance Association (NDA), established first as a dance section in 1932 (within the long-standing AHPER, discussed above and in Chapter 2) and then as a separate organization (within AAHPERD); and, internationally, Dance and the Child

International (daCi; founded in 1978).⁷ The ADG initially began as an education organization, with its emphasis primarily on children's creative dance teachers, but it changed its focus over the years.⁸

Unlike the publication *Impulse*, these organizations put labels on different branches of the field of dance, and many had their own journals that emphasized those labels. All these dance organizations contributed to the establishment of standards for dance within educational institutions and the relatively new discipline in higher education. Therefore, they outlined the branches of dance within the collegiate context; however, the standards were established for each organization independently. Branch definitions created further tension between dance performance and the other focus areas represented in these organizations. Because these developments came on the heels of the explosion of modern dance in the United States, the aesthetic of modern dance became the primary dance subject in academia.⁹ Ending the robust growth period of the 1950s, 1960s, and 1970s, dance became a recognized discipline in higher education, supported by established standards for research and writing, and graduate degrees were subsequently developed to support this growth. The conceptual frameworks for "dance as movement" and "dance as art" developed separately, almost as if two individual disciplines were being created, rather than one.¹⁰ Janet Adshead argued that, as the theatrical purpose of dance is only a small part of the entire field, dance should not be looked at only from the theatrical perspective.¹¹

Impulse, as an annual publication, was never limited to one area of dance. It crossed over into nonacademic fields, with authors including some of the known dance artists and choreographers of its time. Throughout its twenty years of existence, the articles in *Impulse* kept to discussions of dance surrounding a core, rather than separated into branches. It also included dance in many settings, elementary, secondary, and tertiary, as well as within other disciplines and in the professional world. The argument presented here is that the core that was inherent in *Impulse* is called dance education (what Adshead called simply dance), and all these branches emanate from this core.¹²

Tension between Art and Education

Dance education during this period (1950s, 1960s, and 1970s), which was narrowly defined as teacher education and certification, developed into a second tier in higher education, as *dancing* (author emphasis for what became known as concert dance) took priority. During this time, dance remained affiliated with physical education in public education (elementary and secondary), and there was not yet discussion on realignment with arts. "Those who do, dance. Those who can't, teach" became the adage through this liberal/professional split that Thomas Hagood described.¹³ This adage exists in many disciplines even today and seems to cast a pall over the conscious choice to become a dance educator, as if it is the backup plan to the goal of a performance career. It has been present for many years in academia and documented through different types of studies.[14] Discussions ponder the source of this division. It is possibly because dance entered academia through physical education.[15] When creating the conservatory model, as Martha Hill did, this possibly relegated the teaching model to the sidelines, because it emphasized professional aspirations through a college dance degree.

With the creation of the new University of California campus at Irvine, active performers could find employment stability in higher education. However, this confused the nature of qualifications for academic positions. In traditional academic disciplines, the highest academic degree conferred became the criterion for academic employment. However, in dance, the highest performance accolades conferred became the criteria for academic employment, as emphasized in Irvine when Eugene Loring was appointed head of the new dance department. When higher education dance faculty included both those who entered through physical education and those who entered through the professional performance world, a clear hierarchy emerged, shifting education to a lower tier. Job descriptions today still allow for expertise as a performer and/or choreographer to be a substitute qualification for degree conferral for those who are heavily recruited in dance departments in colleges and universities.

Though formal scholarship and formal education are not requirements for teaching positions in the non-formal sector, as stated, the lines become blurred when those with prestigious performance backgrounds are qualified to be employed in the formal setting on the basis of that performance background. In higher education, a goal (of some) to ensure that dance is centered in the arts became conflated with the idea that the technically proficient dancer is necessary to achieve that goal. As this higher education model moved further and further away from the public elementary and secondary model, dance education became confused with dance training. Additionally, it shifted the public perception of the goal of the arts in formal schools to one of training and caused stakeholders to be concerned that artists were using schools for training and not for the full education that society considers when creating formal educational contexts in dance.

A range of issues concerning the emphasis and placement of concert dance in higher education have been recognized for some time. Noted scholar Joann Keali'inohomoku stated:

> In the past, and even to this day in the twenty-first century, the usual course concentrations in dance departments have been on concert dance forms derived from European classical ballet and the form ambiguously labeled "modern dance." The newly discovered wider world of dance is a revolutionary breakthrough, a bursting of the narrow ideas about

dance that have bound the minds and bodies of dancers from mainstream Europe and mainstream North America.[16]

Emphasizing the Need for Education

The term dance education, since dance has been included in academia, has been misused, misunderstood, and dismissed as dance has flourished in higher education. When discussed in contrast to all the other branches of dance in academia, dance education most often refers to physical training sometimes to the field of dance teacher education, and not the full definition promoted here. Equally limiting are the branches of dance themselves, as they tend to consider scholarship within a narrow range and focus only on the branch as stated. Recently, the former Society of Dance History Scholars and Congress on Research in Dance have combined to create the Dance Studies Association. This clarifying move broadens the outreach of scholarship, but it is still not entirely inclusive, though dance studies as a field attempts to create a comprehensive profile.[17] Dance studies is described as an overall categorization of all areas of dance scholarship that are in the academy (higher education), and this title was seemingly created to give these scholars an equal standing with other humanities-based academic disciplines. Making a case for dance studies as a discipline more than twenty years ago, Randy Martin argued that discipline formulation in the academy (higher education or tertiary education) is a response to social and political movements and also to the general discussion of what defines knowledge.[18] Not intentionally, this concentration of dance studies, as defined by Martin, excluded any actual dance education, further separating the field rather than broadening it.

Dance education resides at the periphery of this definition of dance studies, because it is both applied and has an important research component. Dance education is a definition used with all ages and in all settings. Dance studies resides only in higher education (tertiary education) and involves research. Dance education has its own scholarship, but this has been sparse.[19] So, dance education looks to the field of education for scholarship, turning its focus on scholarship away from dance studies. This creates and reinforces a narrow view of dance education within its multiple settings, as well as a separation of dance education and dance studies within the academy. As mentioned in Chapter 2, this narrow view of dance education also results in a lack of shared ideas and history across the various branches of dance within higher education.

One demonstration of the disconnection of information between dance in all its aspects is the scholarship concerning Rudolf von Laban and the history of dance in Germany leading up to the Second World War. Dance studies scholars question Laban's activities and moral grounding; dance education promotes Laban's ideas from its applied perspective, without acknowledging the historical research. Issues of the body and discussion about the body in dance are further areas of disconnect in all areas of dance scholarship. Jill Green passionately argues that, "only through an understanding of how we can explore categories and boundaries of dance scholarship without leaving behind any one particular field of study can we enrich the total literature on the body in dance."[20] The particulars of Laban and his theories are not presented here, as they are discussed in Chapter 2. He is included here as an example of disconnect between areas of dance scholarship.

It is clear that all areas of dance, in various contexts and including all iterations of the definition, will benefit from sharing scholarship, knowledge, and concepts, thus furthering the entire profession.

Purpose of Education

Historical Influences

When dance entered formal educational systems and professional performers became involved, dance lost sight of its initial educational purpose in this context, ignoring the fundamental ideas of Margaret H'Doubler.[21] Physical education began when medical doctors from Harvard University originally decided to bring exercise systems into schools for health reasons. Dance education grew out of physical education in schools and then became closely associated with the progressive educational movement. This aligns the original goals of dance education with those of progressive education—the education of the whole child (mind, body, and spirit) in order to be a member of a democratic society.

The legacy of formal public schools in the United States dates back to Thomas Jefferson, one of the authors of the Declaration of Independence, which is the founding document of the United States. In the ideas he expressed, both in the Declaration of Independence and in the school system he founded in Virginia in 1817, education was interwoven with ideas of democracy and was established for the public in order to ensure the continuation of that democracy.[22] Through all of its many changes over the ensuing 200 years, the goal of formal education has been "the humanizing of each new generation," rather than "socializing," "instructing," or "teaching."[23]

Over the decades, physical education within schools started to amalgamate with sport and competition, just as music education in schools began to amalgamate with performance. This is similar to what is now occurring in dance in formal educational systems. All these focus changes are moving away from the amateur model, which is how music and physical education, followed by dance education, first entered formal schooling. Randall Allsup refers to this as closed and open systems within music education.[24] A closed system is the master–apprentice model in which the education of the student is not central, but rather emphasis is placed on the emulation and replication of the master. The open system is one in which the possibilities and outcomes are open-ended, leading to multiple possibilities rather than one outcome. Allsup goes much further in his analysis and proposes that these closed systems come from forms, leading to the history of the form, which then leads to hierarchy. (In Allsup's example, the form is a music form. In this text, it is a dance form.) Allsup also addresses that this closed system or codified thinking is inclusive of all the elements that arts education adheres to in education, including assessment and certification. He concludes that music education, in a discussion of education, is losing its way because it is being directed by prescribed outcomes.

The progressive education movement, which was very prominent in the early to middle 1900s, led to a much more holistic concept of education, also providing an opportunity for dance as a discipline to exist in education. Both the First and Second World Wars brought shifts to educational goals in response to much more utilitarian needs. As stated in Chapter 2, those needs were more immediate in Europe (owing to the physical proximity of the conflicts) than in the United States.

The Cold War (following the Second World War) created a scientific focus in education through the ideas of competition in different arenas, such as military and space exploration. During the Cold War there were individual advances on social fronts, including the desegregation milestone in the United States and the purported egalitarian focus within the Soviet bloc.[25] However, it also became clear that there were constant shifts between utilitarian outcomes and holistic outcomes of education over many years. Specifically, these can be seen as shifts from education for particular utilitarian outcomes such as skills training to education for the holistic and complete development of the student. These shifts in educational outcomes are still seen today in contemporary education.

Public education started without the skill outcome as its primary purpose. The next major influence was the progressive education movement, and that movement has returned many times over the years, as other movements have gained prominence and then faded. With the social upheavals of the 1960s, progressivism returned to education but became infused with critical pedagogy and social justice, leading it in a much more radical direction. Elements of all these shifts in focus are evident today in education.

There were differences between how progressivism was seen in Europe and in the United States. "The American approach was founded on a totally different philosophy which rejected the correspondence theory of truth and belief in a fixed external world: it was, moreover, first propagated by university professors and then taken up by teachers and their professional associations in the public schools. Its aim was the radical transformation of society."[26]

"Education for the masses," or public education, has gone through cycles of purpose, depending on the prevailing consciousness of the time. Any discipline within education responds accordingly. This has also resulted in different trends. Public education originally began for the purposes of democracy and engagement with the citizens. An extension of this becomes education for freedom, and this concept is emphasized over education for practical outcomes. The concept of democracy is "more than a way of government" and is actually a "way of life," leading to discussions of socialization and release from oppression, as well as critical thinking so that people can participate in the construction of democratic life.[27]

Philosophical Influences

Allsup's discussion of the value of arts education and many other discussions return to educational philosophy when debating the aspirations of education, and arts education in particular. As stated earlier, the work of John Dewey has been inspirational and directional in creating the space for dance education to enter formal education. Dewey's influence definitely traveled to England and, to an extent, to China, so it can be said that he influenced educational philosophy in a global arena. Following Dewey's seminal work, Maxine Greene made clear statements on the need for arts in the full development of the person, that one needs "wide-awakeness" in order to attend to the world.[28] By "wide-awakeness," Greene was referring to the ability to be present and be aware of all that is around one, both tangible and intangible.

Dewey's first philosophical contribution was rethinking pedagogy as

> the method of reflective thinking, with its five steps of problem, data collection, hypothesis, testing and confirmation, as an alternative to the five Herbartian steps of preparation, presentation, association, generalization and application. Whereas Herbart provided a method of instruction for the teacher, Dewey put forward a method whereby the teacher could help the child solve the kinds of real problems that life presents.[29]

Dewey's reconception of pedagogy led to his philosophy of child-centered teaching.[30] The concept of reflection was widely used by H'Doubler when she began dance courses at the University of Wisconsin.[31]

Dewey's movement away from Herbartianism can be thought of as the movement of educational philosophy away from the scientific method to a more human, post-positive approach to educating the whole child.[32] This continued through the twentieth century in different time frames according to the social structures of the times and the influences of world issues, especially the economic crash of 1929 and the two world wars. A more detailed study of these trends and changes can be found in the Bowen text referenced here.[33]

Another contribution from Dewey was the elimination of the dualisms that had existed in education such as bourgeois vs. common, mind vs. body, utilitarian vs. conceptual, positivism vs. post-positivism.[34] He wanted to view education as more human and holistic, and the various dualities became reductionistic. The removal of dualism also brought unity within education closer, leading to "equality, relevance and responsibility."[35] The move away from mind/body dualism is an important tenet of dance education. (Ironically, many other dualisms include those that confuse the definition of dance education.)

Dewey's most significant contribution to educational philosophy is the concept of the experience, which needs active engagement from the student and an interactive process, rather than passive acceptance of ideas or concepts on the part of the student. He developed the idea of the experience as the center of the educational event. The educational event should look ahead rather than be caught in history, though history is a foundation, and "this condition is satisfied only as the educator views teaching and learning as a continuous process of reconstruction of experience."[36] He described experience as a continuum, with not everything on the continuum being positive, so that educators should be aware of those experiences called "mis-educative."

Maxine Greene continued Dewey's ideas in the latter part of the twentieth century. She extended the discussion of experience into active engagement with ideas and concepts and developed this into aesthetic education, encouraging active engagement with works of art. She was clear to emphasize that aesthetic education is not to support learning in non-arts subjects, but rather to open awareness, sensitivity, and perception in the learner. Thinking of education as a holistic event, this awareness could be present in all learning, but has to be cultivated.

Beginning with the idea of the experience, the concepts, for Greene, develop into ideas of imagination. Greene's idea looped back to Dewey's concept that education should not live in the past, as a repetition of old knowledge, without somehow moving it to the future. Greene conceptualized imagination as a way to envision (or imagine) what is possible and where individuals and the world can be, or, as she wrote, "Imagination may be our primary means of forming an understanding of what goes on under the heading of 'reality'; imagination may be responsible for the very texture of our experience."[37] This concept clearly hearkens back to the idea of education and democracy as an active process to engage with and participate in democracy for freedom and with free will. As Greene's ideas are important in relation to the purpose of education, they return at the end of this book as continual grounding for developing concepts of dance education.

Dance in Education

Dance as Steps, Dance as Ideas

Some dance within non-formal settings has primarily been about skills acquisition alone and has become confused with a "dance education" process. However, the setting alone cannot define the dance or dance education that occurs. It is defined by the values. Dance in formal education was introduced with the holistic values expressed in Chapter 2, but shifts to skills acquisition have also been described. Throughout the shifts of educational focus described earlier, dance could never be "repurposed" for a war effort or for the scientific race. The general education outcome of a skill set that was the focus during times of war or times of scientific exploration also indirectly infused the outcomes of dance in formal education. In Chapter 7, arguments will be presented to state that the skill set that dance now seeks, within non-formal settings, is that of a "workforce." Dance in formal education has responded best when progressive ideas were prevalent and has suffered most when utilitarian ideas were strongest.

Dance in formal education has had internal conflicts since its very inception. First it was the conflict with physical education and how to simultaneously remain in alignment with physical education and establish its difference as an art form. This caused gradual shifts away from physical education. Then the conflict was dance as a discipline and the question of whether it should be a holistic education of mind, body, and spirit, or it should be focused on the creation of the professional performer. The conflict that originally moved dance away from physical education to alignment with the arts then became a conflict of professionalism versus amateurism. These conflicts have been resolved in an either/or fashion, rather than by inclusiveness. The conflict of qualifications to teach in higher education has also been in place since the beginning (from the mid-1900s) and is still very prominent today.

Dancer as Subject/Dancer as Object

From Eeva Anttila's perspective, instead of the dancer or student being thought of as an object, they should be thought of as the subject.[38] Many other perspectives come from this shift. This allows for student-centered pedagogy. It allows teachers to respect and know each student as a fully-fledged person and to assist students in valuing who they are.

Academically, Anttila emphasizes that this concept of dancer or student as subject is already present in research and academic presentations, but is more difficult to find in practice. One obstacle is that, as discussed earlier, strong dance research is found in the field of dance studies, which is neither related to nor relatable to dance educators as practitioners. Dance educators in academic positions should work to create practical suggestions on the basis of dance studies research.

Writing from a dance studies perspective, Randy Martin describes the subject/object binary as a political act and a continuation of control of ideas exercised by political entities or movements, perpetuating capitalism.[39] He relates this back to the hold modern dance has in tertiary education because it emphasizes the formalism and structure of the institution. Though he is referring to the earlier styles of modern dance, Martin also points to their appropriation of other cultures while they create a sense of "universalism" in their approach, so that the concept of subject/object becomes further mired in political and power struggles that are beneath the surface of current dance education.

Mind/Body Holism

Consideration of the dancer and dance student as more than objects has deep-seated roots in neuroscience and other forms of movement. This echoes the discussion of whether mind and body are connected or separate. The concept of separate entities dates back to the time of French philosopher René Descartes (1596–1650), who famously stated, "I think, therefore I am," leading to the concept that people operate with mind and body separated.[40] This has commonly been referred to as Cartesian dualism.

Physical educators began to argue against this dualism in the early part of the 1900s; consequently, this argument made a natural segue into dance education, which was supported by physical education at the same time, as discussed in Chapter 2.[41] As a follower of John Dewey's educational philosophies, "Wood believed in holism."[42] Because Thomas Wood, along with his physical education contemporaries in the early 1900s, made many statements about holistic education and education for the full development of the person, there was a direct influence on the development of dance education in the same holistic mold.

Antonio Damasio argued against mind/body dualism from a neuroscience perspective and has revisited this argument many times.[43] Damasio's argument came from outside the realm of movement education, making it important to physical educators, dance educators, and specifically somatic educators, who had been arguing in favor of the holistic person for some time. Now holism was argued for by scientists, philosophers, and movement educators, all reaching the same conclusions.

Physical activity philosopher Scott Kretchmar extended the original concepts of holism to be more complete than when originally advocated for in physical education in the early 1900s.[44] In doing so, he also extended the concept of the multiple intelligences (as a concept developed by Howard Gardner[45]) and spoke about holism as a web of interconnected intelligence, rather than multiple types. Kretchmar's definition of holism is that "we are free rather than constrained, creative rather than unimaginative, and unpredictable rather than patterned."[46] Kretchmar continues: "We do not educate for the life of the mind. We educate, train, and habituate for the life of the whole person."[47]

Hierarchy of Forms

Underlying some of these latter conflicts and infused with the overarching theme of expertise has been the naming of dance forms. Dance entered formal education first through physical education as folk dance. When formalized as a dance subject, the form natural dance was emphasized, but then modern dance became the priority as a response to the new forms of concert dance being created at the time. Initially, ballet was not considered appropriate for formal education because of its rigidity, whereas first natural dance and then the original modern dance ideas included free expression. Seeking the "right" form of dance to introduce resulted in a conscious decision to move away from the strict gymnastics systems originally found in physical education, which led to the original rejection of ballet. However, as ballet evolved, with the introduction of the Balanchine method in the United States, as well as the inclusion of professional modern dancers in the curriculum, ballet was reinstated in the curriculum. Right from the beginning of dance in higher education, there was territorial conflict between the emerging modern dance forms (such as Graham's and Humphrey's) and Margaret H'Doubler's ideas of movement expression. In addition, H'Doubler was not choosing forms she liked, but taking a much more pragmatic view of what would be acceptable to her physical education colleagues in order to have her first curriculum accepted.[48] Though H'Doubler objected to the inclusion of formal types of dance (discussed in Chapter 2), dance in formal education created its first point of conflict with this hierarchy of forms, including the hierarchy of professionalism.

Beginning with the 1930s and the creation of more departments of dance, ballet and modern dance, representing current standards of professionalism in the United States, became the curriculum model. Creative dance was immediately (and perhaps forever) relegated to the second tier. The forms that mostly remained in physical education and in community settings, such as folk dance, ballroom dance, and tap dance, were also relegated to a tier below ballet and modern dance. According to Keali'inohomoku, "folk dancing seemed to confirm elitist ideas that polarized art dance, thought to be superior, with 'traditional' forms."[49] Non-Western and non-concert dance forms, not yet introduced into the West, were relegated to an even lower place and were not included in the Western curriculum until much later, when both integration of student populations and the multicultural focus of student populations became concepts. But folk dance seemed to have a slightly higher place in the hierarchy owing to its European lineage, compared with non-European traditions.[50]

When non-Western forms were finally included (somewhat) in Western formal education, they were often placed in a noncentral position. Though present, they were not primary, whereas ballet and modern dance formed the core of the curriculum. There have been minor attempts at a neutral relationship between dance forms, most notably the creation of the world cultures curriculum in dance at the University of California Los Angeles. In some other instances, such as at Dennison University, African dance is offered in a comparable, parallel form to modern dance.[51] Though a large number of university dance departments in the United States have a statement about diversity, the actual curriculum leaves non-Western dance forms on the periphery.[52] Some of this standardization of dance forms, based on ballet, can be traced to dance competitions, where the focus and judging criteria are based on the clarity of ballet lines. Even in this arena, when forms other than ballet are introduced, ballet standards are applied to those forms, maintaining ballet at the pinnacle of the hierarchy.[53]

Ballet reached this point in the dance consciousness as a consequence of colonialism. While those who promote ballet are no longer the colonializers, the concept that ballet is the pinnacle of technique continues. This is not meant to denigrate the beauty of the art form, but only to view it from a fresh perspective and see that, like any art form, there are blind spots. The vestiges of colonialism, in the United States, have settled into systemic racism, and this is difficult to separate and view from a clear perspective. Brenda Dixon Gottschild brings this into clear focus:

> The issue at hand in our field is not yet perceived among many white faculty as what it is: cultural and systemic racism that is responsible for a growing chasm separating dance programs, particularly graduate programs, from individuals emerging from and/or working with underserved dancers and communities of color. Their spheres of interest and they, themselves, are rejected when they apply for advanced degree programs, while doctorate-granting dance departments are moving away from the populist perspective that sees dance as a measure of society (and potential arena for social justice) and toward the elitism of dance as a measure of theory. This is a contested narrative, frequently with Diasporan (black) dance scholars/students on one side, and white dance scholars/professors on the other.[54]

Ballet remains a staple in many dance programs in higher education, and yet it continues to struggle with inclusivity, diversity, and featuring dancers of color. While modern dance offers more of an opportunity for student voice and personal expression, young artists of color still struggle to see themselves and their experiences reflected in a curriculum and faculty that believe that ballet and modern are the foundations of dance. This hierarchy of forms also returns to the conflict that H'Doubler felt from the beginning, that she did not want to name schools of modern dance that were just beginning at the time. Her initial focus in creating a dance curriculum was to learn about oneself, rather than to learn forms or systems of dancing.[55]

No dance form is better than another, just as no setting for dance is better than another. To conceptualize dance as consisting of Western concert forms, in preparation for the concert stage, narrows the possibilities for the art form to develop the person. This restricting perspective is the result of long-term evolution from the either/or that has been discussed in the history of the development of dance in formal education. Rather than either/or (either physical education or dance, either one form or another), dance offers the possibility for inclusion, acceptability, and openness that is available to people all over the world.

Summary Leading to Definition

Once dance entered formal education, the term "dance education" was commonly used. However, the definition was ambiguous and subject to change according to the setting, and the term was applied without regard for its meaning. This does not imply that dance education began only with formal dance education. Subsequent chapters of this text will explore how dance education exists in all settings and has existed for longer than the definition. Naming, however, necessitates definitions. Definitions have surfaced through different sectors as the need arises, leading to the confusion discussed in this chapter. Some of that confusion has occurred through considering some either/or possibilities, rather than a holistic approach, which will be proposed here.

Education is a right all citizens should be able to embrace to their full capacity and with full participation. A progressive education structure with student-centered learning, as envisioned by John Dewey and modeled by Margaret H'Doubler in dance, places dance education at the center of a fully realized education. Dance education is inherently a student-centered process that engages the student in a holistic and integrated mind and body process, offering the student a full range of expressive capabilities.

The creation of educative and engaging experiences necessitates complete engagement with "wide-awakeness," an opportunity to be aware, broaden one's scope, and fully engage with the world. Dance education, as an opening process, affords a platform for students to explore their imagination about a world and life to be lived to the fullest potential, regardless of specifics. Dance education is "For the development of the whole child—one who is fully expressive, who encounters and understands the world in many ways, and who integrates those experiences into shared meaning."[56] Dance education is the holistic, integrated process of a progressive, student-centered education, with the engaged body and mind central to the process. The student learner is engaged with self, others, and the world around them in order to encounter and understand self, others, and the world around them.

4

Pedagogy and Philosophy of Pedagogy

Introduction and Definition

Application of pedagogical theory is one defining factor when differentiating dance education from dance training in Western contexts. At its core, dance education employs conscious pedagogical ideas supported by complex learning theories to provide a complete education. Conversely, dance training focuses on the *steps*, with replication of those steps as the driving emphasis. Yes, there is pedagogy in all teaching and learning practices, but the focus is where the definition resides, that being focus on the person or on the content. It is important to note that both dance education and pedagogical theory as presented in this volume are Western concepts, so they can only be examined here in the context of Western ideas. Later in this volume, dance education as not defined from a Western perspective will be considered. Chapter 3 began to introduce some pedagogical theories that directly influenced the definition of dance education.

Pedagogy is the series of actions that allow learners to acquire, engage with, and contextualize knowledge. Even as this chapter explores the Western concepts of pedagogy, it is important to think of these series of actions as integrated with the context and particulars of the students in a specific setting, as well as holistic acquisition, engagement, and contextualization of the knowledge acquired. Pegge Vissicaro has said, "learning involves a reciprocal exchange of information, which requires negotiation of meaning. This suggests that we develop our personal world view and cultural knowledge system through the activity of learning."[1] According to Edward Warburton, "instruction itself" is "socially constructed."[2] Though this presentation is focused on Western concepts of pedagogy, ultimately pedagogy and learning are culturally situated and involve the transmission of culture.

Pedagogy is the type of teaching that intends to influence learning. Sometimes this relationship is called the teaching and learning relationship. The types of actions that are used for teaching are based on theories, rather than on random ideas. These actions can be as varied as "direct, general, explicit, implicit, verbal, nonverbal, didactic, collaborative" and others, including dialectic.[3] Pedagogy only becomes a series of actions when these theories are put into practice, guiding the interactions between student and teacher. Without conscious actions, there is no conscious pedagogy, and then "teaching" becomes "giving knowledge," which truncates the learner's ability to grow. This chapter will begin with a survey of pedagogical theories that include critical pedagogy, specifically ideas that were promoted by Paulo Freire, and those who have continued to develop his ideas.[4] Some theories will specifically relate to the pedagogy of movement, which has not always been applied to dance. However, from a dance philosopher's perspective, "the pedagogical base of modern dance technique has not been critically examined in all of its eighty-odd years," and so it is important to begin that examination here.[5]

In any discipline, there is pedagogical knowledge and content or discipline knowledge.[6] In dance, the content knowledge is either the technique, form, or movement material that is being taught, all culturally situated. What is frequently exercised in dance training is the emphasis on content knowledge alone, without any conscious attention paid to pedagogical knowledge, though, within certain settings, there is the "problematic assumption that content knowledge can then be transformed into pedagogical knowledge."[7] Switching attention to pedagogical knowledge means first knowing the students and choosing the pedagogical approaches that are appropriate to the students, the setting, and the content. These variables (students, setting, and content) must be integrated into the choices made.

History of Pedagogical Theories

Pedagogy as such is not completely separate from formal education, nor is its history. Throughout this discussion, many concepts examined in the history of education will reoccur. Pedagogy was initially developed in the field of educational psychology. Its philosophical groundings are in the sub-discipline that combines the disciplines of education and psychology. This is critical, as psychology is about humans' inner workings, and the various pedagogical practices are ultimately dependent on the students. Learning is measured by changes in the knowledge of the student, which resides in psychology, but can only be measured by representative product. Therefore, learning is only an inference.

The overarching construct that has strongly influenced pedagogy is the concept of post-positivism. The concept of positivist empiricism influenced the scientific method with its search for objectivity, control, and replicability. All new disciplines developed along this model, but, as education, psychology, and other social sciences developed, it became clear that a new perspective was needed. Evolving from positivism over a long period of time, this new perspective (around the 1960s) came to be called post-positivism, and some of its subcategories are constructivism, structuralism, and critical theory. Though the focus of this discussion of the evolution from positivism to post-positivism is mostly on formal research, the theories apply to the entire social science spectrum because the post-positivism perspective acknowledges that people cannot be looked at exclusively from an objective stance. Post-positivism also challenged power structures, forcing a re-evaluation of educational movements that had already been long accepted.

The progressive education movement introduced a large pedagogical shift, changing from the focus on content to focus on the student or child. This was discussed earlier but, in summary, the focus shifted from teacher-centered to student-centered pedagogy. Central to this concept is that the student is not a passive receptacle of knowledge, but an active participant; therefore, the student engages in active, lived experiences of which learning and knowledge are the products. Within progressivism, the theory continues; without the active experience, there is no pedagogy.

Western pedagogical theories can be organized as classical (Plato, behaviorism), problem solving (Dewey), biological (Piaget), social (Dewey, Vygotsky), and structural (Bruner).[8] Classical forms suggest that the learning is passive and that the student is the recipient intended to be molded. In some arenas, this is still called didactics or the didactical method. At its root, it is teacher-centered and is defined as the teacher holding the knowledge and delivering it to the passive or inactive student. In contrast to didactics is the dialectical method, which originated with both Plato and Socrates. It is sometimes called the Socratic method and involves a dialogue between two or more people with two or more positions. There is, then, a reasoned discussion between these points of view. Another way to contrast dialectical and didactic is to say that the "dialectical method is the only way to avoid the substitution of verbal memory for intellectual habit. It always puts questions before answers."[9]

The molding of behaviorism is well known through the work of Pavlov, then Thorndike, and finally Skinner. Behaviorism posits that behaviors are shaped by external stimuli. This concept is applied to learning. For example, if a student is presented with an idea that is associated with a reward, the learner will absorb the idea because the student craves the reward, which is the stimulus. These concepts reside in the positivist perspective that can measure and predict human behavior.[10] Mortimer Adler would say that didactics are a form of behaviorism.[11]

Piaget developed his theories from a biological point of view and suggested that people construct knowledge, leading to the theory of constructionism.

He was also involved in the moral development of the child, and, in some ways, this was a continuation of the work of Montessori and Vygotsky.[12] However, critics of Piaget argue that he did not consider the social aspects of pedagogy.

Problem solving in a social setting is what led to the Deweyan concept of experience. Vygotsky developed the concept that this engagement needs to have a zone of proximal development (ZPD) in which learning takes place through social engagement between the student and the more knowledgeable other (MKO). Bruner contributed theories on the structural concept of a curriculum that led to the spiral curriculum, which is the structure of a discipline building upon itself in an increasingly systematic and complex manner, as appropriate for the student population.[13]

Critical theory began in response to the turbulence of the 1960s. In educational and pedagogical theory, this was expressed most clearly through the work of Paulo Freire.[14] In the overall sense, critical theory represents the growth or continuation of progressivism, in response to social problems that are seen largely in Westernized societies.[15] Marxism had a strong influence on these theories as there is a lot of discussion of class divisions which created disenfranchised groups of students. In Freire's theory, articulated by the title of his seminal book *Pedagogy of the Oppressed*, he hypothesizes that disenfranchised populations are oppressed through pedagogy, specifically by the "banking system," where students are made to "bank" or remember and recall the information deemed important by the powerful elite. This is another version of the passive reception of knowledge that progressivism aimed to end. Whereas progressivism was a discussion against this type of teacher-centered education, Freire's theory goes further, examining this approach as a power and control mechanism exerted by a stronger population over a weaker population.

Another perspective emerging from critical theory includes feminist theory, which entered dance through the work of Sherry Shapiro, Susan Stinson, and Isabel Marques.[16] Most importantly, feminist theory moves away from a dichotomy of traditional education vs. progressive education and advocates for a further embracing of the student's voice, more than is present in the Deweyan perspective. If the student is encouraged to invent an "ideal" world through the creative process, is the student really reflecting lived experience? There are many more concepts in pedagogy that are not mentioned here, specifically from underrepresented groups and voices. This brief overview has been presented to demonstrate that there are relationships between many theories, but theories are only as good as their enactment. The teacher should have a developed philosophy and not choose strategies abstractly. From a teaching perspective, the theoretical grounding needs to be congruent with the students, the setting, and the purpose of education within that setting. Furthermore, pedagogy needs to remain flexible and change with changing times; otherwise, it is simply perpetuating a static and isolated view of the world, rather than reflecting reality. Returning to

Dewey, in summarizing the application of progressive education, he stated that, "the mere instructor ceases and the vital teacher begins at the point where communicated matter stimulates into fuller and more significant life that which has entered by the strait and narrow gate of sense perception and motor activity."[17]

Play

Drawing on many pedagogical theories is the notion of play, which arises mostly with developmental psychologists. Play was also important to physical educators Thomas Wood and Luther Gulick, mentioned in Chapter 2. Their approach was never recognized in an educational context broader than physical education, because the concept of play arose through physical education, and general educators had a narrow definition of playground games. However, notions of play are clearly applicable to dance education and are present in dance education, even if not named "play."

The developmental psychologists who researched and promoted play included Lev Vygotsky, Jean Piaget, Jerome Bruner, and Erik Erikson. They and many others encouraged the incorporation of play into all education because it encompasses values that are not present otherwise.[18] Play has a defined role in creativity, thus making it an important aspect of dance education pedagogy.[19] Dewey also considered play in the pedagogy of the creative process saying that: "art originated in play."[20] Play also involves basic socialization and carries cultural values. These are important elements of formal education that exist beyond specific disciplines. Play creates the ZPD and, through imagination, creates abstract thought.[21] As a form of instruction, play also contributes to the development of the child.[22] Play provides the type of "liberating pedagogy" that allows students to experiment, which was a pedagogical value promoted by Piaget.[23] Sometimes these are called "soft skills," leading to their lack of value in formal educational settings.[24]

A critical component of play which is inclusive of educational value is that play is a voluntary activity.[25] So, it will certainly be employed differently in a pedagogical context. Another important element of play is that versions exist in many cultures across the world. There is no single definition of play, just as there is no culture of "ownership." Within each culture, play takes a different form. The anthropologist Eleanor Leacock stated: "What we call children's play is in great part the consciously patterned ways in which children relate to, and experiment with, their social and physical environment and their own abilities." Leacock continues: "theorists of progressive education have continually stressed that free and 'playful' manipulation of their environment is important for children's learning."[26] In this statement, Leacock connects play back to the pedagogy promoted by Dewey.

Applications of Pedagogy for Movement Instruction

All of the pedagogical theories discussed earlier can be applied to any content, but there are specific applications created just for movement. These can be applied in tandem with any of the above theories and are more about the manner in which movement, specifically, is instructed.

Spectrum of Teaching Styles

Most movement education does not have theoreticians working with pedagogical ideas. However, a commonly known scheme was developed specifically for physical education by Muska Mosston. The Spectrum of Teaching Styles defines pedagogy of movement in terms of decisions made by both the teacher and student and how those decisions interact.[27] This spectrum is both useful and thorough because it encompasses many of the theoretical constructs of basic pedagogy, as discussed earlier, and applies them to the specifics of creating teaching situations for movement.

A critical element of the Spectrum of Teaching Styles is that it offers a range from direct instruction to indirect instruction. This means that the purpose of the instruction can range from directing "learners to reproduce the specific skills or information presented by the teacher" to "dealing with higher level cognitive functioning" which is supported by the "indirect (heuristic) instruction."[28] The effective teacher knows how to use the entire range when responding to student needs.

Motor Learning

Commonly called motor skills, movement skills teaching has its own way of discussing learning, based on motor learning. Motor learning is a psychological and physiological process by which motor (movement) skills are learned. The actual skill demonstration reflects the learning, which cannot be directly measured. In other words, the skill demonstration is called performance, and the learning is inferred from the performance.[29] Though this is not specifically a pedagogical theory, it is important to consider when applying pedagogies to the teaching of movement.

When performance demonstrates learning, the use of the word "performance" does not necessarily mean on the performance stage. It refers to the actual execution of the skill, regardless of the setting. A common issue in motor learning is that a skill or series of skills executed or performed well in a studio will not necessarily be executed well in a different setting, such as the stage. This is known as transfer. When performance is not consistent from one setting to another, this can be based on lack of transfer. It can also be based on psychological interference of the performer. Psychological interference can manifest as lack of self-esteem, stage or performance anxiety, and internalizing negative thoughts. This returns the discussion of movement learning to the human qualities that are present in all learning and links this discussion to pedagogical theories that recognize the human component in learning.

The developmental stage of the learner is a vital component in learning. When discussing motor learning, motor development is critical. In all learning, the age and developmental stage of the learner will shape the capacity of the learner and, in motor development, the capacity of the movement. Clearly, all students of all ages should not be taught the same, be it a movement activity or any other type of subject. Developmentally, students also differ in range of ability, categorized through the spectrum of disabilities.

Teacher Feedback as a Pedagogy Component

Feedback is an important element of motor learning, as well as all other teaching and learning settings. Feedback can come from the teacher or a variety of other sources, including the student's own senses (specific to movement), video or recordings of any type of student presentation, and other students. The widest variety of teacher feedback is available for movement learning. The types, timing, frequency, and scope of feedback are dependent on the theoretical perspective of the teaching. Ultimately, feedback is one of the applied elements of any given theory.

Types of teacher feedback used within dance are:

- Verbal
- Written
- Demonstrative (nonverbal)
- Tactile (nonverbal).

Feedback can also be supportive, punitive, or corrective. Feedback is most effective when it can lead to perceived change, meaning that feedback is also most effective when it occurs more than once during the learning experience.

Verbal feedback is present in all disciplines and can be as simple as a response such as "good" or "nice," or as complicated as an entire description of what the student has accomplished or not accomplished. Figurative language, metaphor, and imagery are important aspects of feedback. Written feedback can be in the form of a grade or a longer response to any written or other activity. Any feedback, including written or verbal, is least effective when offered only at the end of a course, because there is no way to measure its impact on change, which is how learning is measured.

Demonstrative feedback occurs when the instructor demonstrates a movement or asks a student to demonstrate an aspect of a movement. It may or may not be accompanied by a verbal explanation. Tactile feedback occurs when an instructor guides or touches the part of the body that needs attention during the performance of a skill. The teacher can also verbally direct the student to apply tactile feedback to him- or herself or to a partner.

For all types of teacher feedback, students' capabilities are important to consider, including those of students with disabilities. The content of the type of feedback may need to be modified according to the individual student's disability. There are additional pedagogies specific for these populations that are beyond the scope of the discussion in this text.

Sensory Feedback

Feedback coming from the student's own senses can be auditory (what the student hears), visual (what the student sees), proprioceptive (what the student feels within the body), and tactile (also what the student feels, but in relationship to outside forces such as the floor and air). Though the teacher does not control the student's perception, instructions can prompt and encourage the student to gain sensitivity to this feedback so that the student can then respond to it. Within the larger discipline of dance is the field of somatics, which focuses on heightened sensitivity to the student's response to this type of feedback (internal or proprioceptive).

The movement explorations of Rudolf von Laban (mentioned in Chapter 2) are sometimes taught in the field of somatics. Within modern educational dance, Laban's work was developed into a movement analysis form. The differentiation between this analysis and what the teacher perceives is that accurate performance of these movement skills is assessed not by outward appearance but by the inner sensations of the mover. It can be used for analysis of one's own movement as well as movement of others; however, problems arise when Laban's movement analysis is considered universal and is universally applied. So, again, this is purely a Western construct and should be used only in that context.

The discussion of artistry—the concepts of the student's senses—rather than academic presentation of a skill is an area that is ill defined. Some will call it artistry; some will call it the *je ne sais quoi*, or that which cannot be articulated or known. In many disciplines there are assertions that artistry cannot be taught. However, what can be taught is sensitivity to internal feedback so that the student can heighten the artistic expression with which he or she performs.

In summary, feedback is not the actual instruction per se, but the supplementary material that encourages the student to reengage with the original content at a deeper level. Instruction is not necessarily a comment on performance, but feedback is always in response to some performance.[30] However, without any feedback, no pedagogy has actually been implemented. The result is a presentation of the movement, rather than pedagogy.

Application Summary

The entire field of motor learning, physical education pedagogy, and all that this research has to offer dance education are not frequently discussed by dance educators. This is one of the drawbacks of the separation of dance from physical education, which was discussed in Chapter 2. Much of the separation came about because the discipline of dance wanted to celebrate and focus on its artistry and not be identified as an aspect of physical education. The irony is that some of the very elements of motor learning that could help enhance and develop artistry were also separated from dance within formal education. The holistic development of the dancer through dance education needs to be inclusive of all the knowledge of the human body, internal and external, in combination with all the theories of teaching, movement, and ideas, all applied in a reflective and sensitive fashion. Only then is true pedagogy practiced, leading to the full growth and development of the student. This can apply to students from all backgrounds and of all capabilities.

According to Sheets-Johnstone, from a philosophical perspective relating to dance, it is queried whether, rather than learning "to master certain rhythmic or special coordinations, should the major focus be on learning to move oneself?"[31] This also reflects the discussion in Chapter 3 of the definition of dance education. Though discussions of history, definition, and pedagogy are presented in separate chapters, they are all aspects of a larger discussion that will continue throughout this book: the discussion of dance education. The discipline of dance education is itself a holistic concept and will be woven in layers and continually developed through this book.

Culturally Responsive Pedagogy

"Because no pedagogy is neutral or culture-free it is important for teachers to reflect on whose assumptions are operating in relation learning, what counts as legitimate knowledge, and ways of organising classroom communication."[32]

Culturally responsive pedagogy is a concept that originated in the United States, specifically responding to the failure to adequately address the needs of African American and Latinx students in schools. Once it became known, it spread first to other marginalized populations in the United States and then took hold around the world in marginalized populations, who are mostly indigenous. In all settings in which students' needs are addressed through culturally responsive pedagogy, the process is complicated by past concepts of colonialization that in many cases must also be addressed. Past colonialization is responsible for stripping identity from marginalized populations.[33]

Culturally responsive teaching or pedagogy is a concept that has been discussed in general education for some time but is only recently being discussed in dance education.[34] Zaretta Hammond defines culturally responsive teaching in general as "The process of using familiar cultural information and processes to scaffold learning. Emphasizes communal orientation. Focuses on relationships, cognitive scaffolding, and critical social awareness."[35] There is no script or clear directions for this practice, but Hammond illuminates a pathway by articulating "The Four Practice Areas of Culturally Responsive Teaching":

- Awareness: to develop awareness of the differences among our students and that some differences come with socio-political power.
- Learning Partnerships: "building trust with our students across differences."
- Information Processing: helping "students process what they are learning."
- Community Building: "creating an environment that feels socially and intellectually safe."[36]

Without discussing dance, alternative forms of pedagogy were originally conceptualized in order to respond to dominant and suppressive ideologies within pedagogy. For example, critical pedagogy, based on critical theory, moved in this direction long before dance considered these concepts. These theories were generally influenced by Marxism and focused on challenging power structures, content, and methods. The more current approach to this is culturally responsive pedagogy.

The pedagogical discussion thus far has been based on a Western construct of movement-skill acquisition and performance. Though not specifically discussing dance only for the concert stage, most dance education in the West is centered on forms that are based on performance in a concert setting. There are many dance forms all over the world that are never intended for a performance setting. As there is not a single purpose or perspective of dance (as discussed in Chapter 1), there cannot be a single type of pedagogy. A variety of pedagogical theories and approaches have already been discussed, and yet the discussion does not explore a non-Western paradigm. In addition, in this globalized world, students from many different backgrounds can be together in the same teaching and learning situation. This was mentioned earlier in this chapter in the context of individualizing instruction according to theories, but sensitivity and awareness of students who may have been exposed to non-Western pedagogies and are integrated into learning situations with students who have experienced Western pedagogies must also be included. According to Vissicaro, "learning involves a reciprocal exchange of information, which requires negotiation of meaning."[37]

The pedagogy that is most prominent in non-European dance forms involves imitation and repetition.[38] With these pedagogical forms there is no verbal instruction and no articulated breakdown of movement components, just the practice of imitating those who are more experienced. Though this practice was developed long before the theory, it can be considered a version of Vygotsky's ZPD in which the MKO guides the learning.

What happens to a non-European dance form when taught in a European context? The traditional European dance teaching context has mirrors in a specialized studio used expressly for dance. A non-European dance form may have been practiced and learned in many different contexts. Perspective, intent, and focus are compromised when a non-European form is taught using a European pedagogical perspective. The expectations of the students are also Westernized with this perspective. However, "how students are taught is culturally formed," and so the pedagogical methods need to be culturally contextualized and not independent from the dance.[39] All pedagogy is "culturally situated."[40] The aspects of dance that are still considered in the domain of physical education (as discussed in Chapter 2) are sometimes better situated to be taught outside of the dance studio and can be explored through culturally responsive pedagogy.[41]

Culturally responsive pedagogy is critical because it shifts the focus away from dance forms (as in what dance content is being taught or discussed) and turns the focus toward the students. It is responsive to both form and students equally and a pedagogical direction chosen in advance. It is not new or different from pedagogies that have been discussed so far, but rather an acknowledgment of sensitivity that takes all the cultural markers into account, including the cultural markers of the students.

The innovation in this concept, culturally responsive pedagogy, is that it is specifically about pedagogy and not about dance content in general. In the past, there has been the inclusion of non-Western forms of dance, within the Western classroom, leading to multicultural dance education "that serve[s] to exoticize diverse students as 'other.'" But this is not truly culturally responsive teaching, which is "designed to problematize teaching and encourage teachers to ask about the nature of the student-teacher relationship, the curriculum, schooling, and society."[42] Multicultural education should not be confused with culturally responsive pedagogy, because multicultural education remains on the surface, as discussed in Chapter 1. Dance scholars, for some time, have been grappling with these very ideas when writing about dance in any form or approach. Isabel Marques theorized in this direction with the development of "context-based dance education" as a way to acknowledge the learner and where he or she is culturally situated.[43] As eloquently stated by Diedre Sklar:

> In summary, based on the premise that movement embodies cultural knowledge, I am advocating an approach that considers movement performance not just as visual spectacle but as kinesthetic, conceptual,

and emotional experience that depends upon cultural learning. Since we all inevitably embody our own very particular cultural perspectives, we must do more than look at movement when we write about dance.[44]

Sklar's ideas can be extrapolated to the concept of teaching dance, that it is not only about movement but about the entire cultural perspective of both the movement and the mover—in other words, valuing difference through dance. A succinct summary from Vissicaro:

> Just as we have multiple identities to which we can relate, there also are multiple ways to label and categorize dance. Depending on one's perspective, different identification tags may be used to help us organize and manage dance information. A danger in classifying dances is the possibility of situating our own value system in a position of power, leading to derogatory views toward other people's dances. It is also valuable to critically assess media representations which often encourage sweeping generalizations and stereotypes. In every case, the best formula is to study dance cultures around the world by using labels and categories that are context specific, creating equality for all dances, dancers, and dancing.[45]

Valuing Difference through Dance

This section will emphasize valuing difference through dance by returning to Jerome Bruner and his concepts of the culture of education. Bruner's theory is about general education but can be applied to dance education and help those grappling with these questions of education, culture, and culturally responsive education. Bruner claims that evolution led humans "to utilize the tools of culture,"[46] meaning that "learning and thinking are always *situated* in a cultural setting."[47] Continuing, intersubjectivity allows humans to negotiate between cultures, but "our Western pedagogical tradition hardly does justice to the importance of intersubjectivity in transmitting culture."[48] In other words, when engaging in a Western-framed pedagogy, culture is ignored. This occurs regardless of where learning takes place, creating a larger pedagogical sphere beyond formal schooling. Bruner ultimately emphasizes the learning process as an indispensable way to gain self-knowledge, which includes group and self-definitions as people.

The full variety of dance, values, settings, purposes, and possibilities are what define humans and differences. Dances are learned within a culture as a vehicle for continuing and engaging with cultural values and mores. Dances from diverse cultures are learned as a way to gain an inside perspective into the values and mores of those who developed the dance content, often when different versions of "otherness" are closed. The true value of dance as a way to honor or to value cultural diversity has yet to be fully realized, even as there are so many avenues to engaging with people around the world. Some items that have infringed upon this possibility are hierarchical categorizations, colonialism, appropriation, and simple lack of awareness. The sensitivity of pedagogical approaches discussed here can lead to the true value of dance as a way to honor cultural diversity. Bruner purposefully does not become involved in policies or directives, but rather takes the approach to value all people, see how those different from oneself value their own cultures, and emphasize the education and learning process as the location of how one defines oneself as a human, willing to thoughtfully engage with the world. This approach can expand the value of dance and human capabilities for nonverbal expression by taking steps back from particulars and looking at education in a holistic manner.

Summary

Pedagogy is therefore a complex interaction of educational theory, content, teacher, and student choices and resides in both the setting and particulars of the students. Particulars of students can include age, background, range of ability, and physical location. This results in a holistic event in which there can be no "recipe" for or guarantee of success, just the confidence and sensitivity of the teacher that occurs in real time as the events are unfolding. Movement pedagogy, encompassing dance education, includes the increased complexity that the learning is expressed through the body and is, therefore, subject to additional considerations. One of those considerations is the development of artistry, if the specific dance education values artistry as an outcome.

Non-Western contexts may not have named pedagogy as it exists in Western conversations but, in analysis, pedagogy does exist. Theories of pedagogy and analysis of pedagogy cannot be universally applied. Finally, most of these theories and concepts have been developed in Western contexts, even though some version of pedagogy exists in every possible context. Culturally responsive pedagogy was summarized to emphasize this focus. Multiculturalism was addressed in relationship to pedagogy and introduced in Chapter 1.

SECTION II

Dance in Educational and Life Settings

Introduction

The following chapters go into detail about three types of teaching/learning contexts (formal, non-formal, and informal), as defined by UNESCO. These will be approached using a variety of voices. Each chapter will begin with an academic discussion that defines all the particulars of these three teaching/learning contexts. In order to illuminate these types of contexts and make them relatable, there will be "closer looks," which will be written in the personal voice of someone who has either taught or learned in the context being discussed. These are presented as personal stories in order to make each context real.

The section begins with Chapter 5, which summarizes a research project that examines and clarifies the three UNESCO-defined types of education—formal, non-formal, and informal education—in dance education contexts. This is followed by three chapters that investigate, in depth, each of these three types of education, with a focus on dance.

Chapter 6, "Formal Dance Education," includes two closer looks, one from the perspective of someone in tertiary education and one from someone in secondary education. After Chapters 7 and 8 comes a whole chapter, Chapter 9, which takes a closer look at all three types of dance education—formal, non-formal, and informal—through the personal story of one dance educator, John-Mario Sevilla. His background includes experience learning in all three contexts, and so this powerful story is included because it also articulates how the delineations between formal, non-formal, and informal education are fluid. It also illuminates dance education in one life.

5

Global Dance Education

A Research Summary

Ann Kipling Brown

This qualitative study begins with a survey, followed by in-depth interviews which are analyzed and coded. The findings are contrasted and compared with official distinctions of dance learning, as defined by UNESCO and as exemplified through local standards, to ascertain whether dance teaching is consistent with students' comprehension of dance learning. This research is deepened with individual interviews, and these stories represent the conflict that has been imposed upon the participants by those who teach in formal settings, who have denigrated informal learning as inferior learning. Arguably, informal learning in dance is powerful for the individual's identity formation and becomes significant when considered in the context of life choices and direction.

Though identified as global, this research was authored from a Western perspective and included subjects from a wide network. This research is ongoing, with the outcome intended to broaden into unrepresented areas, especially Asia. One of the limitations of Asian participation was language, and so the researchers are investigating use of translation to aid accessibility. Illumination of informal learning in dance was an unexpected outcome, but one that the researchers intend to explore further as this research continues.

Introduction

Four researchers (Ann Kipling Brown, Canada; Susan Koff, United States; Jeff Meiners, Australia; Charlotte Svendler Nielsen, Denmark) came together through their interest in and dedication to dance education to seek answers to what is being learned when participants engage in dance activities in specialized learning contexts or personal settings, and what is significant to people who pursue dance as an interest or career. Each of the researchers came to focus on dance education because of their interest in teaching; for instance, Susan's interest was always teaching, but initially she only wanted to work with the gifted and talented. However, circumstances provided her with opportunities to work with children who expressed a joy that seemed to supersede everything else. She found herself interested in dance education only when her definition of who the student could be was broadened and became inclusive rather than exclusive. Ann, as a high school student and then a young student in a teacher education program, was introduced to Laban's theories of dance and movement and his beliefs that dance is for everyone. These studies and her own journey, where dance was a solace and means of expression, guided her to strive for a transformative and democratic dance education for students. Charlotte had been teaching gymnastics since she was fifteen. She loved teaching and, after immersing herself in modern dance, knew that her teaching career should be in dance so she could convey similar life-changing experiences to her own students. Jeff's interest in dance education stems from his childhood and adolescent experiences that led to his long-standing and current work as an educator concerned with social justice and with transforming schools through dance and the arts. He reflects that dance education was intrinsic to his changing personal and professional identities at different stages of his life—as a boy, as a man, and as a classroom teacher with primary-aged children, as a dance consultant in schools and pre-schools, and as a university lecturer with pre-service teachers.

Their commitment to the research reflects their strong interest and desire to communicate with others what is possible through dance, that dance is more than learning a set of steps, and that dance can provide life-changing and continuous enjoyment, meaning, and well-being for many. The researchers identify that recognition should be given to the involvement of children, young people, and teachers in dance from a variety of cultural perspectives in order to understand the depth of those embodied experiences, promoting pedagogical changes and relevant curriculum initiatives and programs. Considerations echo the writings of Anu Soot and Ele Viskus that outlined how the relationship between teacher and learner changed to be a relationship that recognizes and supports the unique characteristics of each learner, creating a dialogue between the teacher and learner to think physically and to develop skills in dancing, dance-making, and appreciation of dance as an art form.[1]

This collaborative research endeavor is located within the discipline of dance education which has emerged over past decades. The researchers' interest was often a consequence of earlier involvements in dance, various teaching and study experiences, and developing philosophies regarding curriculum and pedagogy. They were intrigued by the power of dance to support the development of young people's cognitive and affective domains of learning. They believed this research would provide a voice for those who have not been represented in dance literature and for those who have not had access to a meaningful dance experience, advocating in particular that dance should not sit on the periphery of education but should be a core subject, together with science, engineering, technology, and mathematics.

Conversations and planning for the project between the four researchers and dance colleagues began at the 2012 Dance and the Child International & World Dance Alliance (daCi/WDA) Summit in Taipei, followed by more in-depth conversations and planning in Finland at the 2012 World Alliance for Arts Education Global Summit: Cultural Encounters and Northern Reflections, and then in Germany at the 2013 World Summit on Arts Education, Polylogue 11. At those gatherings, the researchers were able to consult with educators from various dance contexts and from many countries. Concurrently, the researchers began preparing a structured and methodical investigation. Detailed findings of the research have been communicated in various publications and conference presentations (Appendix 1). This chapter brings together those findings and sets them in the context of the discipline of dance education.

Research Project

The design of the research project resulted in three phases. The aim of each phase of the research methodology was to develop knowledge and understanding of what dance education experiences are being offered to young people in formal, non-formal, and informal settings. Researchers also inquired how young people engage in dance and how these dance experiences contribute to their chosen lifestyles and careers. The articulation of what is learned through dance has been advocated by many dance and education theorists and practitioners as essential to understanding the holistic benefits of education in and through dance.[2] In particular, the research drew upon the work of Susanne Keuchel, which highlights UNESCO's definitions of "different fields of education."[3] Keuchel suggests that "'formal learning' is concerned with curriculum offerings within education and training institutions; 'non-formal' learning is acquired in addition or alternatively to formal learning; and, 'informal learning' is learning that occurs in daily life, in the family, in the workplace, in communities and through interests and activities of all individuals.'"[4] It was considered that drawing upon knowledge from life and dance experiences of participants would provide strong and effective information about what is relevant and meaningful for students and teachers in dance education.[5]

The three phases of the research were as follows: in Phase One, a Dance Learning in Motion survey questionnaire was sent to a network of dance educators from several countries; in Phase Two, Dance Learning in Motion qualitative focused interviews were carried out with selected respondents representing geographic diversity and different experiences in dance; and in Phase Three, an examination of dance curricula was undertaken to discover what dance experiences were being offered to young people and whether there were any similarities and differences in the context of the presented curricula.

Phase One: Dance Learning in Motion Survey Questionnaire

The survey questionnaire, accessed by an email link, was drafted and sent to leading dance educators in the researchers' network from the following countries: Finland, Ghana, United States, Denmark, Germany, Australia, Canada, the Netherlands, New Zealand, Taiwan, Brazil, and Hong Kong. These lead educators then distributed the survey questionnaire email to volunteers who were members of groups as tertiary university dance students, recent graduates, or teachers from various institutions. The introductory email explained that volunteers were sought to participate in a research study that aims to ascertain where and how young people engage with dance in various settings and how it is experienced. The email communication added that the researchers were aware that dance does not always have the data to support the importance of dance in education, recreation, or professional contexts, and that their response would help to both plan and advocate for dance. The researchers assured the participants of their anonymity and tabularized their responses by a number so that anonymity could be preserved.

The survey questionnaire involved fourteen questions (Table 5.1), which asked the respondents about their experiences in dance and the significance of dance in their lives and the lives of others. All responses were collated into one document and were reviewed by each researcher. First, the Likert scale responses and explanations regarding age, skill, and experience in dance were collated. Second, using Max van Manen's hermeneutic phenomenology, which recommends three stages—"a wholistic reading approach," "a selective reading approach," and, finally, "a detailed reading approach"—the researchers reviewed the detailed responses individually and then together.[6] In this second analysis themes were identified as being important characteristics of dance learning.

The first set of questions (Q. 1–6) asked the 176 respondents to provide information about themselves and their involvement in dance. The respondents included participants between 18 and 70 years of age, the majority of whom were full-time or part-time teachers of dance or university undergraduate or graduate students, some of whom had recently completed a university

TABLE 5.1 *Dance Learning in Motion Survey Questionnaire*

1. What is your age group?
2. What do you do? (student, teacher, etc.)
3. On a scale of 1–5, how do you rate your skills and knowledge of dance?
4. Dance is an important part of human experience (scale from agree to disagree)
5. Dance should be a part of all primary/elementary school students' learning experiences. Please explain your response in a few sentences.
6. Dance should be a curriculum option for all secondary/high school students. Please explain your response in a few sentences.
7. Why have you chosen that dance should be a part of your life?
8. Please tell us about any important dance experiences you've had.
9. What kinds of dance experiences do you recall at home?
10. What kinds of dance experiences, if any, do you recall during your time at elementary or high school?
11. What kinds of dance experiences, if any, do you recall outside school?
12. If you have ever taught dance in any capacity, please give details.
13. What can be learned through dance? (One sentence)
14. Please give your city and country.

degree. The remaining respondents were administrators, consultants, health practitioners, performers, or choreographers. All described their ability in dance as skilled and of high quality. It was positive that there was a wide variety of careers and how the respondents identified themselves, which proved invaluable to the researchers' investigations. The analysis revealed that participants had dance experience in formal, non-formal, and informal settings, including elementary and high schools, dance studios, university dance and dance education programs, community settings, homes, and other events. Many expressed how dance had been a very positive element in their lives. A mature respondent wrote:

> I am healthy, happy, physically and mentally aware of who I am, and all of this was discovered through my dance experiences. I have built confidence and ownership of my body and mind through the experiences I have had with dance (66).

The responses to the questions about the importance of dance in people's lives and the education of young people were overwhelmingly supportive of dance being available at all curricula levels of formal schooling. One participant explained:

> Dance develops the creative abilities of children, calling for the use of imagination and communication through a diverse vocabulary of movement. It allows the development of psychomotor ability, cognitive ability, and emotional and social capacity (84).

Further comments added to the significance of dance experiences, some explaining "Dance is art and we need art in our lives to know what it is to be human" (10), and that dance "promotes healthy living" (119). The majority also identified the maximum benefits of a dance education and agreed that dance should be part of primary/elementary school students' learning.

The next set of questions (Q. 7–14) invited the respondents to talk about their particular experiences in dance at home, at school, and outside of school, and any teaching experience. The questions focused on how important those experiences had been in their lives. A final question asked them what could be learned through dance. The analysis of these questions through the process of hermeneutic phenomenology revealed four themes about the characteristics of dance learning: embodiment, culture, holistic development, and communication, confirming that the respondents were passionate about dance and desired that all young people should have dance in their lives.

The theme of embodiment was identified with subthemes of kinesthetic awareness and mind-body connection revealed through such statements as "Dance is my way of being, it is my way of living as a person in this world" (63) and "It is good for my physical and emotional well-being" (36).

The theme of culture was identified with subthemes of connectivity, community, awareness of differences of others, identity, openness, and social skills through assertions that dance "is important to the development of the cultural sense, aesthetic sense and social sense of the child, adolescent or adult" (84) and "is a form of personal and cultural expression" (52).

The theme of holistic development was identified with personal (including sense of self, self-esteem, confidence, knowledge of feelings) and physical (including coordination and motor development) subthemes. One person wrote, "Dance is my way of being, it is my way of living as a person in this world" (63), echoing the sentiments of many respondents who wrote that dance changed their life, gave them a sense of freedom, and helped them to find their way in the world.

The final theme, communication, was defined with subthemes of creativity and expression. Several expressed the opinion that dance provides the opportunity to express oneself and provides "a form of expression for societal issues" (131). One respondent explained, "Through dance I can express myself from my deepest impulses and bring out who I am. I also feel deeply connected in my dance community and a sense of togetherness" (64).

The researchers consider that the survey questionnaire provided an initial step in ascertaining how people experience dance in formal, informal, and non-formal settings, and that the four themes with subthemes—embodiment, culture, holistic development, and communication—confirmed for the researchers the importance of dance education and its significance for the development of young students to help them do well aesthetically, academically, and socially. One respondent summarized the themes, saying, "Dance is an essential part of the human experience; is a means of socializing, communicating, expressing, exercising, developing coordination, enjoyment, teaching, learning, sharing, explaining, and emoting" (22). The respondents clearly revealed the power of dance in the informal, non-formal, and formal settings and the significance of dance in their lives. It is clear from the responses that dance is not offered as a curriculum subject in all schools at elementary and secondary levels. It is also evident that many people who dance in an informal context experience more than in other, more formal, settings, and that not all young people have access to specialized settings, such as dance studios. Studying dance could be the way to success where students engage in creative activities, collaborate with others, and problem solve ideas. Such creative practice teaches originality and various methods of thinking and communication, provokes imagination and possibilities, and is central to the arts/dance but also vital to our rapidly changing world and the skills required in the twenty-first century. Unequal access can have unequal consequences.

Phase Two: Dance Learning in Motion Interviews

The researchers recognized that the survey questionnaire provided some insight into dance learning. However, it was considered that more could be discovered through more in-depth, qualitative, focused interviews (Table 5.2) with selected respondents representing geographic diversity and different experiences in dance. Using the results from the survey questionnaire, three current dance educators (Cassandra, Berenice, and Markos) were invited to participate in in-depth interviews that were conducted and subsequently coded and analyzed in the same way as the survey questionnaire. The interview questions (Table 5.2) probed further into their dance experiences and asked about their recollection of first dance experiences in informal, non-formal, and formal settings. They were also asked to talk more about why they had chosen dance to be part of their life.

Cassandra and Berenice had their first experiences in dance studios, whereas Markos's first dance experiences were in community-based dance activities. When talking about initial influences, Cassandra described how she quickly became discouraged through lack of affirmation at the studio and home

TABLE 5.2 *Interview Questions*

1. Tell me about your first recollection of dance experiences?
2. Discuss the conflicts or disconnects that might have existed when you began formal dance, and how you reconciled these.
3. In the survey you gave a number to this statement: Dance is an important part of human experience, agree to disagree. Please now elaborate.
4. Why have you chosen that dance should be a part of your life?
5. Please tell us about any important dance experiences you've had.
6. What kinds of dance experiences do you recall at home?
7. What kinds of dance experiences, if any, do you recall during your time at elementary or high school?
8. What kinds of dance experiences, if any, do you recall outside school?
9. What can be learned through dance?

when she began dancing in a dance studio at the age of six. Later, in her teen years, she returned to dancing with a school friend and that inspired her to continue her studies in dance and dance education. In comparison, Berenice and Markos were actively encouraged by their parents to dance and began dancing at an early age. All three participants had studied dance and dance education at university level, and Berenice and Markos were studying at graduate level. They agreed that dance was an important part of the human experience, explaining that dance "is essential to everyone" (Berenice), "It's a great gift my family, my parents, gave to me, it's part of who I am, it's now part of my personality and who I am" (Markos), and "I look at it from a physical, emotional, energetic, spiritual aspect" (Cassandra). They cherished the experiences that dance had given them, "travelling to different places to dance and study" (Berenice), "using dance to facilitate different forms of empowerment in disadvantaged communities" (Markos), and "working at a school that has so many kids with different languages, or different traumas, I find that that's the universal language" (Cassandra).

In the analysis of the interviews, the themes of culture, holistic development, and communication were revealed. The theme of culture was identified with subthemes of identity, community, and awareness of the difference of others. Berenice explained, "I remember being also engaged and actively encouraged to dance because my parents are avid dancers . . . It was such a joy and such a great moment in just feeling close with my family and enjoying having that as an extra opportunity." Markos described missing his friends and that, "The reason why I miss them is not because

I don't see them anymore, but it's because I have memories about those moments that we had creating music and dance together."

The theme of holistic development was identified with subthemes of a sense of self, lack of confidence/having confidence, and self-esteem. They all agreed that dance could be a cathartic experience and could help to build confidence. Cassandra's comment reflected that dance can help that sense of self: "I do believe that dance is essential for everyone and just being inside that experience helped me to reflect on the many ways that it has made me a better person, a better human being just being connected to other dancers and not only in the romantic sense of it." Berenice identified the confidence that dance affords as "it has the ability to kind of pull down all the barriers and boundaries for us to venture out and interact with more experiences."

The final theme of communication was identified with the subtheme of expression. Cassandra believed: "It means speaking truthfully and being authentic and living a life that is passionate" and "it's a way of life; it's a form of so many different kinds of expression." Markos further explained:

I came from a culture where dance happens the way breathing in and out happens in daily life so it's not taken seriously as an academic subject or even a professional career. So within those contradictions and strictures, I was personally able to locate how dance can be essential to my personal life and the communities that I set out and aspired to serve.

The interviews also revealed a further theme, one of disconnect. Each of the respondents identified that there was a lack of continuity or a disconnect between informal and formal dance experiences, that in many cases formal learning contradicted informal learning. Markos described a disconnect: "learning dance in formal settings did not allow me to work closely and connect with others using dance as a space." He further clarified that this was, "Because we ended up working towards getting a good grade, or competing with each other to get a good mark and be rewarded through quantifiable grading and assessment." Many dancers express a disconnection when they join dancers from the mainstream dance forms, such as ballet, jazz, or modern. Berenice explained her previous experience was in folkloric dance, and that a disconnect emerged when she entered undergraduate studies and did "not perceive myself as a strong dancer in relationship to the techniques or styles that were present, were offered, in that setting." She believed, "It is actually a cultural thing because I have that feeling that you are not a dancer unless you can hold your leg up here, or you can do so many pirouettes, or you can do this and that or you can do those amazing tricks." Cassandra's early experiences in jazz dance led her to reflect that, while "watching some of my instructors in a jazz class and thinking something—what is the disconnect for myself and trying not to judge them. And really, when I look back, it was because it was outdated. I was doing the same routines, like outdated jazz, for seven years."

Findings of the Interviews

The findings of the interviews supported the themes and statements found in the survey questionnaire, providing more in-depth discussion of dance learning. In particular, the themes of culture, holistic development, and communication were clearly revealed. Even though the theme of embodiment was not as evident through the interviews, there were some references to the importance of kinesthetic awareness and mind-body connection. The final theme of disconnect that emerged from the interviews described situations that occurred for many respondents when experiencing dance in formal and non-formal settings, such as lack of recognition and respect for different dance forms and teaching contexts, out-of-date dance syllabi, focus on skill training, and no opportunities to create or communicate with others. Specifically, those informal learning experiences are supported by the work of Sherry Shapiro who initiated the debate on traditional practices in the dance class and encouraged educators to recognize that the lived experiences of the students are embedded in all that they do and thus are a reliable source of knowledge.[7] Those informal experiences, whether experienced privately or socially, inform the formal and non-formal dance learning contexts. Therefore, it is important to recognize that all dance experiences are important to the training and development of all dancers, whether in educational or professional contexts. Educators need to acknowledge that informal experiences are invaluable to the identity of the dancer, and recognition of students' dance roots may foster dance learning in a different and new context. Becky Dyer recommends somatic practice in student-centered classes, thus "exploring the uniqueness of each individual's moving body and movement attributes" (113).[8] The development of culturally relevant classrooms recommended by Liz Melchior, as well as Doug Risner and Susan Stinson, is of paramount importance.[9]

Phase Three: Dance Curriculum

The researchers recognized the importance of referencing the writings of dance scholars who focused on curriculum development and pedagogy. Additionally, it was also important to review selected dance curricula to assess what is happening in dance education. It was fortuitous that two particular developments were available: first, the International Arts Education Standards—a review of standards, practices, and expectations of thirteen countries and regions—and, second, the Curriculum in Motion project.[10] Finally, a review of the above and the themes identified in the Dance Learning in Motion survey questionnaire and interviews was undertaken.

The writings of many dance scholars and dance curriculum writers advocate that curriculum development and pedagogy should provide students with a good dance experience, enable them to learn more about others and themselves, and prepare them to actively participate in society in a meaningful and artistic way.[11] They assert that it is paramount that the curriculum is culturally sensitive and responds to today's complex classrooms, which include students of different backgrounds, abilities, race, ethnicities, and faiths who have different needs and desires. It is important to accept that young people bring with them knowledge of and experience in dance, knowledge of contemporary popular culture and media, and the ability to employ technology to create and communicate globally.

The examination of the review initiated by the National Coalition for Core Arts Standards, the International Arts Education Standards review of standards, practices, and expectations of thirteen countries and regions, revealed:

> which arts disciplines are most and least represented in arts standards and curricula worldwide; which habits, skills, abilities related to arts teaching and learning are most commonly emphasized in these documents; how those expectations are articulated for educators; and, where applicable, what guidelines exist for measuring student achievement of the standards.[12]

Thirteen countries were examined, nine of which provided examples of dance standards which connected with the most prevalent themes for learning in the arts: cultural understanding, critical and creative thinking, problem solving, communication, pleasure and enjoyment, and a sense of well-being.[13] Generally, these standards in dance involved making and performing dance, communicating meaning through dance, applying critical and creative thinking skills in dance, demonstrating and understanding dance in various cultures and historical periods and other art forms, making connections between dance and healthy living, and making connections between dance and other disciplines.

The Curriculum in Motion Project was led by Susan R. Koff, United States, Charlotte Svendler Nielsen, Denmark, Cornelia Baumgart, Germany, and Ivančica Janković, Croatia. It encouraged participants from different countries to share dance curriculum experiences and ideas and to consider how educators might learn from each other and work together to shape the development and implementation of a high-quality standard of dance education, particularly in schools. The project reflected the major aims of many dance organizations, such as daCi and WDA, which provide dance professionals with a forum to discuss research as it pertains to students in educational or training contexts. The project was held at the daCi/WDA

Global Dance Summit in Taipei in 2012, where delegates were invited from selected countries and were asked to present their specific dance curricula, followed by other participants sharing curriculum developments in their countries. It was evident from these presentations that not every country designed and implemented curricula in the same way. Table 5.3 identifies the responsibility for curriculum development, those who teach the dance curriculum, and the emphasis and competency areas identified for the programs.

Curricula were prepared by the state, province, or country, making comparison sometimes difficult; however, it was possible to identify major learning competencies. Competencies were generally identified as students being able to create, perform, and appreciate dance, and a few focused on specific dance forms that were to be experienced. Dance was taught mainly within arts education, with a few examples where dance was part of physical education and/or music, and those teaching dance ranged from generalist teachers, mainly in the primary school context, and dance specialists and artists in the secondary school context. There was an emphasis on dance as an art form, with students undertaking personal study and connecting to life experience. A few placed importance on the dance product. In the

TABLE 5.3 *The Curriculum in Motion Project*

Country	Characteristics of Dance Learning
Australia	Culture, holistic development, physical, communication
Canada	Culture, physical, communication
USA	Culture, holistic development physical, communication
New Zealand	Culture, holistic development, communication
Finland	Holistic development, physical, communication
Croatia	Physical, communication
Estonia	Physical, communication
Germany	Physical, communication
India	Communication
Jamaica	Culture, physical
Portugal	Physical
Slovenia	Physical
Taiwan	Holistic development

comparison of the characteristics of dance learning (Table 5.3) presented by the Curriculum in Motion Project and the review of the International Arts Education Standards, there were many similarities with the themes identified in the Dance Learning in Motion survey questionnaire and interviews, such as expression, body, social, emotional, and creative benefits. The researchers appreciated that the review of the curriculum initiatives and documents and comparison with the findings of the survey questionnaire and interviews revealed the significance of dance learning for those participants and confirmed how important dance experiences are for participants in various learning environments.

Conclusion

The researchers' intention to explore learning in dance in various dance settings has produced some meaningful data regarding how dance is experienced; what is and can be learned in, about, and through dance; and what is important about how people are engaged in dance. The survey questionnaire and interviews provided insight into how dance is experienced and uncovered the deeper personal meanings of people staying involved in dance. The review of dance scholars' writings and investigation of selected dance curricula supported the importance of recognizing and supporting students' experiences in dance and providing relevant and respectful programs for diverse contexts and populations.

This research study contributes to discourses of dance education with a particular focus on the embodied, performative nature of dance as significant lived experience. The motivation to continue the research after Phase One largely came from this finding. When they arrived at the finding of "disconnect," the researchers were motivated to uncover more details and to examine the nature of this disconnect, as well as implications for future teaching and learning. The clearest implication so far is, first, that dance educators in formal and non-formal sectors should be informed about the value of informal dance learning and supported in valuing this past learning of their students within their formal and non-formal classrooms. In some ways, this is implied within culturally responsive teaching.

These findings may be constructive for researchers and others in the educational field who are identifying future policy directions for dance education. Further research in this area could have wide application across early childhood education and elementary, secondary, and tertiary sectors of education. Research outcomes might provide evidence to support renewed attention to the value of dance for government policy, focusing on citizens' artistic and social engagement, health, and well-being, all the while enforcing this value within all sectors engaging with dance, especially the informal sector.

Appendix 1

The findings of the survey questionnaire and interviews, together with the discussion of dance curricula, were reported and presented in the following publications and conferences:

Kipling Brown, A., Koff, S. R. Meiners, J. and Svendler Nielsen, C. (2014). "Dance learning in motion: global dance education. Contemporising the past: envisaging the future." In *Proceedings of the 2014 World Dance Alliance Global Summit* (http://www.ausdance.org.au)

Kipling Brown, A., Koff, S. R. Meiners, J. and Svendler Nielsen, C. (2015). "Shaping future directions for dance education." In *Exploring identities in dance. Proceedings from the 13th World Congress of Dance and the Child International.* Available online: http://ausdance.org.au/publications/details/exploring-identities-in-dance

Kipling Brown, A., and Koff, S. R. (2017). "Dance Education in Grassroots Dancing." Presented at the *World Dance Alliance-Americas Conference, Dancing from the Grassroots Conference.* Memorial University St. John's, Newfoundland, July 23–28.

Kipling Brown, A., Koff, S. R., Meiners, J. and Svendler Nielsen, C. (2018). "Culturally responsive pedagogy: Taking the project global dance education to the third level." Presented at *Panpapanpalya 2018. 2nd Joint Congress of daCi (Dance and the Child International) and WDA (World Dance Alliance) Global Education and Training Network.* July 8–13.

6

Formal Dance Education

Introduction

Formal dance education within existing broad educational institutions (elementary, secondary, and tertiary education) began first within larger educational contexts in higher education and has evolved from courses in physical education departments into, at times, conservatory training. Through this evolution, dance became aligned with other arts, as well as moving to other levels of formal education (elementary and secondary). This alignment strengthened the voice of dance in academia and within public education, thus providing dance the arts education advocacy that led to dance teacher certification (qualification) and dance standards throughout the United States and in many parts of the world. This chapter will discuss the many ways in which formal dance education takes place throughout the world. At the conclusion of these three chapters on formal, non-formal, and informal dance education, a summary will contrast and compare the many common topics that are found in formal, non-formal, and informal dance education. The topics, which will be covered indirectly through these three chapters, include:

- Who are the teachers?
- What are their qualifications?
- Who are the students?
- What are their qualifications?
- What is the curriculum?
- Who oversees the education in this setting?
- Is this education for profit or not for profit?

Definition and History

The terms formal, informal, and non-formal education were used in Chapter 5 (and somewhat in the first section of this book), but they will now be discussed in more detail in this chapter and the following two chapters. The simplest description of formal education is the concept or model that is most familiar: schools that have a set curriculum, regardless of age, which usually results in formal assessment (leading to grading) and possibly culminates in some form of credential. This credential can usually lead to admission to additional formal education and ultimately to a profession. This description is built upon the formal learning definition that is applied in this text to dance education:

> The **formal field of learning** is concerned with curriculum offerings within education and training institutions: "Formal learning takes place in education and training institutions, is recognised by relevant national authorities and leads to diplomas and qualifications. Formal learning is structured according to educational arrangements such as curricula, qualifications and teaching–learning requirements."[1]

The history of formal dance education is relatively new in settings that have a full range of education, which is covered in detail in Chapter 2. As a summary of this kind of education, naming formal dance education is a predominantly Western concept and was initiated through the discipline of physical education. Though formal dance education is now present all over the world, in both Western and non-Western settings, the structure and outcomes in (mostly graded) general educational institutions first appeared in the United States, followed by England and spreading primarily through the English-speaking world. The initial version was merely copied when it moved on to the non-English-speaking world. Though the origin was in physical education, the most widely emulated version within higher education, which can still be seen today, is the conservatory model. As these models spread to the non-English-speaking world, they were centered on Western concert dance forms, mainly ballet and modern dance. Though the spread of Western concert dance forms to non-Western countries was not viewed initially as a form of colonialism, looking at it from a Western perspective today, it appears as colonialism. In retrospect, the spread of Western concert dance forms suppressed the value of much older dance forms in the curricula of non-Western countries' formal dance education.

Dance in Formal Training Settings

However, there is also formal dance education that existed long before dance entered general education. Some well-known schools of specified dance forms throughout the world are the Noh schools in Japan, which have been in existence for hundreds of years; the Paris Opera Ballet School, founded in the 1700s; and the current tradition of the hālau hula (traditional hula school), in Hawaii.[2] Hula began as a religious practice long before there was any permanent record of it. With the colonialization of Hawaii, it was banned, then revived under court patronage, and is now independent of both religion and government.³ In contrast, formal dance education in general education began as a Western idea and was not affiliated with any religions. Dance education in dance-only formal schools is a worldwide phenomenon and has much more international reach than formal dance education in general education settings, as well as a much longer history. In indigenous, religious-based dance, colonialization influenced the development and movement from setting to setting.

Ballet, which began in France, moved to many other European countries (including Italy, Russia, England, Denmark, and beyond) over hundreds of years. Ballet exists in formal general educational institutions (such as universities) and also in stand-alone formal educational schools (such as those affiliated with professional ballet companies). However, modern dance, which began in the United States and Germany, has a much shorter history. The introduction of modern dance into formal general education gave it a platform to spread more rapidly throughout the world through formal educational settings. With the emphasis on the conservatory model, this training became another form of colonialism, as both ballet and modern dance were held in higher esteem than local indigenous forms of dance, because these Western forms were included in degree-granting programs. Through this domination, a stereotype developed which perpetuated the myth that ballet and modern dance are the foundations of all dance. This stereotype is still present today in formal dance education, as discussed in Chapters 2 and 3.⁴

Formal dance education lies on a continuum, from formal education to non-formal education. There is no strong dividing line where one begins and the other ends. For the purposes of this discussion, formal education will mostly be limited to settings with all educational subjects included and those that generally lead to graded outcomes.

History of Dance Teacher Education

Dance teacher education (in formal general education institutions) first began in the field of physical education and was not a separate area of teacher education until dance was considered a separate field in public, or as it is known, pre-kindergarten to grade 12 (PK-12), education (meaning, primary or elementary and secondary education). As discussed in Chapter 2, dance teacher education for PK-12 teachers followed the development of dance education majors in tertiary education. Dance teacher education is dependent upon several factors:

- That there are dance standards for PK-12 primary and secondary schools
- That dance is taught as a discrete subject in PK-12 schools.

In some countries, dance teacher education is still not separate from physical education. Furthermore, dance in some PK-12 settings is taught by those without any dance teacher education. Finally, there is no formal dance teacher education for tertiary education. In some instances, formal teacher education in a formal specialty school of dance qualifies as preparation to be a tertiary dance educator in a general tertiary educational institution. As mentioned in the earlier chapters, in some instances, membership of a formal professional dance company qualifies one to be a teacher in tertiary education. This hearkens back to the earliest days of dance as a discipline in tertiary education. Chapter 7, on non-formal education, will cover dance teacher education in the private sector.

Dance Teacher Certification

Dance entered formal education (for the first time as its own discipline) in the United States in Wisconsin as dance education. This eventually led to teaching credentials for public, PK-12. This is formal dance teacher education. Dance in formal education has necessitated the continuity of dance education, leading to a teaching credential that can be appropriate to a specific educational setting. Initially, the teaching credential was in physical education, as there was no such credential specifically for dance. Since dance has been included in formal educational settings, teaching credentials have followed local standards and customs. The inclusion of dance in formal education in the United States led to a split in teaching credentials between formal public education (PK-12) and higher education. Higher education, regardless of the discipline, mostly requires higher degrees as a teaching credential. However, as was discussed in Chapter 2, the introduction of dance into higher education in the United States coincided with the beginning of modern dance as a profession in the United States. Higher education became a location for these early modern dancers to seek steady employment, regardless of their degree credentials. The professionalism of the dancer was a substitute for any other qualification. This practice continues today and is seen quite consistently in job qualification lists as "M.F.A./M.A. in dance, or equivalent professional experience in the field." Though the necessity for pedagogical content knowledge has been discussed for more than thirty years in general formal education, dance joined this discussion much later than other educational disciplines.[5] Still, there are areas in the conservatory model where pedagogical content is never discussed, and the focus remains instead on professional experience (or content knowledge) as the requirement for the position of a teacher in higher education.

Historically, public education (PK-12) in all disciplines has adhered to more formal pedagogy requirements for teacher education than higher education. This is the same in dance. Initially, when dance was introduced into public education through physical education, the formal education requirements were those for physical education. As dance began to separate from physical education in the United States, it followed a similar pathway to any country in which dance was also introduced through physical education. The teacher education credential was acquired through a higher education institution, often as a combination of the disciplines of education and dance or physical education.

Dance teacher certification (or qualification) is always dependent on local laws and customs but generally includes both dance content and pedagogical content. This is a direct contrast to the varying qualifications for higher education employment, which rarely include pedagogical content, if at all, in any discipline. There are formal rules in higher education that surround teaching, including assessment, curriculum development, structure of degree programs, and continuity of faculty positions. Again, these rules are dependent on local laws and customs.

Turning to an official definition, formal qualification when completing a program recognized by government is defined by UNESCO as:

> The official confirmation, usually in the form of a document, certifying the successful completion of an education programme or a stage of a programme. Qualifications can be obtained through: i) successful completion of a full education programme; ii) successful completion of a stage of an education programme (intermediate qualifications); or iii) validation of acquired knowledge, skills and competencies, independent of participation in an education programme. This may also be referred to as a "credential."[6]

History of Dance/Arts Standards

For as long as there have been standards for teaching physical education in the world, some aspect of dance has been included, usually folk and social dance forms. Many countries have included dance in some form of standard, either in arts or physical education. Though this list is not meant to be fully inclusive, these countries include: Australia, Canada, Finland, Germany, Jamaica, New Zealand, Portugal, Slovenia, Taiwan, and the United States.[7]

As with the history of dance teacher certification or qualifications, all dance/arts standards are controlled locally. In countries where folk and social dancing are strong aspects of physical education, dance standards began and possibly remain in physical education. However, many countries have been influenced by UNESCO-organized events, such as the various international meetings and events concerning arts education. One of these events resulted in the Seoul Agenda, which called upon "UNESCO Member States, civil society, professional organisations and communities to recognise its governing goals, to employ the proposed strategies, and to implement the action items in a concerted effort to realise the full potential of high quality arts education."[8]

In the United States, the migration of dance standards from physical education to their affiliation with the arts was instigated by advocacy combined with other arts education organizations (visual art, music, and theatre). This advocacy occurred both with and among organizations focused on curricula for higher education and those focused on curricula and teaching in PK-12 education.[9] Models for these arts standards were initiated by research supported by the Getty Center, a non-profit arm of the J. Paul Getty Museum, which created the Discipline Based Art Education (DBAE) model in the 1980s.[10] Though the Getty Center no longer promotes DBAE, the structure of it is evident in initial dance standards documents in many countries.[11] The strength of the initial model was to look at any art form as much more than only production of the art. Each art form includes aesthetics, criticism, and history. However, a failing of the initial DBAE structure is that it became so teacher-directed as not to include the student voice.[12] This teacher-centered curriculum fell into the model of "banking" education, as described by Freire.[13] Recognition of this weakness has been a driving force in curriculum and standards revisions over the years. A recent revision was the initial National Standards for Arts Education in the United States, which were subsequently revised to be the current National Core Arts Standards.[14] New curriculum documents have also been written in Australia and New Zealand.

The world over, many countries' standards documents were influenced initially by this more rounded model, as exemplified by DBAE and perpetuated mostly by English language dance education theorists. Jeff Meiners sees a downside in that, "creating (composing or choreographing), performing (presenting) and appreciating (viewing and responding) appears as a regime of truth shared by various curriculum authorities."[15] This has led to the exclusion of cultural and indigenous forms from formal curricula and also exclusion of the student voice. As dance has adapted to all the structures of formal education, there have also been limitations as to what aspects of dance translate into the context of formal education.

The combined advocacy that led to the affiliation of dance with the arts in the United States and had a ripple effect in other countries was motivated by recognition that dance remains expendable as an element of the curriculum. Though dance as a subject has been on the fringes of formal education in many countries and for many years, it is still not considered an important or integral aspect of formal education.[16] All the elements that have been summarized thus far, including the history of dance in formal education, the history of dance teacher certification or qualification, and the history of dance standards, have been the results of exhausting efforts made by countless people around the world working toward creating legitimate recognition of the importance of dance in formal education. The mere confusion about the definition of dance education, as discussed in Chapter 3, has thwarted some of these efforts. International financial changes and international competition have also influenced the recognition of dance as a fundamental aspect of formal education. It is still not fully recognized, world over, as an essential part of the curriculum.[17]

Formal standards do not exist in the same way for tertiary education. The PK-12 standards that have been discussed here are usually developed under government and local control. In tertiary education, control is even more localized, in individual institutions. In an effort to counter this in the United States, an accrediting organization, the National Association of Schools of Dance, was created to establish suggested standards for an undergraduate dance degree. This organization was one of the later outcomes from the Development Conference on Dance mentioned in Chapter 3.

Dance Curricula

There is wide variety in the ways that curricula have been researched, discussed, and named.[18] Curricula represent not only what the experts in any discipline consider should be taught, but also the overall values of the community.[19] Dance curricula "are a product of the socio-cultural-economic community from which they emanate."[20] Ralph Buck goes on to discuss the balance that must exist between visionary ideas and practical implementation. Without a well-prepared teacher, and a supportive local community and context, wonderful curriculum documents are useless. Not only is dance situated in varied settings (within the arts or within physical education) dependent on the local context, in some instances, dance is delivered through general education in elementary grades and specialist education in secondary grades. Both teacher preparation and curricular emphasis vary widely. Another interesting observation from Buck is that countries or locales that have been most directly influenced by England (Australia, New Zealand, Hong Kong, and Singapore, for example) have been more progressive than England in moving dance into alignment with the arts.[21] This move to align with the arts has resulted in more holistic outcomes being described for dance in the curriculum.

Having dance in alignment with the arts in curricula is an area that is both unclear and sometimes problematic.[22] As an advocacy alignment, this has been helpful for dance education (and theatre or drama education) which has historically had a weaker voice than music and visual arts education. However, if alignment with the arts leads to integrated curricula, so that each art form does not have its own identity, then the very recognition that dance education was seeking within the curriculum is lost. Additionally, these art forms do not have identical practices of pedagogy and expected or desired outcomes. So, again, dance is at risk of being marginalized when included in a performing arts grouping. If these groupings are bureaucratic structures and not curricular, then this issue can be alleviated.

Standards and curriculum are not the same, though the words are used interchangeably in many parts of the world. Generally, one should pay attention to how these words are used in order to discern meaning. Standards focus on the outcomes that reflect a well-rounded curriculum. Curricula need to be developed according to the values of the local context, as well as influenced by the location in which dance resides at the educational level in that context. The outcome focus of curricula is what dignifies dance in an educational context, indicating that there is an entire discipline to be taught. Finally, the outcomes of a curriculum can be assessed, leading to clear indicators of the progress of students engaged in that curriculum.

No sharp division exists between curriculum and pedagogy, meaning that a curriculum cannot exist without pedagogy, or the teaching of the curriculum.[23] Curriculum is further delineated as "institutional curriculum," which "expresses a perception or a paradigm of what schooling should be with respect to society," and the written curriculum which makes content available for teachers.[24]

From an arts education perspective there are:

> three distinct orientations in visual arts curricula: the rote, teacher-centered orientation; the open-ended student-centered orientation; and the higher-order cognitive orientation. Each of these orientations implies different assumptions about the nature of art and arts education. Each shares different views of teaching and learning, implying its own set of goals, contents, pedagogies, and evaluation practices. The first orientation is imitative, perpetuating the general academic curriculum in its goals and structures; the second is complementary, trying to compensate for teachers' perceptions of an imbalanced academic curriculum; the third is expansive, aiming to enhance the curriculum in ways that are advocated in the scholarly literature, and incorporate into it a variety of intelligences and modes of thinking.[25]

These orientations are then supported by the worldviews and different pedagogies discussed in Chapter 4.

Donald Blumenfeld-Jones and Sheaun-Yann Liang present a different delineation of curriculum and standards, as well as the different aspects of curriculum, by articulating the following categories: explicit/formal curriculum (content/standards), operationalized curriculum (as it is actually taught), experienced curriculum (from the learner perspective), hidden curriculum (what is taught beyond the discipline), and null curriculum (what is absent in the curriculum but becomes implied).[26]

The hidden curriculum and null curriculum are those least considered by dance educators, but each participates in a large part in the way that dance is perceived in the formal curriculum. The null curriculum can exclude "entire disciplines to the omission of particular bits of information"[27] within any discipline. The dearth of formal dance curriculum research weakens the position of dance education in formal educational settings that include other disciplines, and then dance education does not participate as actively in curriculum discussions.[28] In all formal educational discussions and research (curriculum, pedagogy, and assessment), dance is a less active participant, which devalues dance overall in formal education. Stating that dance is different, or cannot be looked at in the same way as non-arts disciplines, is not sufficient and leads to one of the reasons this book was needed.

Presenting dance education as an important aspect of the hidden curriculum is one way to achieve a more central status in formal education. "This [hidden] curriculum alerts us to the fact that schools teach more than academics and skills. They also teach how to live in the world."[29] These attributes are inherent in dance education, as outlined in Chapter 3, and are definitely what separates dance education from dance training. These are the very skills that emphasize working well with others, developing creativity and imagination, and valuing and perceiving difference without making negative value judgments. Some formal schools might call these skills "life skills," and they are the very skills that have lost focus with the shifting emphasis on assessment and testing in all forms of education. In Chapter 4, they were also mentioned as soft skills that are learned or acquired in the context of play.

Susan Stinson considers that the hidden curriculum can have both positive and negative effects.[30] In this she is speaking perhaps to both hidden and null curricula. In her line of reasoning, the hidden curriculum is that which is "taken for granted" but not articulated. Her research has focused on gendered behavior in dance and both positive and negative outcomes of that behavior. Pedagogy, as the enactment of curriculum, places the behavioral expectations in the classroom.

The null curriculum can have far more insidious effects than the hidden curriculum. It can be defined as "the options students are not afforded, the perspectives they may never know about, much less be able to use, the concepts and skills that are not part of their intellectual repertoire."[31] It can include implications about certain body types that are favored in the dance classroom and implications about societal standing. For example, a dance teacher who places the more advanced students at the front of a class might think that those students are there to provide an example. But the less experienced students could perceive that they are not "good enough," which is exactly what the null curriculum is about. It might or might not have been intended, but the students perceive this negative implication nonetheless.

In this instance and in many others, knowledge of curriculum theory can allow teachers to consider all the implications of what transpires in the classroom, and they can make conscious decisions about every issue, rather than default to the most expedient decision. Finally, one aspect of the null curriculum that has been discussed earlier, without this identifier, is the inclusion of Western dance forms as the core of the curriculum, with any non-Western dance forms as elective or on the periphery. This is what was referred to earlier as omission. This placement of dance forms at the core or on the periphery of the curriculum makes a statement about what is valued and clearly values Western dance forms above all others. It continues the hierarchy of dance forms, mentioned in Chapter 3.

Summary

This chapter has covered formal dance education in all settings, meaning PK-12 and higher or tertiary education. However, the three preceding sections, on certification, standards, and curriculum, were primarily focused on PK-12. These three very important elements of education are regulated mostly in the public education or PK-12 sector. Higher education or tertiary education comes under much less scrutiny and, in some instances, seems to resemble the qualifications and controls of non-formal education that are listed in Chapter 7. This disconnect has been mentioned in many other places, but bringing it into focus here makes it glaring.

In addition, two types of formal dance education have been presented here: that found in broad educational contexts (discussed thoroughly in this chapter), and that found in a single dance school affiliated with either a professional company or a specific type of dance. Dance education within the single affiliated school will be discussed more fully in Chapter 7, on non-formal dance education, as some of the particulars fall into that definition. Dance education in broad formal education contexts is involved in and influenced by all the particulars of formal education and learning, which include standards and curriculum, as well as local values and contexts. The expertise in these areas spans from theorists to researchers to practitioners, and the students who are influenced are in elementary, secondary, and tertiary education. The wide span of expertise, as well as that of populations influenced by formal dance education, naturally lends itself to a wide range of ideas, concepts, and forms of implementation. The purpose of this chapter is not to explore these ideas, concepts, and forms of implementation in depth, but rather to paint a picture of the larger scope of this type of education. Only in this way can the complexity be clear.

This chapter does not delve into the actual practice of formal education. The practice is pedagogy, which was discussed in Chapter 4. Now that the complexity of formal education is clearer, actual implementation has to be even more complex in order to adhere to all the standards and other parameters in terms of local context. It is also complicated by outside forces that control quality, which is also a local concern.[32] In the two closer looks that follow, a small window is opened onto the reality of all these issues in practice and the effects upon those who teach in these settings. These two "looks" are situated here not only to illuminate the actual practice of formal dance education, but also to present a contrast between secondary and tertiary dance education.

A CLOSER LOOK AT DANCE IN THE TERTIARY SETTING

Ralph Buck, Head of Dance Studies, University of Auckland

As Head of Department, Dance Studies, University of Auckland, I have an open door policy, where I aim to keep in touch with all of my students and staff. As such, I have many interesting personal and professional conversations in my office, but also out of my office.

I was with a group of third-year students touring International schools in Shanghai, China. We had been in a school all day teaching and performing, and then having dinner together, where my open door policy took on new meanings. One of the students asked, "So, how do you get to be a Head of Department. How do I get your job?" Another student said, "sshhh, you can't speak to Ralph like that he is the HOD, and . . . but yeah, how did you get into your job, I mean you travel lots, and well you know it looks pretty good."

I replied, "Yes I do enjoy my job, but it is not easy and, you don't really see what I do." I continued, "So while you were teaching today, I was doing emails. Today, my job included: organising a trip to India for my Dean, where we are to meet other Universities and establish curriculum, teaching and research exchanges; I helped new staff prepare for the delivery of the new Masters in Dance Movement Therapy; finalised marketing budgets and strategy for the year; set up contracts for new casual staff; approved doctoral scholarships; organised a staff retreat where we aim to discuss graduate profiles and directions for the next few years; chatted to a staff member about her maternity leave; approving course outlines and assessment criteria for summer school courses and so on."

One of the students, asked, "Didn't you watch us teach today?" I replied, "Of course I did. I needed to know what you were teaching, and that you delivered it in an appropriate manner and you were pitching your lesson at the right level. I got all of this in the first five minutes and then I focused on my OTHER work."

We ordered our pizzas and then the student asked again, "So, how did you get your job, I mean, what do I need to do?" I paused and said: "First, get qualifications that follow your heart, study what really interests you; in every job be reliable, consistent, organised and be prepared to flex; always do administration accurately and quickly; offer solutions to problems; be a team worker and be willing to step up and lead when required; be transparent, honest and have standards; own your work and help others to own their work and to plan for their future."

I realised I was speaking about "what" I do and "how" I do it, much like when I teach. I went on to speak of being a good networker in conferences and being out there engaging with the community, and making your work relevant and count for something. I finished my rant by emphasising that you had to always be a learner and be open to new ideas and people.

I could see that their eyes were glazing over. I realised as I finished my beer that my job is complex. It is about people and ideas, and how to help others learn—staff, students and colleagues. I laughed and said to my students, "I aim to provide you with an education, such that you feel confident to replace me." I got up and went to bed, exhausted from another full day.

A CLOSER LOOK AT DANCE IN THE SECONDARY SETTING

Shirlene Blake, Certified Secondary Dance Educator, New York City

Teaching dance in public schools can be both rewarding and challenging. You can find yourself in numerous scenarios which can often be dictated by the school's philosophy. Wherever you find yourself, the opportunity to expose large numbers of students to the benefits of a dance education is extremely rewarding. I have predominately taught in high schools, and the opportunity for young people to feel comfortable in their bodies, feel good about themselves, make connections to their life or some other subject matter or just have the pure joy of moving are some of the outcomes of knowing the importance of this work.

The challenges come when you are faced with numerous parameters to do your job well. In the convenes of the classroom, magic can happen. It's the planning of curriculum and lessons when there is no consistency in how you may see students. In a performing arts high school setting in which I had the opportunity to teach, students had year-long independent classes in technique (ballet, modern, jazz) as well as independent classes in improvisation, dance history, kinesiology, and master classes in tap, African, hip-hop, and the list goes on. In a school where I teach dance as general education, I may see a student all four years of their high school tenure or I may see a student once or twice over the course of that tenure. I may even see students who have no desire to take a dance class. Thus, I have made a choice to teach in what I call truncated units. I plan the curriculum so that the student who takes my class for all four years does not repeat a unit, but if a student only sees me once, the unit is as holistic as possible. Students experience dance physically, historically, and culturally. This may sound obvious, but not always practical. It is important to understand and also give up the notion that you can't teach everything. I want students to have opportunities to learn choreography and create choreography. And ultimately, I want them to feel comfortable in their bodies and have an understanding that everyone dances.

7

Non-Formal Dance Education

Dance in Studios and Other Settings

Introduction

The expansion of formal dance education has led to the proliferation of private dance studios. They have become extensive in the era of reality dance shows. But non-formal education existed long before this current explosion of private dance studios. This chapter will illuminate the focus of non-formal dance education and its many settings, including the social impact of dance as articulated in those settings. Some of these non-formal settings are commercial, and some are not. Non-formal settings sometimes have no set standards regarding teacher qualifications, which can lead to a variety of dancer outcomes. Non-formal settings also tend to have socio-cultural impacts, as these settings, largely commercial, are then limited to those with the financial means to participate.

Non-formal dance education is complex and cannot be totally articulated in one chapter. It is a worldwide phenomenon/occurrence with its own deep and varied history. There are many good dance history texts that offer a more comprehensive look at dance through this lens.[1] The purpose of this chapter is to describe it as a whole, rather than focus on all the smaller parts. However, much more current versions of non-formal dance education, competition and commercialism, will be detailed more here because of the extensive outreach and implications of those directions.

Definition

"**Non-formal** is learning that has been acquired in addition or alternatively to formal learning. In some cases, it is also structured according to educational and training arrangements, but more flexible. It usually takes place in community-based settings, the workplace and through the activities of civil society organisations."[2] This definition is quite wide and encompasses many different types of settings. In unpacking this definition further, it indicates that, "Education that is institutionalised, intentional and planned by an education provider . . . Non-formal education mostly leads to qualifications that are not recognised as formal or equivalent to formal qualifications by the relevant national or sub-national education authorities or to no qualifications at all."[3] Based on this definition, the long-standing schools that were mentioned in Chapter 6 are included here as non-formal education. Sometimes, non-formal settings are referred to as private sector teaching and learning, in contrast to public sector (formal settings).

There are a wide range of settings that can be included in non-formal education and learning, of every possible size. These can be after-school programs, community programs, private studios and education centers, and schools recognized as international centers of a certain style (very popular with codified ballet styles). These many locations can lead to professionalism or can be purely recreational. Sometimes there is an affiliation with a formal educational institution (for example when an artists-in-residence program takes its work into a formal educational institution). All ages can be served through non-formal education. There is no set standard or curriculum throughout all non-formal education; however, there can be an accrediting organization or professional organization that sets standards within that organization. The financial structure of non-formal education centers can be proprietary (for profit), non-profit, or government-related.

The key element that defines non-formal education is that it is in addition to formal education, but there is some structure of institution and classes. The definition lies between the definitions of formal education and informal education. In one person's definition, a formal ballet school affiliated with a professional dance company is formal dance education. In another person's definition, this very school is defined as non-formal education. One element, present only in non-formal education, is the concept of dance competition, which is usually seen in ballet and dance sport (ballroom). Competitive ballroom dance having the title of "dance sport" additionally confuses the separation of dance from physical education that is discussed in so many forms of dance. Dance competition has extended to television, and in this location wider varieties of dance styles are included.

Access to non-formal education is varied and contingent upon an organization's discretion. There are institutions that merely require payment, meaning anyone who can pay will have access. At the other end of the spectrum, there are those institutions which are accessible only through audition, or membership in a certain class or structure in society or religion. This range of access is controlled locally as well. Examples of local organizations are Dance Masters of America (in the United States, including modern dance, ballet, and Western concert forms), National Dance Teachers Association of America (covering most ballroom dances),

One Dance UK (providing standards in the United Kingdom across all sectors), International Society of Teachers of Dance (providing standards and teacher accreditation in theatre dance within and outside the European Union, as well as Dancesport), and World Dance Sport Federation (housed in Switzerland and centered on competitive ballroom dancing). Teacher standards, learning standards, and standards of competition are covered by these varied organizations but are usually organization-specific and outside the purview of governmental controls.

On the continuum of formal to non-formal education are those schools that have an established structure but specialize in dance alone; they will be discussed as offering non-formal education. The following is, again, a list of topics that are common to the three educational categories:

- Who are the teachers?
- What are their qualifications?
- Who are the students?
- What are their qualifications?
- What is the curriculum?
- Who oversees the education in this setting?
- Is this education for profit or not for profit?

The responses can be summarized as follows:

- Who are the teachers? What are their qualifications?

When dance is taught in a formal school, but one not leading to the general education of students, there may or may not be credentials required of teachers, or there may be no consistent standards to those qualifications.[4] If the goal in this setting is technical proficiency leading to professional status in the dance form and a professional company affiliated with the school, many times the qualification to be a teacher is having a high-achieving professional performing career. It is this very qualification that has become confused since dance entered broader educational settings, such as universities and public schools.

- Who are the students? What are their qualifications?

Generally, in a specialized school, the students are those who seek a career in that dance form, if it is a professional school. The qualifications are that they complete and pass an audition to enter that school. In some instances, there are additional auditions or exams to pass in order to progress in the school. In some parts of the world, qualification can involve being a member of a certain part of society or a member of a specified family lineage. The qualification for students in some settings, usually recreational in outcome, is the willingness or ability to pay for the classes and to make a commitment to attend those classes.

- What is the curriculum?

The curriculum in this type of setting is often set by the overarching profession of each dance form, such as ballet. Individual schools establish a curriculum specific to their educational philosophies or values. In some settings, this is called a syllabus, rather than curriculum. Some programs do not have a curriculum, just a list of steps that should be taught. As was presented in formal education, the word curriculum is interpreted differently according to each setting.

- Who oversees the education in this setting?

Often, this setting is overseen locally, by the organization or company that has created the school or the curriculum. An example of this is the Royal Academy of Dance, which began in England, but its curriculum is implemented throughout the world. The education in these types of schools is often outside of government control.

- Is this education for profit or not for profit?

The profit/not-for-profit definition varies depending on this education's local context.

Non-Formal as a Worldwide Setting

Both non-formal and informal teaching and learning in dance began long before formal teaching and learning in dance. South Indian training of dancers in a non-formal setting dates back to the sixteenth century.[5] Chinese, Japanese, and Cambodian non-formal dance training can be traced back even further, as well as many dance practices within the Pacific region. In many of the early settings of non-formal dance teaching and learning, they existed in conjunction with religion and can be found throughout the world associated with older religious practices. Though many of these dance practices have now been reconceptualized outside religion, they are still being taught and learned in non-formal settings.

Internationally, some schools have been affiliated with governments and, in some instances, have actually either perpetuated a political agenda or have been closed because of a political agenda. This has occurred in both China (perpetuating a political agenda) and Cambodia (closed because of a political agenda), as some brief examples.[6] As ballet flourished in Russia, it became an aspect of propaganda for the Soviet regime. The same schools still exist, post-glasnost; however, there is now a more open attitude about who can study there and what they are able to do with their training.

Dance Studios/Private Study

A common notion about private dance studios is that no generalizations can be made. Within the formal dance education setting, standards are set by governments regarding curriculum, qualifications for teachers, and general safety and well-being. Governments have not, as a general rule, created any educational standards or controls for private dance studios. As private businesses, studios must be in compliance with business standards and practices, but not educational standards. The organization of the studio, the teacher background and qualifications, and the plans for the students are only regulated at the individual discretion of the studio. Studios can also range from very amateur to very professional in focus for the students. They can be organized in a manner whereby a student registers for an ongoing course, such as at a specified time each week, and the student pays for the entire session of classes. There can be drop-in classes such as at professional studios in New York City (Steps, Peridance, Broadway Dance Center), London (The Place, Pineapple Dance Studios), and many other cities around the world. It is finally the market (commercial dealings) that keeps these studios viable and operating in their own locations.

Smaller private studios outside of professional training, focusing on recreational dance, developed largely during the early part of the twentieth century as an outcome of the voices of women being heard in society for the first time.[7] Students' (mostly women's) ability to participate in these dance styles was supported by changes in women's fashion which softened clothing from previous restrictions. These studios largely catered to women and children. Those who were at the forefront of professional dance at the time created mail-order ideas for lessons and teaching. Most notable in this group were Ruth St. Denis and Ted Shawn, two pioneers in the development of modern dance in the United States during the early 1900s.[8] Dance Masters of America, a convention group still active today that began in 1926, was a way for these mail-order lessons to be marketed or promoted. The Fred Astaire and Arthur Murray studios for ballroom dance followed in the 1940s.[9]

Private dance studios and training were the only options for any type of dance training prior to the beginning of formal dance education, as articulated in Chapter 2. The dance forms that were taught in one sector influenced what was happening in the other sector, as also discussed in Chapter 2. When modern dance was first created in New York and in Germany, those who were experimenting in these new forms were also operating their own dance studios. World-renowned ballet companies have operated schools as a direct pipeline supplying their companies for a much longer period of time.

Examples worldwide include the Royal Ballet School (London), Paris Opera Ballet, Bolshoi Ballet Academy (Moscow), and Teatro alla Scala Academy (Milan). These are the very studios that could be considered closer to formal dance training on the continuum of formal to non-formal.

Dance Competitions/Conventions

A relatively newer aspect of the private studio dance world is the creation of dance competitions and conventions. The origins of competition in dance, which began in ballroom dance, lie in the unclear separation of dance from physical education in the earlier part of the twentieth century. Ballroom dance, in some locations, remained within the domain of physical education, making competition a more central part of the culture, as competition was present in sport. In later years, this competitive ethos became centered in the private studio realm, and organizations have developed to support this direction. Prizes that are awarded in competitive ballroom dancing (called DanceSport in Europe, Australia, and Canada) are supported through the dance studio system.[10]

The organization of competitions being fed by a studio system was popularized first through dance competition organizations (initially mostly ballroom) and then globalized through television dance competitions such as *So You Think You Can Dance* (emphasizing contemporary dance styles, with versions in twenty-five countries) and *Dancing with the Stars* (emphasizing ballroom dance). Dance competition is globalized through outreach, but not dance forms or styles. Both these shows have British roots and are copied in many other countries around the world. The precursor to many of these televised dance shows (though not in a competition format) was MTV (music television) and music videos. Dance forms other than ballroom on television did not initially begin as competitive, but the value and global reach of the ballroom dance competitions seeped into other dance forms, leading to the world of dance competitions and conventions.

The dance convention circuit, which includes classes (which are categorized as non-formal dance teaching and learning) and competitions, is also fed by private dance studios. The private studios that participate in these systems are organized to send their students as a group to competitions that are part of their circuit. This happens internationally. Some examples are Jump Dance Convention, located in the United States and Latin America; Youth America Grand Prix (YAGP, which is actually international), focusing on ballet; and hundreds of other groups around the globe. It is important to note that not all competitions are the same, and YAGP also leads to scholarships and professional ballet contracts.

In the United States, dance studios and competition are closely connected, as is indicated in the research article titled: "Dance and/as Competition in the Privately Owned US Studio."[11] Though there are no government educational standards applied to the dance convention/competition circuit, one observation is that, in order to create some level of standards on which students can be assessed, the socio-cultural grounding of any dance form is ignored in order to make it fit the standard of the organization.[12]

Commercialization

A succinct definition of commercial dance is "dance used in service of selling a product that draws from a blend of jazz, hip-hop, and contemporary styles that is performed in the entertainment industry by heteronormative, highly gendered, young dancing bodies."[13] Dance competition and commercialization are not identical, but are very entwined owing to overlapping values between the two.[14] A distinguishing factor between the two is that competition tends to be recreational in intent, whereas commercial dance is a professional career route. They are both about marketing and selling a product.

Commercialization of dance has led to widespread awareness about dance, but has not had an influence on elevating the status of dance in relationship to other curricular areas.[15] The formal sector of dance education is relatively small in relation to the non-formal and informal sectors, and so commercialization through the non-formal sector tends to influence attitudes about dance in general, regardless of the sector in which it appears. This very element of commercialization is what influences the low status of dance in formal education because commercialization does not make a compelling case for dance as an essential aspect of the curriculum. Commercialization has been exemplified by the previously mentioned conventions, competitions, and television shows, as well as by the proliferation of dancers on stage in large music concerts (mostly pop and hip-hop). The global appeal is that these television shows are in multiple countries, and the music tours are worldwide. *So You Think You Can Dance* has versions in thirty-nine countries, and the format has led to the development of several other commercial dance television shows as well. Though commercialization of dance and dance competition are not identical, the explosion of commercialization has been supported through the many dance competitions that exist in both live practice and on television.

Commercialization: Politics

Commercial dance can have sociopolitical implications, as competition in dance and its popularity have influenced the public perceptions of dance:

> In all these ways, the competition format reiterates and reinforces key values in the neoliberal, globalized economy. As Randy Martin has succinctly observed, neoliberalism is "a triumphant ideology that replaces

state with markets, public with private values, and a liberal consensus with a conservative hegemony." Where the dance studio formerly institutionalized a community's process of transmitting the knowledge of dance, it now functions as the training ground for entry into the labor force of dance, replacing a community function with a market function. In place of the dance recital format that supported a notion of public good through its collective presentation of shared understanding about dance, the dance competition substitutes a machinery of the marketplace that privileges individual accomplishment, replacing public with private values.[16]

Through this analysis, dance as emphasized through commercialization has created two perceptions: that dance is about a "workforce," and that dance is about the perpetuation of a societal philosophy that is motivated by the conservative forces of the time. Dance becomes about creating the same or similar performances that fulfill the very ideals perpetuated by commercialism, which then negates individual expression or development but moves toward continuation of the commercial sector by creating the very types of dancers it values. The combination of workforce demands and neoliberal values contradicts development of human or individualized expression. As discussed in Chapter 4, those who advocate for culturally responsive pedagogy will also state that neoliberalism is just a current manifestation of colonialism, returning society to the practices of erasing local culture in place of an "ideal."[17] By extension, practicing competition in dance is the new colonialism as well.

Though television dance competitions are highly produced and are presented to the world in a scripted fashion, the pedagogical implications are transmitted back to the very studios that participate in dance competition. This becomes a cyclical process, which does not include formal educational values. Also, those who study and teach in formal education are influenced by the very values that are perpetuated through mediated dance as seen on television, lessening the values that define dance education as articulated in Chapter 3. "In Marxist terms, competition in dance replaces its use value as a form of personal self-expression and creativity." Foster continues, "Thus, instead of finding emotional fulfillment through dancing, satisfaction comes from the amount of effort that the dancer puts into its execution. Movement itself is no longer expressive; movement, with its familiar shapings, times, and coordinations of parts of the body, is a kind of shell into which one can pour greater or lesser amounts of drive."[18] The only type of individual expression that is allowed or encouraged in this commercial sector is the effort or simply work that is done.

An additional problem for formal dance education is that Foster's clearly articulated critique of commercial dance is directed at and discussed through the world of dance studies research. This returns to an earlier discussion in Chapter 3, the separation of dance branches, limiting this important viewpoint to a discussion among those in the sub-field of dance studies. The clear critique of commercialism in dance has direct implications for dance education, as articulated earlier: Commercialization is influencing the type of education occurring in private dance studios and it is influencing the larger public perceptions about dance. It is therefore important for those in dance education to create and continue the conversation and research to counter the images perpetuated by commercialization in dance. Those in dance education are not engaging sufficiently with this conversation, though they are beginning to, as exemplified by Schupp's research. But this also contributes to a separation of the sub-fields of dance, leading to the emphasis on some in the traditional dance research areas limiting their association with those in the applied areas of research.

Commercialization: The Body

The portrayal of commercial dance is about the body and not embodied learning from a philosophical perspective. Commercialization in dance has also led to negative connotations about the use of the body. From the time of Isadora Duncan, when she threw off her corsets and danced in a free fashion, along with all the women who tried to move beyond the Victorian canons of the 1800s, dance has been under scrutiny in many areas.[19] There was a time in the 1800s when patronage of ballet dancers was a thinly veiled form of prostitution, as in the Paris Opera Ballet when wealthy male patrons were known to proposition dancers and had a room in the building in which to do this.[20] Dancers in Egypt in the eighteenth century were also involved in prostitution.[21] Dance as a performing art has gone through many periods of being considered sexualized and lower class throughout history.

Focus on the body, and who has agency over the body, exists in dance research in all sectors of dance, both commercial and non-commercial. It also exists in somatics (mentioned in Chapter 4), critical pedagogy, and cultural studies. Intersections with Freirian perspectives, as discussed in Chapter 4, are brought into focus as the discussion becomes about power and who has power over a person's body. For a more complete discussion in this area relating to non-commercial dance, see work by Jill Green.[22]

Coming into a more current focus, the proliferation of dance competition and dance on television has included discussions of the "sexualization of prepubescent girls."[23] This seeming sexualization of prepubescent girls occurs because those in competitions are emulating often older, highly successful performers in the commercial world of dance and related fields. The public's concern relates to this attitude among those who are young, and yet very little conversation exists about the over-sexualized costumes and movements that are perpetuated throughout commercialized dance, regardless of the age of the dancers. The attitudes, approaches, and costumes that are popularized on these shows are then reflected throughout the non-formal sector that aspires to imitate these shows. The cycle continues. Some of the many issues that those in the private sector of dance face is that they are responding to market forces because they are a business. As a business, it is important to attract customers and to run an organization that meets customer expectations, which is part of this cycle.[24] Clark names this issue "sexploitation" and suggests that it results from market forces as well as lack of focus on child development in the teaching process. As discussed earlier, a degree in teacher education is not usually a requirement to teach in the private sector, and so child development knowledge may not be present either.

The Journal of Dance Education had two special issues on "Dance & Sexuality" in 2004 and 2005. Clearly this is a concern, as represented by these focused issues. Yet, those working in the commercial sector are responding to the market and not to educational research. So, there is a different type of disconnect, between those who are academically prepared in dance and those who are not.

Additionally, the commercial presentation of dance, as exemplified by televised competition shows, has become exclusionary, limiting the types of people (as indicated by their body shape, size, and color of skin) who are able to enter and perform. There is no room for expression of anything other than heteronormative presentation. Though the commercialization of dance leads to popular awareness of dance, it also excludes any but a small group of select people who are able to participate.[25]

As Ralph Buck states:

> Through utilizing the process of making and remaking community, we as dance educators have potentially powerful roles to play in education. Our role in meeting some of the global challenges as outlined by UNESCO is tangible and real. We work with people, their bodies, their minds, their feelings and their culture. If we as dance educators cannot play a role in addressing the challenges abundant around us and outlined by UNESCO, then we are not honoring the power of dance.[26]

Commercialization in dance moves the focus away from the power of dance for the person and focuses on outside views of the body and where the body belongs in the sociopolitical context. As Schupp stated, commercialization with competitions promotes a narrow vision of dance that "is entertaining, specialized, and beguiling." She continues, "Dance competition culture and commercial dance are not simply venues for entertainment; they are microcosms of US social and cultural values."[27]

Socio-cultural Impact

The emphasis on commercial dance in non-formal dance teaching and learning has also separated dance into different socio-cultural sectors. The large, commercial dance sector both is expensive and favors white, Eurocentric dancers and dance forms. These become "pedagogies of privilege."[28] In addition to separating access by perceived class, the commercial sector is widely accessed (mostly through television), which then directly contradicts the advocacy for dance as a fundamental aspect of education. Those who are making decisions about including dance in the public, non-commercial sector do not have a ready example of what dance looks like when it is inclusive, egalitarian, and representative of our different sectors of society. The ready examples are commercial and exclusionary, as perpetuated by dance on television.

Competition in dance has influenced pedagogy in the non-formal locations (usually private studios) that participate in these competitions. The driving force has shifted away from pedagogy and toward business and marketing. Those students who are interested in participating in the competition aspect of the studio (and who are accepted) are required to attend a significant number of classes per week at these studios, creating a higher cost to participate. This is in addition to competition fees, as most competitions are held by profit-making organizations charging high fees for participation. The studio also may want to be an advertiser at these competition events (seeking more students), and so the studio has additional fees for advertising, which can cost upward of US$2,000. Studio owners will find some way to pass along these costs to their students. Many additional businesses, all with a profit-making model, are involved in this complex competition structure: those selling costumes or advertising, convention spaces, and itinerant choreographers (who travel to studios to create competition choreography). According to Foster, "students' training, along with the competition fees, can cost anywhere between $5,000 and $30,000 per year [US dollars]."[29]

This model of for-profit dance teaching and learning creates large socioeconomic separation between students and those who do not have the finances to become students. Profit-making studios tend to be located within communities that have the financial means to attend. The socioeconomic disparities of dance education are increasing, along with the global awareness of dance through mediated transmission.

Summary

Dance education considered in the non-formal realm is quite a large field, spanning history as well as geography. The most current iteration, commercial dance, is most widely known, but has not replaced all the non-commercial forms and locations. Commercial dance has only homogenized concepts, not actual forms of non-formal dance teaching and learning. Those forms have been present for a much longer period of time and have provided the true consistency of dance education within non-formal settings, but they are being eclipsed by the financial power and visibility of commercial dance. However, the focus on gender, ethnicity, and social status is not new in the non-formal sector.[30] Commercialization and competition in the non-formal sector have overtaken other issues that have been present for much longer. A closer look will illuminate the non-commercial aspects, as these are not so readily present currently.

A Closer Look will be given in Chapter 9. A personal story, which incorporates many aspects of this non-formal learning and the discussion of informal learning in the chapter that follows, will be in Chapter 9, which follows the chapter on informal learning. Though this story cannot illuminate every issue and concept presented here, it brings many concepts to life through an autoethnographic perspective.

8

Informal Dance Education

Introduction

As described earlier, informal dance education has existed possibly longer than formal dance education but is less recognized owing to the locations in which it takes place and the lack of curriculum. This very unstructured shape is what creates the impression that no education is occurring. This chapter will broaden the definition by including all the locations of informal dance education and how it has been treated; it is often marginalized by those working in formal and non-formal dance education. It is important to address informal dance education so that those with formal preparation as dance educators are aware of prior knowledge gained by their students from informal learning. Informal dance education is described here in detail; in previous chapters, it is contrasted with other forms of dance education. It will be discussed through the following sections:

1. Definition of informal education/operational definition
2. Marginalization of informal dance education
3. Who is the teacher? Who is the student?
4. Unconscious pedagogy/culture or person is the focus.

Definition of Informal Education

Returning to the definitions of the three types of learning, "**Informal learning** is learning that occurs in daily life, in the family, in the workplace, in communities and through activities of all individuals."[1] "In some cases, the term experiential learning is used to refer to informal learning that focuses on learning from experience."[2] This definition was clarified for dance through the theme of the 2017 World Dance Alliance Americas meeting, which stated that, "Dancing from the grassroots—as self-governed, amateur, participatory, community-based: local, translocal, and virtual—can be a public source of pleasure, inclusion, social networking, health and wellbeing, and intergenerational community building."[3] Informal dance education is all the learning that occurs when formal class structures or even formal teaching and learning are not in place. Chapter 1 discussed all the different meanings and uses of dance. Through those definitions it becomes clear that a discussion about informal dance education is about when and where dance occurs, rather than specific techniques or movement styles. Expanding on the definition of informal learning, the Organisation for Economic Co-operation and Development (OECD) states, "Informal learning is never organised, has no set objective in terms of learning outcomes and is never intentional from the learner's standpoint. Often it is referred to as learning by experience or just as experience."[4]

Dance that is learned through the informal process is "the most common way people around the world learn dance culture."[5] The settings can be familial and communal; however, this is neither planned nor organized learning, though it can be a planned or organized event, such as a party or a celebration. A distinguishing element of informal learning is the lack of feedback and pedagogical practices discussed in Chapter 4.

Informal dance education can occur at an organized event (such as a celebration) when those in attendance begin dancing to the music. It can also be entirely spontaneous, such as starting to move when listening to music or watching someone else who is moving. Informal dance education is often closely tied to music, ritual, and religion, as occurs in many of the original locations of dance and movement. It can also occur in a simple social context such as a nightclub or music venue. Some of these examples have been discussed previously and are impossible to list, as a list would be limiting. Therefore, informal dance education is probably more widespread than any other form of dance learning. It is available to all people and all types of experience, but is not often referred to as dance education/learning.

An arts education scholar from Namibia has a clear perspective on informal education as "that which uses the surrounding world and its meaning as curriculum."[6] While informal learning takes place mostly outside formal settings, it can also take place in formal settings. Multiple arts education researchers identify play as an opportunity for informal arts education, but this aspect of learning is often undervalued.[7] The social construction of education, as emphasized by Lev Vygotsky and discussed in Chapter 4, is also considered an aspect of play and as important to informal learning.[8] Play can occur during any part of education, and, in that way, informal education occurs during formal and non-formal education. The critical element is for educators to value what is occurring during these times or moments of play (or informal aspects occurring during formal education) and to recognize that play can occur at any age, in any setting; can influence social-emotional development, cultural development, creativity, and the participants' understanding of others;⁹ and can lead to the development of soft skills or life skills.¹⁰

From a journalist's standpoint, informal learning is an expression of "collective joy" that is seen around the world in many different settings.¹¹ Barbara Ehrenreich covers a diverse range of spectacles, including ancient Greek and Hebrew events, as well as contemporary rock concerts. What they all have in common is the "communal celebration" that is open to all participants. She traces this story through history and anthropology. The common thread is that the outside world does not view these celebrations as dance.

The issue that occurs when informal dance learning is defined is that, whereas the forms of dance that are learned or experienced through this process are well documented through dance history and dance anthropology, the teaching and learning of these forms are ignored. From a traditional dance education perspective, these dance forms may not exist or may have already been marginalized. Secondarily, a dance form that might be learned in a formal class (salsa, for example) is not considered to have been learned if the only exposure to salsa is through a community event, such as at a *quinceañera*, the celebration of a girl's fifteenth birthday which is popular in the Spanish-speaking Americas. The definition of informal learning is then lost. This very issue (teaching and learning of forms of dance that arise from community or religious events) was discussed in Chapter 3 as a product of the separation of dance into branches or subdisciplines. When considering informal learning, the issue of dividing dance into branches becomes clear. But the OECD still makes a case to recognize informal learning by saying: "The assumption behind the work reported here is that all learning has value and most of it deserves to be made visible and recognized."¹²

Marginalization

To take a closer look at the context of informal dance education, it is important to consider the marginalization of indigenous cultures, as this has a direct influence on the manner in which informal dance education is perceived. The marginalization of indigenous cultures has a long history. This history began with colonialism, which occurred when colonializers appeared to conquer one group and proselytize religious beliefs. This is the history of the Maori people in New Zealand, the Aboriginal people in Australia, the First Nations in Canada, the Native Americans in the United States, the Polynesian people in the Pacific Islands, many different tribes in South Africa as well as all throughout the African nations, and numerous other cultures around the world. Colonialization led to the stripping of these indigenous religious practices and cultures, which in most instances included dance.¹³ The dance practices of many marginalized cultures were relegated to a lower status than the practices of those who colonialized—hence, the introduction of ballet throughout the world, as well as the creation of a hierarchical alignment of dance forms, mentioned originally in Chapter 1.

The effects of this marginalization are still seen today in formal dance education settings, as discussed in the research summary in Chapter 5. The research discussed the perceptions of those who felt a "disconnect" between their prior dance learning and formal dance education. Participants in this research discussed that their prior informal dance education was not perceived as valuable within the formal dance education setting. From a student perspective, the participants in this research were articulating these very issues with the type of dance that is taught and valued in formal education. This is a different perspective on an ongoing conversation.

Categorization can also lead to marginalization. However, in the instance of the definitions of formal, non-formal, and informal learning, this categorization does the exact opposite: it opens up a discussion so that types of teaching and learning are no longer ostracized.[14] The many indigenous cultures that were marginalized through colonialization have continued to pass their values and customs to new generations, despite the many historical obstacles, which are too long to list. Learning about these traditions mostly remains in the informal realm, whereas any formal dance/movement education has also imported the colonializing concepts. Looking at these forms from an outside perspective and trying to categorize them according to "evaluative criteria" then lead to further marginalization.[15]

New dance forms actually developed through colonialization and the restriction of the original forms. Original forms and practices—for example the religious practices and movement of the Yoruba from West Africa—were blended with Catholicism in the New World; thus, new religions were born along with new movement practices. Voodoo and Santeria in Caribbean nations are examples of these new practices. As the world has become more globally connected, new dance forms are constantly evolving and blending traditions from many different dance practices.

Teacher-Student Relationship

Returning to the OECD definition of "learning by experience," there are no defined roles for student or teacher in informal learning in dance. As stated by an anthropologist when analyzing dancers in discotheques, "They are their own masters of what they do and how they do it."[16] Informal learning is devoid of all the rigid or strict structures that exist within formal education. There are no roles (of teacher and student), no set location, no curriculum, no standards, no assessment, no qualifications (for either teacher or student). The lack of all these parameters is exactly what makes informal teaching and learning invisible. But there is pedagogy. As discussed earlier, the pedagogy mostly consists of imitation or mimicry.[17] The roles of student and teacher are not defined and can even be fluid, so that a teacher becomes a student, and a student becomes a teacher in a seamless fashion.

The lack of roles and any other formal structures returns to the discussion of Chapter 5. Without formal structures present, informal learning is not respected or valued in other educational contexts. This lack of recognition is intimately tied to the concept of marginalization and hierarchies. The assumption becomes that, if learning is formally organized and named, then it must be superior to any other type of learning. So, this very devaluing is perpetuated.

UNESCO attempts to value this informal type of learning:

Today, in a complex and fast-changing world, it is necessary for individuals to acquire and adapt competences (knowledge, skills, and attitudes) through all forms of learning to cope with various challenges. However, qualifications systems in many societies still focus on formal learning in educational institutions. As a result, a large part of individuals' learning remains unrecognised, and many individuals' motivation and confidence to continue learning is not well promoted. This leads to a huge under-utilisation of human talent and resources in society. Therefore, the learning outcomes that young people and adults acquire in the course of their life in non-formal and informal settings need to be made visible, assessed and accredited.[18]

Informal learning, by its nature, can never be formally organized; however, as stated earlier, it can occur within the context of formal education. It can be recognized and valued for its contributions and for simply existing. The spaces in which it exists and the opportunity for it to unfold are the only structures that can really be controlled. So, the time to be with others in social, community, and home life settings is of primary importance for informal learning. Time for play is also important for informal learning. It is these very settings that can be nurtured and protected. Additionally, those in the formal and non-formal settings should expand their concept of education to include the value of informal learning in dance. It has much to contribute to formal and non-formal learning in dance, as well as how people value dance.

Contrast/Compare/Summary of Three Learning Settings

Before a closer look at the three types of dance education, consideration will first be given to the following areas as a whole, as they have now been discussed through the chapters on formal, non-formal, and informal dance education:

- Who are the teachers?
- What are their qualifications?
- Who are the students?
- What are their qualifications?
- What is the curriculum?
- Who oversees the education in this setting?
- Is this education for profit or not for profit?

Through this summary, it will be clear to see that, while there is a continuum, as expressed earlier, to the outsider, formal and non-formal dance education are closer on the continuum. The experience from the student perspective is not the focus in this discussion, but, if the student experience was emphasized, it would make the three types of learning much more evenly spread along the continuum.

Who Are the Teachers? What Are Their Qualifications?

As discussed in the two preceding chapters, teachers are clearly defined in both formal and non-formal education, but qualifications are what separates formal from non-formal education. If a government or a larger entity creates the qualifications, it tends to be formal education. If the individual school creates the qualifications, it tends to be non-formal education. In many instances, qualifications rest on past experiences and not on pedagogical content knowledge or teaching proficiency. This leans more toward non-formal education on this continuum. Informal education does not have a defined teacher. Anyone can be a teacher in this setting, perhaps not even knowing that they occupy this role. Someone can inadvertently take the role of a teacher by stating "I'll show you" or "just follow me." So, the teacher role is quite fluid in informal education.

Who Are the Students? What Are Their Qualifications?

As with teachers, students are clearly defined in both formal and non-formal education but may not realize they are students in informal education. In informal education, one person may inadvertently begin to mimic or follow another person's activities, and that imitator has become a student in this setting. In formal education, the student is the one who qualifies for the larger educational setting. In non-formal education, depending on the setting, there may or may not be a qualification, but qualifying might involve an audition or the ability to pay for the education that is offered.

What Is the Curriculum? Who Oversees Education in this Setting?

As discussed in Chapter 6 on formal education, the curriculum is defined and may be set by a governmental authority or some entity larger than the dance unit itself. The complication in these instances is that the entities setting the curriculum may have no knowledge of dance themselves, in which case they should consult those with the appropriate knowledge base. Non-formal education has a curriculum that is set by a local school, studio, or professional organization that oversees that type of dance. Unlike non-formal education, in formal educational settings those defining the curriculum have complete knowledge about student learning and growth. The specific discipline (dance, in this instance) is set within that general knowledge. In non-formal education, those with professional performance experience set the curriculum and generally do not incorporate knowledge of general student learning and growth. In other words, curriculum setting in this context is more heavily based on discipline content knowledge, with little to no emphasis on pedagogical content knowledge. Informal education has no curriculum, and its very unstructured shape is what creates the impression that no education is occurring. Overseeing education in each of these settings is done, usually, by the same entity that creates the curriculum. In the instance of informal education, with no curriculum and no oversight of the education, there is again the perception that no education is occurring.

Is this Education for Profit or Not for Profit?

Generally, formal education is not for profit. Non-formal education can be either, depending on the setting. The full commercialization described in Chapter 7 is for profit. No money is exchanged in informal education, and so this is not discussed in that setting.

Summary

Informal dance education and learning are least understood, but can hold the key to a holistic definition of dance education. In the past they have been marginalized through colonialization, categorization, and formal education. Informal dance education is present in many of those areas of life that include cultural education and values. Though inconsistently documented, informal dance education is the oldest, and most widespread, form of dance education. Language has done a disservice to its recognition, as discussed in Chapter 1.

Chapter 9 takes a closer look at all three chapters on formal, non-formal, and informal education. Its beauty and eloquence show that involvement in dance education is both a personal as well as an engaged experience and, more often, integrates all three forms of education, without strong barriers between them. The human process that an individual experiences, as evidenced by this personal story, is in essence the process of becoming a dance educator and a fully realized integrated being.

9

The Formation of a Dancer

John-Mario Sevilla

This chapter is an autobiography that exemplifies the three types of dance education—formal, non-formal, and informal. This shift of voice and author is to give insight into how these three types of learning can actually manifest, beyond theory. A reflection on the author's life and engagement in dance also shows that there are no formal delineations between types of learning. As discussed in the introduction, John-Mario Sevilla recognizes the influences of colonialism on his practices, has gone through many versions of reflection on his life, career, and influences, and has lived a life in spite of "othering." This chapter summarizes through a lived practice how this book may be embodied throughout one's deepening dance education and formative human development.

Birth and Becoming: An Informal Dance Education

It wasn't until after I had a performance career that I had a formal dance education. I was in my mid-thirties, and it was at Teachers College, Columbia University. Already a dancer by profession, this was the first time I had studied dance in an academic environment. Curiously, before and since Teachers College, I've had signifying experiences, both in and out of studios and classrooms, that have indelibly sustained and inspired a dance life.

Whenever I'm asked when I started dancing, I say, "When I was born." My dance education began on the island of Maui with my mom, Frances Fortunata Arcilla Sevilla, right after birth, when my body, in attunement with hers, received the attention that ensured my survival and well-being during that critical stage of my developing self. What, if not through the actions of the body, was I viably sensing, tasting, feeling, hearing, seeing, thinking, and learning during those initial months? What did I, an infant, an emerging being, experience during those inklings of cognition? Was she informing me then, leading me on a pathway, a curriculum of her design?

Her motherhood embodied foundational intentions and ambitious visions of a future me that she had expressed regularly to anyone. These proclamations are ingrained in my memory to this day. She declared that I needed to be learned and articulate. Both she and my father insisted that hard work and educational success would elevate our social standing. She would compare us with more economically successful ethnic families and noted how we needed to strive to be as good, if not better. I understood from an early age that I was to be a manifestation of these aspirations, and she did everything in her power to push me toward those explicit goals and objectives, to get the schooling that she—a child laborer of the Great Depression—did not have, in spite of her aptitude. Paired with these clear notions of success, nonetheless, were somatic sensibilities that were less defined and more felt, and, in reflection, not only about my future but as much about our past and present. Her parental expectations may not have resulted in the profession that she had imagined for me. They nevertheless informed the person I am today, a dancer, choreographer, producer, educator, and a lifelong-learning citizen of our planet.

Born in Pepeʻekeo, Hawaiʻi, Frances was also the daughter of immigrants from Cebu and Leyte, Philippines. Her dance with my infant self—soothing, rocking, and bouncing—included clapping rhymes and songs of her parents that connected me to her, to my family history, to my expanding world and cultural legacy. She had studied hula with one of Maui's most renowned *kumu hula* (hula master) and musical composers of her generation, Aunty Emma Farden Sharpe. I am certain that during those critical swaying moments of human development she imparted the kinesthetic and emotional flow of the dance such that hula has always felt innate and natural, like I was born to do it. In truth, I was born *into* it. These messages of motion, melody, and pulse—dances of my earliest being and knowing—initiated deep habits of mind and body that I still feel today and connect me with her and the elusive, potent history of Hawaiʻi. Throughout this transmission of kinesthetic sensations, motion was meaningful.

Hula: An Informal and Non-Formal Dance Education

For my early childhood care, as the "baby brother" of five siblings, I was given over to my older sisters, Linda, Lolita, and Rosita. They studied the hula with Leimomi Tokunaga and Robert Kalani as well as Spanish folk dance with Tito Cesar, a charismatic teacher who had found his way to

Maui to start a disciplined troupe of children that featured the three Sevilla girls. I soon began openly staging my own hula pageants in my father's grocery store. My older brother, Duke, denounced these performances and proclaimed me a "sissy." So, in this hidden curriculum, I also quickly experienced the fraught gender issues of the dancing male body. At that time in the 1960s, hula was not considered the venerable art it is today. Though it was the beginning of the Hawaiian renaissance, when *kanaka maoli* (Native Hawaiians) began to affirm their rich history and political rights through the resurgence in cultural practices, especially through hula, the dance was still not considered something boys should do.

I quit my public dance presentations and satisfied the urge to perform in the seclusion of my parents' bedroom. My dance education became surreptitious. Ashamed of the ridicule from my brother and who-knows-who-else, my studio and stage, behind the closed door of my parents' bedroom, was figuratively a closet, where literally the voluminous, dramatic costumes were stored.

More than a decade ago, I joined a *hui* (group) of New York City (NYC) hula dancers, led by Michelle Nalei Akina, Janu Cassidy, and the late Keo Woodford. Today, I'm a proud dancer of hula. Since leaving my full-time job as an internationally touring concert dance performer, after completing my formal education in two graduate programs (Teachers College and University of Wisconsin, Milwaukee) and while directing dance education and performance programming at New York City Ballet and 92nd Street Y Harkness Dance Center, I've returned to the practice of hula, somewhat in the traditional model of hula learning, with a *kumu hula* in a *hālau* (school). Since the days with the NYC *hui*, I have studied with Kumu Hula June Kaʻililani Tanoue of Hālau I Ka Pono, who comes from the Aunty Maiki Aiu Lake lineage of hula. I now am a *haumana* (student) of Kumu Hula Hōkūlani Holt, from the island of Maui, who inherited knowledge of this cultural practice from many generations of her *kupuna* (elders) and *ʻohana* (family). As a hula practitioner, this naming of one's genealogy is a serious responsibility.

My education in hula is also non-traditional; as Kumu Hōkūlani lives and teaches on Maui and I reside in Stockton, New Jersey, my study is online and virtual. Via monthly Skype, Zoom, and Google classroom sessions, I watch video of her other *haumana* and share video of my own practice. And, when on the *ʻāina* (land) of Maui, I join her weekly lessons. I am learning the foundational canon of her lineage—the movements that embody fundamental cultural values, the *mele* and *oli* (song, poetry, and chant) that express the dance's purpose and intentions, and *pule* (prayers, blessings, and incantations) that summon meta-energetic forces and spiritual beings to guide us. Through this hybrid form of traditional education, I am trying to practice the holistic form of hula that lives beyond the footwork and gestures, that grounds us to our *ʻāina* and sensitizes us to the elements of nature, of which we hula dancers are their stewards, ever respectful and grateful for our *kupuna*, cultivating *mana* (spiritual energy) and *ʻike* (insight) and living important values, like *laulima* (cooperation and unity) and *pono* (righteousness).

Social Dance: An Informal and Formal Dance Education

My dad, who was known as A.B., joked that the moniker stood for American Boy rather than his real name, Asisclo Baylon. My parents had a deliberate strategy for our immigrant family to assimilate: we had to master the American cultural arts, which, at the time, meant classical music. For the Sevillas, music was required study as part of our social elevation and achievement. A.B. played the violin, Frances played the piano. I had 12 years of private piano instruction and played the trumpet and French horn in middle and high school. Until graduate school, music was my only formal education in the arts.

Dance, on the other hand, was recreation. The Arcillas (mom's side of the family) loved to jitterbug, a dance that I, throughout my childhood, observed them enjoy at weddings. Their fleet, intimate, and intricate partnering provoked awe and longing. Then, the traditional wedding dance, which, in the Filipino version, involved stuffing dollar bills into the kissing mouths of the newlyweds, fascinated me. Later, in my work as a dancer with Pilobolus, where the skill of weight sharing and bearing was one of the innovative traits of this singular company, I was an able partner. I owe my sensitivity to partnering and ensemble dancing to these weekend celebrations with family.

As a quiet child observer of public dancing, I continued to learn and satisfy my need to move from local and cinematic versions of musical theater, *American Bandstand*, and *Soul Train*. TV was the teacher, and my holy day was Saturday when the dance shows aired after the morning cartoons. Decades before such castings were considered innovative on Broadway, my sister, Lolita, played the lead role in her high school musical, *Oliver*, cross-dressing as a British orphan with a multicultural cast of other Asians and Pacific Islanders. "Where Is love?" she sang. In the audience, I wept.

One day, the eldest sister, Linda, brought home from college a new dance, a rocking weight shift from side to side that allowed the free leg to rotate and groove inwardly, accentuating a circular pathway of the knee, soulfully weighted. I watched her teach my other sisters. I recently saw Beyoncé do a quicker, sharper version of this move on one of her music videos. When Rosita, the third eldest, went away to college, she brought home Disco, which was trickier to master without a partner. But she also knew the Hustle. I dashed into my stealth studio to master the line dance alone, along with my growing repertory of other social dances learned from family, film, and television. My masters thesis at Teachers College mined the historical and cultural emanations of a fun 1960s soul dance song, from which the Hustle is clearly derived. The contemplation of an excavation of a popular dance connected me to the tragic African American saga of displacement, slavery, and prevailing injustice.

May Day: An Informal Dance Education

A.B. took the family out of the Catholic Church and parochial school when the nuns at St. Anthony wanted to keep my brother, Duke, back a grade. I was just a dance-crazed toddler at the time. I theorize that the Marianist sisters on Maui, in the 1960s, were not able to diagnose and support a case of hyperactivity. So, we went to public school. I was enrolled at Wailuku Elementary. And though there was never any formal arts curriculum, the years were spiked with formative experiences.

At Wailuku El, my favorite event of the year was May Day, when all the students would perform dances with their classmates. The performance was followed by outdoor games and competitions, like the three-legged race, which pitted the classes against each other. The island variant involved pairs of students racing other couples on *getta* (Japanese thonged slippers) built for two on two-by-fours. In kindergarten, we danced my first sanctioned public hula to a comic *hapa-haole* (a fusion of Hawaiian and Western music) tune, *Puka Pants*, a song about the carefree joys of wearing pants with holes (*puka*). I don't know what else I learned that year, but I can recall the patches my mom had sewn all over my shorts and my coconut hat. In the third grade, we performed a traditional maypole dance, but the fourth graders did something extraordinary. First, they boogied to popular rock-n-roll music. I can't remember the song, but it has since left a surf-rock impression. Near the end of it, everyone danced however they wanted for a few frantic, all-hell-broke-loose, crazy moments, and then they froze. Then they did it again, this time one line after the other, still wild, chaotic, and joyful, but in a sequence. Finally, they again danced however they wanted, together. I was stunned with what I now know were the "free dance," "improvisation," "tableau," and "canon." And, though I didn't know the words for what I saw, I yearned to do it, too.

Philippine Folk Dance: A Non-Formal Dance Education

As part of our familial religious protestation, we became Episcopalian/Anglican, or the Filipino version of it, which is known as *Anglipayan*. The entire service was spoken and sung in my father's language, Ilocano, which I didn't understand. My mother spoke Visayan, a completely different language, so English, the language of the new country, was the only idiom of the house, and we had to speak it well. Yet, I was caught by the sacredness, the mystery, the pageantry, the ritual, the costumes, the gestures, the notions of goodness. I sang in the choir, faking my comprehension of Ilocano. The Good Shepherd Youth Choir was a way to organize the Filipino youth of the church in engaged fellowship. The choir provided no serious voice training. We sang "by ear" rather than by reading the actual notes on the page. The organist/choirmaster, Manang ("big sister") Nancy Andres, relied on our natural youthful voices to render an angelic tone to the hymns. However, when the older boys' voices started to change, she decided that we should also learn Philippine folk dance. We henceforth became a disciplined folk dance troupe, which began my kinesthetic education of my Filipino-American legacy. My first dance, taught by Nana ("aunt") Agrifina Cabebe, was *Rogelia*, a folksy square dance, clearly a colonial iteration of European social dances.

At age 11, we entered Maui's annual Filipino folk dance competition, which had until then included only adult dancers, and won. Our popularity grew, and we visited and performed at churches all over Hawaiʻi. We toured Victoria and Vancouver (Canada), Seattle, San Francisco, and Los Angeles, which culminated with a performance at Disneyland. After we learned most of the folk dance repertory known on Maui, we invited the professor of Philippine folk dance at the University of Hawaiʻi at Mānoa, H. Wayne Mendoza, to teach us. Manong ("big brother") Wayne remains today a life-long artistic mentor.

When I was in the 8th grade, I was invited to perform an experimental interpretation of the *Maglalatik*. Traditionally, this joyous, shirtless, male-only dance with a skimpy costume of coconut shells that are strung on the thighs, backs, chest, and shoulders and percussively struck by the performers commemorates a battle between Christians and Muslims. For this new version, the dance—a trio—was conceived to interpret the Spanish-American War that ceded the Philippines to the United States. Each dancer was to represent one of the countries in that conflict, the United States, Spain, and the Philippines. I was flown from Maui to Honolulu to learn and perform this dance. I remember slides on the scrim, spoken text, and new music. In hindsight, this was my first modern dance. My performance was observed by Lucrecia Reyes (aka "Mommy") Urtula, the charismatic director of the national dance company of the Philippines, Bayanihan, who, after seeing my performance, invited me to study with the company in Manila. My parents refused.

The Good Shepherd Youth Choir appeared often on a TV show, called *Filipino Fiesta*. As I began to be known as a dancer, my adolescent self felt a worry grow, without concrete proof, that my masculinity was being questioned. I don't quite know from where the shame came. It could have been from the moment when choir members lodged the term "gay" against someone. When I asked what they meant, they answered with silence. The taunts of my brother also echoed in my memory. I already knew then that

I was different, softer, and more reflective in temperament, and had an attraction to other boys. Somewhere, in my education as a dancer—a null curriculum of a sort—all of these heteronormative forces and homophobic fears converged. So, I quit dancing before I started high school.

From Philippine Folk to Modern Dance: A Non-Formal Dance Education

After a year of culture shock at Northwestern University, where I joined a popular fraternity of jocks and tried to pass as a straight college guy, I moved to Honolulu. I enrolled at the University of Hawai'i at Mānoa and declared myself an English major. By then, my disco-dancing sister, Rosita, had become a disco-dancing nurse and belonged to a Filipino folk dance troupe, called Pamana, which, in Pilipino or Tagalog, means legacy. Pamana was led by Hana Gomez Trinidad, a former dancer of Bayanihan, the Manila-based company that I'd been invited to study with when I was an 8th grader. *Bayanihan*, which can be translated as the collective spirit and shared vision of a community, created an international stir when it first toured the globe in the late 1950s with its exotic dances of the 7,500+ island archipelago. The company had a run on Broadway. Hana was part of the first generation of dancers, many of whom were just teenagers at the time. They were nevertheless cultural ambassadors on behalf of a country that was then an Asian model of American-style democracy and capitalism.

When I moved to Honolulu, I joined Pamana and, in so many ways, felt like I had come home. I had matured and gotten over most of my fears of dancing. In fact, I finally realized that I needed to dance, that dance brought me absolute, deep joy. Pamana provided a space and community that valued my dancing self. Run like a family, the group was a mix of a social club and performing company. Hana's husband, Corky, who was a political cartoonist, was an artistic adviser; all of their children danced. Weekly rehearsals started with food and conversation that eventually led to the learning of dances. Despite the relaxed atmosphere, Pamana presented professional theatrical productions, in the manner of Bayanihan, with dramatic lighting and costumes. Performances were organized into suites that explained the four major genres of Philippine dance. The concerts started with the Igorot suite that portrayed the earthy dances of the indigenous mountain tribes. The dignified Maria Clara section—which highlighted the noble, colonial dances that were transplanted from European social dance forms—followed. The sinuous and solemn Moro segment portrayed the Muslim clans of the south. And, the finale featured the inventive and buoyant dances of the barrios, which also illuminated lasting European impressions. All of these dances had been taken from their original contexts (the celebrations and rituals of the villages and tribes) and theatricized and performed by trained dancers.

As we were growing up, we thought of them as folk dance. But the more appropriate description of this appropriation for theatrical purposes is folkloric dance.

While in Pamana, I finally got to study with Bayanihan in Manila for a whole summer. When I returned, I was charged with teaching the rest of the company the new repertory that I had learned. A rehearsal was booked in a dance studio in Honolulu, called Dances We Dance. I arrived early to prepare. A dance rehearsal was in process. Two women and one man were traveling through the entire space of the studio, with, through, and around each other, forward and backward, linking and breaking with one another, limping ("piques") and leaping with an urgent flow that I had never witnessed before. Once again, the motion swept me away.

An older woman and man who had been watching the rehearsal gave the dancers notes afterward. The couple had noticed me watching, so they walked over and introduced themselves as Betty Jones and Fritz Ludin. They asked me if I had ever seen this kind of dance. "Concert dance," they called it, and would I like to study it, they asked. I, of course, said yes, and the next day began my education as a modern dancer in the principles of movement—fall and recovery, weight and breath, isolations of the body, the successional flow of movement, etc.—that were promoted by Doris Humphrey, Charles Weidman, and José Limón. Betty had danced with Doris, considered along with Charles Weidman and Martha Graham as pioneers of modern dance. José was Doris's protégé. When José started his own company, Betty was one of the first members. Fritz, who joined the company later, became Betty's partner on stage and in life. Betty taught at Juilliard and studied with Lulu Sweigard, who developed the somatic practice of ideokinesis, which brought to dance a deep attention to the efficient and imagistic mechanics of anatomy. Betty and Fritz moved to Hawai'i in the 1970s and started Dances We Dance, a school and company. Within months of studying with them, I began dancing the company's repertory and soon learned and performed that first choreography of modern dance that had initially moved me to become a concert dancer, Doris Humphrey's *Invention*.

A Dancer's Life: An Ongoing Dance Education

I was an English major. UH-Mānoa had a dance program with BFA and MFA tracks. But while I performed in many student concerts and enrolled in a couple of classes there, my true dance education, which operated on a separate curriculum from my literary studies, was an apprenticeship with Dances We Dance and Pamana. While reading and writing about literature, I was experiencing an unstoppable welling seriousness in dance.

Upon graduation, when it came time to declare my professional ambition, I was faced with a dilemma. My parents explicitly intended for me to go to law or medical school. But I had decided to become a dancer. Despite all of the dance experiences in our family's social and cultural lives, A.B. and Frances still thought dance was a hobby. The dutiful pressure to please my immigrant parents loomed heavily over me at the time. It took my adviser and mentor in the English department, Jack Unterecker, a renowned poet/scholar, to boost me toward the thing that had brought me the greatest satisfaction. He offered an essential question that has encouraged me throughout my lucky life in dance: "What's wrong," he asked, "with making beauty?"

I decided to follow that quest. And I am learning that beauty is kinesthetic, fecund, and cosmic. The process of cultivating these aesthetic sensations through, with, and for the body, while organic and deeply personal, has had ethical, cultural, economic, political, environmental, and metaphysical consequences: life, through all of its quests, trials, and transformations, from dream to reflection, a heartfelt search and discovery of meanings in motion.

SECTION III

Dance in Our Lives

Introduction

Section III includes an academic perspective, but this time it is woven in with the personal stories in an approach to the question, what does this all mean? Chapter 10 is an invitation to Alfdaniels Mabingo, from Uganda, to a dialogue about ethnorelative teaching concepts that are applied to dance education. These conversations developed over time and now are considered in a contrast/compare version of two people who came from such diverse backgrounds who now work in parallel with each other.

From a worldview, indigenous dance forms and values are slowly becoming more acknowledged. However, within the United States, this acknowledgment is much slower than in New Zealand, Australia, and Canada. An invitation to William Huntington to write from an inside/outside perspective about Native American dance forms Chapter 11. It is inside because he has explored some dance forms through his Native American siblings, and outside because he is a Caucasian male.

The final chapter brings all these seemingly disparate discussions together in order for the reader to ponder all these issues, and more, and consider them within the contexts in which he or she will teach or work. The philosophical grounding that was developed in Section I is reiterated and extended, and, with the personal perspective, this chapter returns to the first-person narrative. Nothing is meant to provide definitive answers or recipes that one can follow. Rather, the reader will be encouraged to consider some analysis of experiences past, present, and future in order to honor the presence of dance in our lives.

10

Ethnorelativism in Dance Education

Alfdaniels Mabingo and Susan Koff

Introduction

Dance educators come from different cultural, national, political, racial, social, and geographic backgrounds. The journey to becoming a dance educator is shaped by numerous experiences that an individual is exposed to. These varied backgrounds may include educational opportunities, dance traditions, familial upbringing, cultural encounters, and socioeconomic factors. Exposure to a multiplicity of influences forms preconceptions that frame one's worldview through which the dance teacher develops, rationalizes, and applies pedagogies in different environments of dance education. The world in which dance educators work is becoming progressively complex. The students are more diverse than ever. The environments in which dance is taught and learned are increasingly varied. The functions that dance serves in different communities are ever-expanding. Dance educators have found themselves in working environments that may not align with their ethnocentric worldviews and philosophies. This phenomenon requires dance educators to cope with the ever-changing environment of practice and at the same time retain their professional teaching identities.

This chapter critically examines two professionals' work and reflections on social, cultural, and educational orientations which shape ethnorelative pedagogic philosophies and application. It is necessary to adhere to the view that reflection is "a key means by which teachers can become more in tune with their sense of self and with a deep understanding of how this self fits into a larger context which involves others; in other words, reflection is a factor in the shaping of identity."[1] There is a notion that, "Teaching pedagogy as a subject does not acknowledge that developing a personal pedagogy results from the interaction between an individual's beliefs and skills."[2] This chapter aims to dispel this view by sharing two personal narratives on how reflection on personal backgrounds can transform a dance teacher's pedagogic philosophy. Specifically, this text critically examines how to develop ethnorelative approaches to pedagogical development, rationalization, and application.[3]

The personal narratives of Susan Koff and Alfdaniels Mabingo reveal how the complex schemas of social, cultural, and educational backgrounds continue to evolve the way they see themselves as dance teachers. "In other words, they are continually in the process of fashioning and refashioning identities by patching together fragments of the discourses to which they are exposed."[4] The following question examines the themes of this chapter: How can self-reflection on the cultural, social, and educational backgrounds of a dance teacher lead them to cultivate an ethnorelative pedagogical philosophy? The analysis dissects how the cultural and educational environments that teachers were exposed to during their early days of dance education continue to act as points of departure for teachers to engage in ethnorelative approaches to dance pedagogy. In the context of this chapter, concepts of ethnorelativism represent movement away from cultural biases (ethnorelativism).[5] Arguably, engaging in self-reflexivity on personal journeys and backgrounds can allow a dance educator to explore means to ethnorelatively transform their pedagogies. In this process of transformation toward ethnorelative pedagogies, the dance educator seeks to recognize, accept, and adapt to the diverse environments in which they find themselves teaching.

Ethnorelativism in Dance Education: Agency, Reflection, and Transformation

It is vital to note that developing ethnorelative pedagogical approaches is a transformative experience that entails a dance teacher's agency and reflection. Reflection on cultural, social, and educational backgrounds creates what has been defined as emancipatory knowledge.[6] According to Jack Mezirow, "Emancipatory knowledge is knowledge gained through critical self-reflection, as distinct from the knowledge gained from our 'technical' interest in the objective world or our 'practical' interest in social relationships."[7] Recognizing that reflecting on past experience develops ethnorelative pedagogies is an emancipatory and transformative experience because it creates possibilities for one to develop intercultural competence. Judith Martin and Thomas Nakayama have noted that self-knowledge is considered to be the most important kind of knowledge for intercultural communication competency.[8]

Edward C. Warburton's focus on including pedagogical content with subject content was a central reference and catalyst, illuminating that one's background offers great insight to the construction of one's teaching philosophies.[9] "Learning to teach is an inherently reflexive process. One's assumptions and beliefs are challenged . . . Teachers' beliefs derive directly from personal experiences in a subject. These beliefs have been shown to influence how teachers structure tasks and interact with learners."[10] The beliefs that Warburton is alluding to stem from the encounters teachers have had in social, cultural, and educational contexts. One's personal disposition is central to the way a person performs teaching functions and the tasks that teachers set for students.

When dance teachers reflect on their personal journeys and generate personal stories as a means to ethnorelative pedagogical practices, they become what Carey E. Andrzejewski has referred to as a whole person.[11] In the context of dance education, the "whole person is composed of layered elements including, but not limited to the intellectual, emotional, physical, social, aesthetic, creative, and spiritual."[12] When teachers reflect on their personal journeys, they appreciate how such encounters impact their intellectual, emotional, creative, social, and cultural wholeness.

Engaging in self-reflection is vital in raising intercultural awareness and ethnorelative pedagogical applications. According to Milton J. Bennett, teachers can effectively teach in diverse environments if they first recognize and understand their own worldviews and then use this understanding to embrace the worldviews of their students.[13] Teachers' nature of teaching reveals their stance on their "understanding and interpretation of how the world functions and express[es] how individuals have constructed their worldviews, in other words: their realities."[14] When teachers seek to know themselves, question their beliefs, and reflect on the pillars that support their mode of pedagogic reasoning, they identify areas in which they need to grow. Teachers in today's complex society must acknowledge that, in diverse settings, one of those areas might be intercultural competence and awareness.

Dance teachers need to find moments to question the self. In this case, "Self, then, might be thought of as the meaning maker and identity as the meaning made, even as the self and identity evolve and transform over time."[15] The meaning-making process that drives toward intercultural awareness can be transformative. This is all the more so because self-reflection can push "the individual toward a more inclusive, differentiated, permeable (open to other points of view), and integrated meaning perspective, the validity of which has been established through rational discourse."[16] Teachers' reflection on their beliefs, biases, and interests and the factors that inform them is necessary. It enables them to develop ways to contextualize their pedagogies, especially when they are working in culturally complex environments.

This self-reflection can lead to what Mezirow has defined as perspective transformation, which "is the process of becoming critically aware of how and why our assumptions have come to constrain the way we perceive, understand, and feel about our world; changing these structures of habitual expectation to make possible a more inclusive, discriminating, and integrative perspective; and, finally, making choices or otherwise acting upon these new understandings."[17]

As dance educators who have come from complex backgrounds and taught dance in diverse contexts, Koff and Mabingo found the views from the foregoing literature illuminating. The discourses framed the way they synthesized their reflections and the narratives that form the basis for this chapter. The views expressed in the literature touched on their complex struggles, transformation, agency, and dilemmas which reconcile their backgrounds and development and application of ethnorelative pedagogies.

To arrive at this stage, Koff and Mabingo transformed their own frame of reference, using what Mezirow has termed "subjective reframing."[18] They engaged in a three-part process of subjective framing to arrive at insights that constitute this discussion. First, they critically reflected on their backgrounds and beliefs. In the process, Koff and Mabingo individually pursued the following question: How can self-reflection on the cultural, social, and educational backgrounds of a dance teacher lead them to cultivate an ethnorelative pedagogical philosophy? Second, with broader insights sparked by the aforementioned question, they engaged in discourse to validate the critically reflective understandings. They exchanged views on the points of their reflections, asking each other probing questions and making critical comments about each other's viewpoints.

Their different backgrounds enabled them to make insightful and critical inquiries into each other's reflections on social, cultural, and educational backgrounds. The final stage involved engaging in action. This action centered on generating insightful narratives that captured the essence of reflections on their personal journeys. They specifically invoked their memories about the social, cultural, and educational backgrounds that kindled their ethnorelative pedagogic identities. To generate these narratives, Koff and Mabingo referenced the view that the narratives that teachers create can illuminate their personal and professional teaching philosophies and identities.[19] Following Therese Riley and Penelope Hawe's position on how research can rationalize meaningful data from narratives, they interpreted the themes and meanings inherent in their personal narratives.[20]

Contextualizing Dance Practices

Koff and Mabingo are dance educators who have lived in varied environments that have shaped the ethnorelative ways in which they teach dance. They acknowledge that the journey toward developing and applying ethnorelative teaching philosophies is still continuing as they find themselves working in varied environments and with diverse populations.

> **Mabingo's Story**
>
> As I entered the "mirror room," I had so many imaginations of what the modern dance technique class was going to be like. As a freshman at Makerere University in Uganda, I had no prior knowledge of the "mirror room" and "modern dance technique." When I entered the room, I saw mirrors erected on one side of the room. The teacher opened the class with a brief introduction of the different techniques encompassed in the modern dance tradition. The class proceeded with a 20-minute warm up, which covered stretching of the different body parts and a combination of locomotor movements across the floor. This was the first time I did a "warm up" before undertaking a "dance class." During the technique class, we explored movement routines and body postures while facing the mirror. The focus of the class was body alignment. The teacher emphasized that we needed to see ourselves in the mirror in order to know whether we were "getting the movements right." While standing inside this mirror room, it dawned on me that there was another way of learning and knowing dance—the mirror. It was difficult for me to adapt to this new way of learning and moving. I had no prior experience of this pedagogy. My dance training was deeply rooted in cultural dances, where the processes of teaching and learning dance were participatory. Emphasis was placed on using movements, music, and stories to contribute to the collective experience. The community of dancers was more or less the "mirror." The modern dance technique gave me a snapshot into a new world of dance. My curiosity to inquire into other dance forms grew. My interest in other ways of teaching and learning dance also developed. As a dance teacher in different cultural contexts, I have always leveraged my initial encounter with modern dance technique classes in Uganda to teach students cultural dances.

Alfdaniels Mabingo grew up in rural central Uganda in an environment that is still carrying legacies of British colonialism. Before the advent of colonialism, communities created and performed indigenous dances as part of cultural, social, political, and spiritual expression and practice. These dances were integral to the way of life for these communities. The indigenous communities were able to construct social and cultural identities and realities from the embodied experiences of their dances. Communities practiced dances that spanned different purposes such as worship, rite of passage, marriage, fertility, harvest, funeral, birth, fishing, and many more. Dancing sought to reveal the experiences that people lived as they partook in these different activities. Teaching, learning, and creating these dances encouraged individuals to explore dance traditions and consider new ideas through improvisation. Such inclusive tendencies enabled individuals within communities to have agency in kinesthetic innovation and cultural production.

During colonialism and Christianization, communities were barred from practicing their dances, music, rituals, celebrations, ceremonies, and festivals.[21] Participation in indigenous music and dance activities was considered primitive and devilish.[22] From the perspective of Christianity, indigenous dances were labeled superstitious and sexual, especially because many of them involved movements of the waist.[23] Faith in European religions was held in higher regard than indigenous forms of artistic expression, communication, and interaction such as dances and music.[24] People in local communities abandoned their shrines and dance sites in favor of the church and other places of religious worship.

The indigenous communities lost confidence in their original dance and music practices under the weight of the new forms of religious expression. The missionaries preached that, in order to enter the biblical paradise of heaven, men and women had to rid themselves of earthly evils. Indigenous dances were considered to be part of the evil and darkness. It became divinely abominable for people to practice music and dance and at the same time swear allegiance to the new religious faiths. Consequently, many people were forced to abandon traditional dance and music. In some communities, traditional instruments were destroyed. Individuals who occupied positions of cultural significance abandoned them and became religious converts and adherents.

In the postcolonial period, different communities in Uganda embarked on reviving indigenous dances. Through frameworks such as schools, churches, nongovernmental organizations, dance troupes, orphanages, and arts and cultural centers, among others, communities undertook measures to achieve political, cultural, social, academic, and economic empowerment guided by the principle of Afrocentricity.[25] Indigenous dances were considered knowledge that would empower people to understand and take ownership in creating their local realities, processes, activities, and imaginations.[26] Indigenous dances and music formed a core part of various interventions which aimed at community building, identity construction, and development. These dances have persisted in carrying continuities and accommodating change in response to the ever-changing local environments in which they are practiced.

Mabingo first encountered Western dance in the aforementioned postcolonial, cultural, and educational environments. However, he had been dancing all his life. In universities and the general education system, the standards still ape British education. Emphasis is put on "academic" courses in areas such as law, medicine, technology, business studies, and mathematics, among others. Recently, resources from the government and the private sector have invested in science, technology, engineering, and mathematics (STEM). Because of subservience to the British academic canons and lack of investment in indigenous dance research and education, Mabingo developed a Eurocentric academic and research ethnocentrism. Over the years, he has been transforming his pedagogy to recognize, accept, and adapt indigenous dance pedagogies in academic and nonacademic intercultural settings in Uganda, the United States, New Zealand, Jamaica, and Australia. This process has entailed reflecting and drawing on preconceptions that shaped this ethnocentrism in order for Mabingo to develop pedagogies that honor indigenous dance knowledge paradigms.

Susan's Story

In my hometown, Tucson, Arizona, there was a large **Native American** population that practiced their dance forms. I had little appreciation for these forms and was convinced that they did not belong in any of the spaces in which I studied dance. I lament this attitude today and, when I return to Arizona for visits, I seek Powwows to attend in order to observe the Native American dance practices. The irony of my attitude of long ago is that it was not consistent with my attitude toward other art forms. I valued Native American jewelry over the traditional gold and gemstones treasured in other parts of the United States at that time. So why did I, as a dancer, see Native American dance as less sophisticated but simultaneously see Native American jewelry as fine art?

My initial exposure to dance was in this Tucson community. I began as a student in a studio held at the Jewish Community Center. I was fortunate that, at the age of seven, when I began, creative movement was the approach. Since that time, I have viewed dance as a form of individual expression and have been comfortable creating and finding my "voice" within dance. These creative dance classes made way for formal techniques such as Graham technique and ballet. I disliked the rigidity of ballet (and perhaps the teacher, too) and directed my focus to modern dance. Even though there was a rigidity to the Graham forms, there was room for the expression that I craved.

My childhood was a time of great expansion of the national parks in Arizona. As my family was relatively new to Arizona, we embarked on family vacations exploring those very parks and natural areas. Over 27 percent of Arizona is Native American land, so many of those parks and recreation areas are adjacent to Native American land. Visiting those locations included shopping for Native American crafts (including jewelry) and viewing "entertainment" by Native American dancers. The context was augmented by study in school that included what I now perceive as revisionist history. According to this history, the Native Americans were considered "primitive" before the Americans came into contact with them. The result was that they were "now cultured and not crass." The bits of artistry that we were allowed to view were presented as a result of that "refinement" brought by the European Americans. My lens was filtered through a colonial perspective.

I appreciated the jewelry because it was in forms and shapes I could recognize—that is, earrings, rings, necklaces, and belt buckles. There were many locations to watch the jewelry being made which emphasized the care and artistry that it entailed. There was individuality, which I valued. The dances were completely different from what I experienced in my own education, and so I could not make the same connections. The costumes included leather, feathers, and bells. The movements did not emphasize the same lines and shapes of the body that were valued by ballet and modern dance in my own experience. The music was mostly drumming and what I would call at the time "non-melodic singing." The performances were in a circle, with no proscenium, no formal lighting, and no printed program. So, though it was called dance, it did not seem to have any characteristics that I had learned to call dance. There also did not seem to be any focus on unison. It was interesting to observe, but it was "other," and I continued my own dance training without any connections to what I observed in these Native American dances.

I made no connections between these Native American dances and my own dance background for many years following these experiences. At this young age, I never considered pedagogy, and so there was no reason to think in that way either. It was my impression that these people were different and had been refined by the European presence in these lands. So, my strongest influences in these encounters were the whitewashed narratives that I was learning in school. One of the purposes of this chapter is to examine how we have (or have not) translated these ideas into dance education.

Susan Koff grew up in a modern Jewish family in the southwest part of the United States. Though her formative years were in Arizona, both her parents moved there from New York City and reflected liberal, urban, modern Jewish values. Attending dance classes from a young age was an outgrowth of this upbringing, but it was gender-specific because she attended dance classes while her two brothers excelled in sport. Sport became a family value, but dance remained gendered, with only Susan and her mother attending professional performances together. The family as a whole was also active in attending Euro-American-styled music and theatrical performances. The cultural community values were centered on the Jewish community and engagement with family and friends in New York City, but there was not sufficient cultural exploration in the southwest of the United States, except for family travel to and engagement with the spectacular land and natural environment of the desert. However, the overall family values centered on education, the value of the person above material goods, and the acceptance of all regardless of background.

Though Jewish people were somewhat integrated into the United States, there was the constant reminder that this was not true in the world at large. The upbringing of Jews in the United States does include a strong global awareness as knowledge of others and how people live their lives to their fullest value, which is of the utmost importance. There is the secondary awareness that, just as Jews do not live freely everywhere in the world, there are people of many different backgrounds who may encounter the same issues of discrimination and persecution. These reasons influenced Jews to become heavily involved in the civil rights movement of the 1960s in the United States, which continues to the present day.[27]

The acceptance of others was not as readily reciprocated in parts of the United States with small Jewish populations, such as Arizona. Bigger Jewish populations were centered in New York and larger urban areas in the United States. Simultaneously, racial segregation in the United States continued in many forms. In retrospect, this also led to limited involvement with the Native American and Mexican populations in Arizona, because they were segregated and lived far from any location that Susan normally visited.

Susan continued her dance involvement in secondary school because, in that location, there was an option to enroll in dance as a version of physical education. Dance involvement in all four years of secondary school included many creative and performance opportunities. This made a natural segue to tertiary education because there was a newly formed Bachelor of Fine Arts (BFA) degree in dance at the University of Arizona, which grew out of the former women's physical education department at the university. This classic development from physical education to dance was discussed in Chapter 2, delineating the history of dance in tertiary education in the United States. The focus of this BFA degree was modern dance, with a secondary focus on ballet. Dance history focused on Curt Sachs and had a global perspective, but through a European lens.[28] No indigenous dance forms were included in the curriculum, which reflected the liberal arts focus as discussed in Chapter 2.

Impressions about the "other" in dance and what made a good dancer were influenced by Susan's upbringing in elementary, secondary, and tertiary education and remained with her until more than twenty-five years later, when the narratives in education in general were being revisited and then translated into dance education. At that point, entering a doctoral program in dance, Susan also encountered concepts of critical pedagogy and suppression of minorities through formal education and, most influentially, she studied with Brenda Dixon Gottschild who brought all of these ideas into the context of dance.[29] Armed with pedagogical knowledge and an enlightened perspective, Susan began to seriously reflect on her dance background. While appreciative of the creative expression and individuality that it offered, she realized how narrowly she looked at the world of dance and how many cultures had been erased or suppressed. She began to reconsider her own practice in light of these growing realizations.

Synthesizing Our Stories

Above are two stories by two people from completely different parts of the world (United States and Uganda), with different ethnicities and exposures to the world. Mabingo encountered Western pedagogy, identified as the "mirror room," as an adult when entering university. Western pedagogy was all that Susan knew until she became an adult, and even much later than that. Though their encounters with Western pedagogy are a result of colonialism, being in a postcolonial world makes it seem less obvious. But a bit of deconstruction of these narratives will show how these attitudes formed.

Uganda was colonialized by the British and became a British protectorate from 1894 to 1962. British and French missionaries moved into Uganda, beginning in the late 1800s, and brought Western religion, values, and forms of cultural appreciation. Makerere University was established during the time of the protectorate and then became a part of University College, London. The affiliation ended shortly after Ugandan independence in 1962. However, the British system currently remains in the university.

Missionaries were the original colonializers in what is now Arizona. These missionaries were from Spain and began their missions in the 1700s. Though from a completely different part of Europe, the results were the same in that the missionaries brought Western religion, values, and forms of cultural appreciation. Ultimately, the forms of education that remained also reflected these European structures and values.

Western religions, values, and forms of cultural appreciation still exist in both areas, although, prior to missionary colonialization, there were indigenous people in both locations who had their own religions, values, and forms of cultural expression. However, the Western religions, values, and cultural expressions have remained dominant as, slowly, indigenous forms of expression have re-emerged. Uganda has many smaller indigenous groups who have maintained their own kingdoms, even as the Western governmental structures were created. Tracing the interactions and developments between Ugandan kingdoms and the Western governments is not the focus of this analysis. However, knowledge of this intricate arrangement leads to knowledge of values from different sources existing simultaneously. In Uganda today, the legal government reflects Western values, while indigenous values exist in the kingdoms, which are recognized but have no legal standing.

Mabingo began his first dance and movement expression in a context removed from the "mirror" room and with a pedagogy independent of Western practices. Though he had experienced rich practices since his younger years, those practices were not included in the university education. A hierarchy of ideas was created, so that his earlier learning remained in his community, and this new style of learning remained in the university, which is a structure persisting from the colonialization of Uganda by Britain. The positive outcome is that he was exposed to multiple pedagogies and could differentiate between them but also recognize the value in each. His ethnorelative reflection is the beginning of considering these multiple types of dance education as a part of his holistic self, and this is ultimately what forms his stance as an educator.

In what is now Arizona, the indigenous groups are Native Americans. There are many different tribes, as they are known, each expressing different versions of their own practices. Study of their practices and history is included in all education in Arizona, and yet it is a very "whitewashed" version, developed by the colonializers, that does not express the truth as it is currently known. Their religions and customs have been stripped, and very little of them is presented to the wider world today. What can be observed today, from an outside perspective, is recreated for a Western audience. None of these indigenous practices are included in any Western formal and non-formal education as fully-fledged academic programs, which is what made them seem "underdeveloped" to Susan in her first encounters. Additionally, there was no context to enter into the indigenous forms from an emic or inside perspective, because these indigenous groups, or tribes, are largely segregated on reservations, which was the formal arrangement with the government that still exists today. Susan was not exposed to multiple pedagogies in this setting.

Susan has taken much longer to come to an ethnorelative reflection, because the multiple dance forms she was exposed to in her youth were not an aspect of her own background, contrary to Mabingo's story. However, over this much longer period of time, she began to recognize that the suppression of and limitations to Native American practices was not unlike what had occurred to other cultures in the world, including, at times, practices of her own religion. Though never inside Native American culture, she developed a clearer understanding of what Native Americans experienced and how that suppression resulted in the unrealistic representations she observed during her childhood. This resulted in reflections upon other oppressed minorities and an awareness that this pattern had occurred many times in history and in many parts of the world.

Missionaries in both parts of the world (United States and Uganda) ultimately influenced the structure of education in these locations and created the situations in which Mabingo and Susan encountered formal dance education. These locations were structured similarly, privileging Western dance forms and not including dance forms from indigenous people or any other oppressed minorities. It is interesting to note that, even though modern dance, an important form for both Susan and Mabingo in their own pasts, is not readily considered colonial in its own right, modern dance as a form was colonial because of the many appropriations of other sources of movement, particularly emphasized in Graham technique.[30]

For Mabingo, this encounter with modern dance in tertiary education was in contrast to his earlier experiences in dance. As this Western dance encounter was at the level of "higher" education, he became Eurocentric in his academic focus, not recognizing initially that he was rejecting his upbringing. Susan's entire formal and informal dance education was always Eurocentric, and she was not even aware that there were other options until she was pursuing her doctoral studies. Though living close to those who were oppressed by colonialism hundreds of years before, the narrative about them was also rewritten by the original colonializers, and so she was not aware of the true nature of this oppression. Many years later, in a completely different part of the country, elements of how this past had been rewritten became clear to her.

Conclusion

The field of dance pedagogy is still evolving. This growth is in and includes complex contexts in which dance educators find themselves working. Stories of dance educators who come from different backgrounds and have served in varied cultural contexts reveal the nuanced issues entangled in dance pedagogy in multicultural environments. Particularly when dance educators engage in self-reflection on their social, cultural, and educational backgrounds, they can identify effective ways to enhance their pedagogic practices to better serve in the ever-diversifying teaching settings. Koff and Mabingo shared their personal stories with a view to highlighting how self-reflection on social, cultural, and educational orientations can position dance educators to develop and apply ethnorelative pedagogic philosophies.

Applying Donald Schön's reflective practice as a teacher helps teachers to acknowledge that their past practices could use revisions, once they have realized the sources of their conceptions.[31] Consideration of their own social, cultural, and educational backgrounds causes them to also consider that their students' backgrounds are not identical to their own and need to have a place and representation in the curriculum. Culturally responsive pedagogy, discussed and detailed in Chapter 4, is not a concept that a teacher can employ superficially. Rather, it must be an outcome of this deep and ongoing reflective practice.

11

Giving Thanks to the Land

Indigenous Pedagogies within US Dance Education

William S. Huntington

Introduction

I will start this chapter by identifying myself as claiming German and English-Scottish heritage, my father's family having immigrated from England well before the Revolutionary War (1700s), and my mother's family having immigrated in parts during the late nineteenth century. My younger sister is of Mayan heritage (Guatemala), and my older sister is of mixed Quechua and Mestizo heritage from Perú. I give thanks to the Lenape and Canarsie land on which I conducted the research for this chapter, as well as the Nacotchtank land on which I was born, and the Tunxis, Massacoe, and Wabenaki Confederacy land on which I spent most of my childhood. I grew up Unitarian Universalist in a congregation that drew much knowledge from indigenous teachings and instilled a deep reverence and awareness of indigenous practices and values. I identify all this so that my perspective is considered when this chapter is read, and any biases or opinions are viewed as my own and reflective of my experiences with indigenous peoples and cultural practices.

This chapter will address indigenous pedagogies in dance education in the United States and Canada and the theoretical underpinnings of such teaching philosophies. Writing as a Euro-American, White, cisgender male about non-monolithic philosophies and cultures of which I am not a part presents several challenges such as ownership, authorship, authenticity, access, and control.[1] I present ideas from authors, educators, and artists of various indigenous cultures from the Americas and Oceania in an attempt to disseminate these philosophies and practices to an audience that might not otherwise come into contact with them. In doing so, I hope to encourage self-reflection among dance educators on pedagogical approaches that challenge and inspire. Indigenous scholars have had a deep and lasting impact on me and my conceptualizations of teaching and relationships, and I hope I honor them by offering this discussion to others who might need it. Many authors and artists presented in this chapter frequently acknowledge a lack of place for indigenous ideologies within academia or public education. Indigenous epistemologies consistently value oral histories and ancestral knowledge, which are only just now gaining traction within research and education, over written text or didactic pedagogy. My aim is to synthesize authentic indigenous pedagogies specifically toward the teaching and learning processes in Western concert dance and to address how indigenous dance can inform and deepen educators' critical reflexivity as well as students' development of their own personal identity and that of a dancer.

Background

Writings about indigenous cultural practices, including dance, have been relatively limited. White men and women, usually government and/or church agents, have written the vast majority of texts that exist from the nineteenth and early twentieth century. These legal documents, military accords, religious texts, and popular propaganda increasingly forbade spiritual practices or intertribal potlatches* and laid the foundations for the common stereotypes for most indigenous American populations.[2] Several authors attempted to capture the various dances they observed in the Midwest/Great Plains and Southwest in ways that White Euro-American audiences could readily consume. Bessie and May G. Evans, Reginald and Gladys Laubin, and Jill D. Sweet all offer varying levels of insight into and authenticity of specific dances and their contexts within certain tribes.[3] These authors typically went to tribal functions under various guises to observe and record the movement and music they observed and then explained it or translated it into Western terminology. As video recording was largely unavailable, some of these dancers and anthropologists used Labanotation or Western musical transcription, and others relied on written dance analysis or ethnographic descriptions. Regardless of the methods used, they were distinctly un-indigenous in that no indigenous

---

*Gift-giving feast of Pacific North American indigenous people.

methodologies for passing on cultural knowledge were utilized, and the product and packaging were targeted for an overwhelmingly White upper-middle-class audience.

Jacqueline Shea Murphy takes a different approach and rather traces indigenous dances and their influences on modern dance and ballet in the United States and Canada.[4] Noting how early modern dance pioneers, such as Ruth St. Denis, Ted Shawn, Lester Horton, Martha Graham, and Alvin Ailey, weaved (or colonialized) in-person experiences with indigenous peoples into their individual aesthetics, Shea Murphy goes on to ultimately highlight indigenous artists in the twenty-first century and how indigenous dance and culture are growing and expanding in a digital age. With the help of the internet, indigenous culture is able to assert itself on a global stage, thanks in no small part to the role of Facebook and YouTube in the Standing Rock protest.* Videos of not only sacred dances and drum circles, but also Māori haka and Hawai'ian hula and mele, streamed for thousands of viewers (to such effect that Beyoncé and Rihanna famously had haka dedicated to them during their concerts in New Zealand).

Education in the Face of Colonialization

From an educational perspective, many indigenous populations have faced more direct forms of colonialization and cultural violence through government-run educational institutions that have for many decades defined for indigenous people what is and is not "American Indian" and have strongly called for increased self-determination within education.[5] For many,

> Education remains one of those areas that has been difficult to reconcile. While most Indigenous Peoples would likely concede that some formalized education in the colonizer's system is necessary to survive in the modern world while developing strategies of resistance, there still exists tremendous distrust for the educational systems that have treated our children so brutally. Indigenous knowledge has rarely, if at all, impacted educational institutions responsible for teaching our children even today. Thus, rather than facilitating a liberatory educational experience, the schools are designed to indoctrinate new generations of children with the beliefs and values of the colonizing society, and Indigenous ways continue to be denigrated.[6]

---

*2016–2017 protests over gas and oil pipeline construction through Sioux Native American land in north-central United States, in the Dakotas.

This quote by Waziyatawin Angela Wilson establishes a clear picture for those unfamiliar with Indian residency schools and the extent of loss suffered by indigenous populations and the almost insurmountable challenges young indigenous children still face today. Indigenous peoples have been able to gain stronger footholds in the retelling of their cultural histories and to have their knowledge, histories, and cultural practices represented in public spheres and education.[7] Bolstered by a global indigenous presence on the internet, Western national histories are increasingly taught from a postcolonialist viewpoint that acknowledges human rights atrocities frequently denied by twentieth-century education. Governments are going so far as to implement indigenous educational frameworks within public education in order to redress the centuries of erasure perpetrated on indigenous populations, though much work still remains as these frameworks are tested and refined.[8]

However, in the face of these challenges, Ojibway* Senator Murray Sinclair has said of his work with the Canadian Ministry of Education, "It was education that helped perpetuate the situation we see today for Indigenous Peoples in Canada. We ... believe that it will be education, again, that will be the tool that best addresses all of that."[9] Indigenous pedagogy, its theories and praxis, should thus be seen alongside Paulo Freire, bell hooks, and Joann Keali'inohomoku on an educator's mental bookshelf of reflective and emancipatory pedagogies that disrupt Eurocentric, colonial educational models. These can find immediate relevance for dance educators.

Dance education has simultaneously questioned its own Euro-centrism, and educators in the United States and Canada have sought to incorporate indigenous dance and cultural values into their curriculum.[10] The challenge for many is that most dance educators in the United States and Canada do not know any indigenous dances, let alone a dance artist or teacher who is indigenous. Educators should ask: Which dances do I teach? What is the point of learning these dances? Battiste et al. offer the following:

> the heritage of every Indigenous people is a complete knowledge system with its own concepts of epistemology, philosophy, and scientific and logical validity. The diverse elements of an Indigenous people's heritage can be fully learned or understood only by means of the pedagogy traditionally employed by these people themselves. It comprises all knowledge the nature or use of which has been transmitted from generation to generation, and which is regarded as pertaining to a particular people or its territory.[11]

This passage succinctly lays out a foundational argument for indigenous pedagogy in dance education and for many forms of dance that once might

---

*A North Central Plains tribe that includes both the United States and Canada.

have been taught in an "Ethnic Dance" course.* Reflecting on the non-centrality of White Euro-American cultural forms and pedagogies is crucial for any dance educator in the twenty-first century, as developing a deep respect for and familiarity with a multiplicity of pedagogies will only make for a better educator.

More important to focus upon here are the theoretical concerns of indigenous pedagogy and how these principles can be applied to the teaching and learning of dance in a public-school setting. This discussion draws on theoretical approaches to culturally relevant teaching and learning from several disciplines.[12] Emphasis is given to indigenous scholars and texts to honor their voices in telling the lived experience of indigenous dance pedagogy. Just as "indigenous" is multifarious, so too is indigenous pedagogy, though indigenous research pioneer Shawn Wilson, Opaskwayak Cree, from Northern Manitoba (Canada), found that, "Preparing for and teaching [a course on international indigenous issues] really emphasized in my mind the similarities among Indigenous peoples."[13] Far from proposing or imposing a singular definition, the goal of this text is to prompt educators of all backgrounds to reflect on their own personal pedagogies in order to make space for diversity, inclusivity, equity, access, belonging, and justice within the learning environment.

The first item to address is some sort of a conceptualization of "indigenous pedagogy" while still respectfully resisting a monolithic definition. Sandy Grande, Quechua (Perú), offers the following:

> The quest for a new Red pedagogy is, thus, at base, a search for the ways in which American Indian education can be deepened by its engagement with critical educational theory and for critical theory to be deepened by Indian education. While a Red pedagogy privileges "revolutionary critical pedagogy" as a mode of inquiry, it does not simply appropriate or absorb its language and epistemic frames, but rather employs its vision as one of many starting points for rethinking indigenous praxis. The aim is "to diversify the theoretical itineraries" of both indigenous and critical education so that new questions and perspectives can be generated (McLaren, 2002, 29). Finally, what distinguishes Red pedagogy is its basis in hope. Not the future-centered hope of the Western imagination, but rather a hope that lives in contingency with the past—one that trusts

---

*Fayard notes that best practice for dance educators who do not claim indigenous heritage is to invite an indigenous arts educator into the classroom to teach students, with the primary educator supporting the artist (2017, p. 155). Educators can also bring their students out to powwows or performances if such events are local enough and if there is funding from the school. Educators can also discuss issues of colonialism, historic record, appropriateness of dances in certain contexts, religiosity/spirituality in the arts, and identity through culture and heritage. All of these are valuable and enriching teaching tools for educators within public and private school settings.

the beliefs and understandings of our ancestors as well as the power of traditional knowledge.[14]

Grande draws guidance from traditional indigenous teaching and learning from Gregory Cajete (Tewa) among many others, as well as from revolutionary critical pedagogy as described by Peter McLaren and Marxist theories regarding rights and land commodities.[15] The empowering and generative potentials of Grande's proposal should speak to dance educators who wish to instill such qualities in their students through dance.

Shawn Wilson relates pedagogy to research methodologies as reflective of the value system of the researcher and institution. As indigenous research and education have gained traction within academia, "Indigenous people have come to realize that beyond control over the topic chosen for study, the research methodology needs to incorporate their cosmology, worldview, epistemology and ethical beliefs."[16] Research reflecting the value systems of the researcher is well established in qualitative research, but is still in contention among many quantitative paradigms. It is not hard to see why indigenous researchers would reject classic paradigms from White Western academia that have continually misinterpreted or blatantly misrepresented indigenous peoples. The theoretical basis for indigenous research can be seen in both broad and specific terms, depending on one's own context and the specific peoples involved. Though Wilson's assessment that most indigenous peoples' value systems are largely comparable or overlapping is a broad statement to make, what is clear is, if a non-indigenous educator is teaching in an indigenous context (indigenous population of students, indigenous subject matter, etc.), they should first spend time talking to and especially listening to elders of specific indigenous peoples to help shape their educative experiences.

Values of Ceremony—Indigenous Ideology, Spirituality, and Experience

A crucial acknowledgment for indigenous arts, returning to the quote from Battiste et al. mentioned earlier, is that the process and product are reflections of indigenous ideologies, spiritualities, and experiences, which differ foundationally from Western White practices and can prove challenging, but also liberatory, when melding in an education setting. Knowing that Eurocentric pedagogical paradigms "are just one form of knowledge out of many" (and are largely oppressive for indigenous peoples) is a foundational step for twenty-first-century educators to see and appreciate indigenous pedagogy.[17] Kelly Fayard explains further: "Unlike in Western culture where there is a tendency to think that all knowledge should be knowable, or at least accessible, by everyone, that is not the case [with indigenous peoples]."[18]

Knowability of knowledge can be related to ownability of objects and comes from a European conception of the physical world as subservient to (White) man. This is largely antithetical to indigenous conceptions of knowledge, land, and property in which all things are meant to be shared and gain value the longer they are held within a symbiotic or spiritual loop (see the section on Sovereignty and Stewardship later for further discussion). Battiste et al. further note, "The broad and entrenched assumption of most postsecondary curricula is that Eurocentric knowledge represents the neutral and necessary story for 'all' of us."[19] The very foundation of indigenous pedagogy is predicated on an understanding of place and relationship to others, rather than Western academia's belief in individual exceptionalism, where one can and should know as much as possible, and Euro-American history is the basis for all human history. Scholars and activists have challenged White institutions of education to decolonialize their curricula and for indigenous academics to take leadership in such efforts.

Primarily, indigenous dance and music "emerge from real life, ritual, and social practices across time, geographical regions, and tribal groups ... performed with others ... often, as worship to a higher being."[20] These dances tie individuals to community and peoples to the greater planet, which is reflective of "inclusive animism," a concept stemming from the indigenous understanding that all things contain anima (inner self), have things to teach, and are able to hold dialogue with others.[21] Many ceremonies in indigenous religious practices involve physical activities, as "Native religion tended to be bodily" and does not always reflect a Western religious paradigm.[22] Nearly the same could be said for indigenous teaching and learning. This, of course, changed with European missionaries, forced conversions, and government boarding schools, as many indigenous peoples within the Americas have adopted (or were forced to adopt) religious and educational practices that centralize Christian and (White) European influence.[23]

Contrary to Fayard's notion of "knowability" from Western pedagogies, these dance practices are frequently privileged by indigenous peoples and thus not meant for consumption by public-school-students who do not claim indigenous heritage. Researching and then disseminating such religious or private dances would be highly insulting and colonial in impetus and would more than likely be miseducative, as context and meaning would be lacking in such a lesson. Indigenous educators and scholars readily recognize that much of knowledge is not known or knowable, which conflicts with the Western construct of education.[24] Furthering such challenges, engaging in such explicitly spiritual or religious practices in a public education setting can be met with considerable resistance in certain communities where religious presence in schooling is frowned upon. Removing the spiritual elements of indigenous music and dance, however, poses an equally problematic alternative, as the meaning and stories behind specific movements, songs, chants, and ceremonies gets lost in transmission and thus fails indigenous pedagogy.

However, the approach can be the idea of "teaching as ceremony." Shawn Wilson posits the following:

> In our cultures an integral part of any ceremony is setting the stage properly. When ceremonies take place, everyone who is participating needs to be ready to step beyond the everyday and accept a raised stage of consciousness. You could say that specific rituals that make up the ceremony are designed to get the participants into a state of mind that will allow for the extraordinary to take place. As an Elder explained it to me: if it is possible to get every single person in a room thinking about the exact same thing for only two seconds, then a miracle will happen.[25]

Viewing a dance class as a ceremony is an immediately familiar idea for most Western dancers: the daily task of being in class and going through the movements, rehearsing the elements that make performance possible, the community and relationship (spatial, physical, emotional, intellectual) between dancers, students, teachers, music, musicians, and space—these are all rituals in a ceremony that is endemic to most dance training and education and is fostered within indigenous pedagogy.

Teacher-Learner Relationship

One of the most salient commonalities among many indigenous learning paradigms is the teacher-learner relationship. Most indigenous dancers in the United States and Canada (and surely elsewhere) describe how they learned their dance from a close family member teaching them for years during ceremonies, powwows,* or potlatches.[26] Ann Axtmann notes, "Often a grandparent, parent, or older friend teaches a young child [to dance] as soon as she or he can walk," and this teaching is intended to pass on through to a "seventh generation" in the future.[27] Louis Mofsie, of the Thunderbird American Indian Dancers, insists that dance "has to come through family."[28] Respectfully learning from elders is seen as a very tangible way of honoring older members of a community and strengthens social bonds. Young dancers will spend months or years watching an elder perform at powwows or smaller ceremonies, usually until they are quite sure they can perform the movement well, though some more energetic students will imitate the movement off to the side of the dance area while watching.[29]

---

*North American indigenous festival of food, song, and dance.

Western educators might see this context as informal instruction and thus may reject or marginalize its place in formal education.[30] However, the relationship between the teacher and learner, the actual movement, the context of the movement, the land, and the people who govern the movement are highly codified and foundational elements of indigenous pedagogy. Western dance teachers commonly teach in a Western-style dance studio with sprung-wood floors, rattan or Marley flooring, mirrors on at least one wall, and themselves placed at the front of the room facing their students, who are all facing the same direction.[31] This teacher-centric command style of teaching is well supported in the United States education system as it offers a high student-to-teacher ratio and thus ostensibly delivers the most product (knowledge) via the fewest deliverers (teachers). For indigenous communities, such a capitalist view of passing on knowledge and culture does not honor the relationship that is endemic to indigenous identities and epistemologies.[32] Instead, a direct and deep relationship between one learner and one educator is the classic paradigm for many indigenous dancers, and this relationship is traditional for many indigenous pedagogies. This is not to say that twenty-first-century indigenous dance artist/educators exclusively teach one-on-one with a family member. As times have changed, so have indigenous identities and culture, and one can find many ad hoc workshops (or even fitness classes) that offer indigenous American dances, hula being a prime example, to indigenous and non-indigenous participants and look very similar in pedagogy to a ballet class in an established Western location. However, the fundamental conception of the relationship (Wilson coins the term "relationality") and the responsibilities of those in this one-to-one relationship constitute a distinctly indigenous ideology.

Learning Methodologies

Educational researchers have previously suggested that many indigenous children learn best visually, by "observation, manipulation and experimentation," preferring to observe an activity, process the material internally or even in private, and gain a certain level of confidence in their performance before demonstrating publicly.[33] Indigenous teacher Shawn Wilson calls this "ceremony." This longer and potentially private acquisition period may be uncomfortable for many Western dance educators, who are used to verbally describing and physically demonstrating a movement sequence and asking the students to perform the sequence immediately afterward. Many dance educators would cite a fast acquisition stage, an immediate attempting stage, and speedy perfecting stage as a core educational goal for their curricula.[34] This parallels public schools within the United States today, which value fast verbal acquisition, high testing performance, and indefinite retention. Dance educators must remind themselves and frequently justify to others that teaching dance in a similar way as one would teach mathematics is not the only or even the best way for students to learn. This poses a creative challenge for teachers who only ever present new material verbally to instead explore pedagogies that value visual and experiential presentations.

Indigenous Principals Influencing Pedagogy

Relationality

Shawn Wilson discusses his conception of relationality in the acknowledgment that individuals consist of their relationships to other people, to the land/environment, to the cosmos (which incorporates spirituality, ancestry, and cultural knowledge that is passed down), and to ideas.[35] Practitioners should conceptualize their work in constant relationship with these elements and how their work both affects and effects this "context."[36] Viewed from a theoretical standpoint, context informs the content and pedagogy in classrooms, though it is not always possible to appreciate fully the practical ramifications of context until actually confronted by the classroom.[37] Wilson's framework challenges the *tabula rasa* conception of children and learning by encompassing the contexts of the educator, the individual and collective students, the students' families and communities, the physical space of the studio, the greater institution, the land the school is built on, the community around the school, the ancestors of the educator and the students, the spirituality of the educator and the students, and the actual content to be learned/taught. In education, some of this context is identified as prior knowledge or classroom management, but relationality delves deeper into the teaching and learning process. Wilson reflects on his father, scholar Stanley Wilson, Opaskwayak Cree,[*] in stating that indigenous identity "is grounded in their relationships with the land, with their ancestors who have returned to the land and with future generations who will come into being on the land. Rather than viewing ourselves as being *in* relationships with other people or things, we *are* the relationships that we hold and are part of."[38] Relationality believes that interactions and contexts are profound and expansive, and that humans should treat these actions with this careful consciousness.

Along these lines, relationality manifests in students' indigenous tendencies to learn in cooperative rather than competitive environments.[39] Cooperation

---

[*]Manitoba, Canada.

when learning reinforces the importance researchers found in North American (Canada and United States) schools on reservations, where students were most active during small group learning activities that utilized cooperative goals and participated most when teachers established a more equitable hierarchy in the classroom setting.[40] Many researchers also found strong evidence for the contrary: in expressly competitive and teacher-centric learning environments, indigenous students were less likely to offer individual verbal responses and were more likely to identify that they felt they were struggling academically.[41] Further evidence suggests that, when competition benefits a social group (such as a team sport or powwow), competition is encouraged as it deepens interpersonal bonds and the sense of relationality.[42] Indigenous pedagogy thus embraces students relating to one another in a cooperative and respectful manner that does not seek to pit one against the other, as is similarly seen in most dance education practices in the United States and Canada. Instead, indigenous philosophy embraces equality among peers and a power structure that does not resemble most public-school classrooms.

Relationality also addresses how teachers talk to students, noting that indigenous elders and educators frequently talk to students in a different way than many Western educators. Where Western dance educators might give little time to verbal or physical responses and can be quick to identify an error out loud in front of a full class of peers, indigenous educators frequently give longer periods for students to offer responses and they value privacy and tact when dealing with an error or mistake.[43] Indigenous teachers and elders report that they prefer to discuss student errors in a more private setting or while the rest of the class is engaged in another activity.[44] In this way, educators are able to avoid any kind of embarrassment for the student, which might lead to some level of shame and miseducation. Furthermore, it offers a better opportunity to explain a correct answer while demonstrating respect for the teacher-student relationship as well as the student's social standing within the learning environment.

Consciousness of one's web of relations may not be immediately poignant for many Western dance educators who view interactions as discrete and ephemeral events or who may not come from a family that values cultural/ethnic identities.* Especially for White educators, the Whiteness of dance education is largely invisible and thus unquestioned. Western dance forms are viewed as the standard, and all dance that is not ballet, modern, or contemporary is seen as "other" and "marked."[45] Teaching to honor the story

---

*I use the terms "discrete" and "ephemeral" with the understanding that educators in public-school systems typically view lessons as a continuum over a unit, semester, or year. In this view, knowledge is building or cumulative over a period of time toward the overall educative goals or outcomes. However, the oral history or context of a specific dance frequently becomes secondary to the actual movement, yielding movement that might become void of background or meaning. This is decidedly not reflected in observed practices or literature concerning the transmission of dance in indigenous cultures (Contreras & Bernstein, 1996).

of one's personal dance as well as one's own culture of dance does not appear on many curricula; most educators may not even know the full story of their dance lineage. In the United States, people view themselves with an emphasis on individualism rather than on collectivity or a continuum and thus place more emphasis on working in isolation. Shifting consciousness to encompass not only the moment of teaching and learning but also the before and the after in factors of months, years, and generations is a demanding task, but a necessary one in the twenty-first century. Knowing where one's dance comes from, being a dance anthropologist, and receiving and sharing those stories from elders are fundamental indigenous values for many peoples.

Ancestral Knowledge

Battiste et al. advocate that, "truly postcolonial [education] must begin with guidance from Aboriginal Elders and with the honor of sustaining an ongoing relationship with them."[46] This element of indigenous pedagogy ("Indigenous values . . . directly related to traditional knowledge") is reflective of many indigenous cultures around the world and is frequently at odds with White Euro-American educational theories that prize recent data and research within a university or educational setting over other forms of knowledge.[47] Ancestral knowledge is frequently passed on in the form of storytelling, which comprises many indigenous teaching methods as well as research methods within universities and governmental bodies.[48] Stories carry culture and meaning for many indigenous peoples, and the many processes of storytelling, usually in the appropriate indigenous language, are powerful bases in indigenous pedagogy. Many indigenous scholars and educators note that indigenous knowledge must come from actual elders: one cannot "Google it."[49]

Language

For many Western dance educators, teaching words that go hand-in-hand with movement may not be their bread-and-butter in their studio classes, save for creative movement or musical theatre. However, indigenous dances typically have words, vocalizations, rhythms, and melodies that are not only appropriate for that dance, but necessary. Not knowing them is tantamount to not knowing the movement. Teaching the words to a population that has little to no understanding of the language can be challenging, but indigenous scholars frequently emphasize the importance of reclaiming and preserving language that has been lost to colonialism.* Waziyatawin Angela Wilson

---

*I can report from personal experience that I was (gently) not allowed to perform in any hula kahiko when I was younger until I learned the words, which I did not learn. I was never told to stop dancing when I was watching and imitating, but was held back from dancing with adults

clearly asserts, "Nothing reflects Indigenous worldviews and ways of being more than Indigenous languages."[50]

Communal Identity

Indigenous identity and histories have largely been passed down through oral transmission, paintings and drawings, and what Western dance scholars might call dance-dramas in community contexts.[51] Western academia has only recently begun to consider oral histories as worthy modes of scholarship comparable to written or recorded documents, thus embracing indigenous knowledge as it finally gains ground as respected scholarship. The act of talking-with is a meaningful pedagogical tool for most indigenous dancers who find their relationship with their teachers foundational to their understanding of the movement of the dances. An indigenous dance typically has a story associated with it that tells of the first person who did the dance (or sang the song), of how a spirit or dream showed the dance to an individual or people, or of how the dance depicts the history of a mythical figure.[52] These stories may vary between individuals or people and can speak to the multiplicities of experience between nations or tribes. Knowing the story behind the movement and the words to the appropriate song/music is seen as de rigueur for any performer or competitor and ties the dance to the dancer and the greater community. Sharing these stories becomes part of the fabric of the dance as well, and the story of how one people passed on a dance to another people can vary widely. Such knowledge is meant to be shared when a learner is ready.

This is somewhat at odds with the value Western education places on individual exceptionalism over group participation and believing in standardized evaluation (i.e., the Gaussian bell curve) rather than collective success (i.e., an A grade looks different for every student). There are even dance educators who feel they can lead an entire class without "translating" or "diluting" movement into language by teaching in one mode of instruction, in which they were taught, and are beyond critique or evaluation by their students. These elements, which are largely present in Western education systems, are not designed to create community or foster storytelling in a way that honors each other, families, identities, or ancestors. Many readers should immediately recall being quieted in dance class by a teacher rather than being asked to express themselves in a respectful and communal way. Why is discourse discouraged in these settings, and why are students asked to be only receptacles of knowledge rather than liberated thinkers? Arts education frequently discusses this Freirian paradigm in the arts, as the United States educational system vastly values STEM and other "core" curricular subjects

---

who were performing, and it was explained that I could perform when I was older.

over the arts and vocational subjects that do not fit neatly into standardized testing and correct/incorrect modes of evaluation. This is not to say that the fine and vocational arts have not been forced to adapt their pedagogies and evaluation methods to fit a correct/incorrect model. It is, however, still fundamentally anathema for a dance to be completely correct or incorrect, unlike a math problem, which can absolutely be correct or incorrect. What changes about the arts when viewed in such a black-and-white way?

Though many indigenous experiences and ceremonies are sacred and not meant for discussion, the sharing of stories and the building of community through dialogue are important for many indigenous peoples and can be lost for many non-indigenous young dancers.[53] Individual exceptionalism and notions of genius are valued over community building in dance education in many settings and can leave talented young dancers and even well-established educators feeling isolated within the dance community. The sharing process honors indigenous values, and many cite a talking circle as a particularly meaningful way to share with others. A talking circle consists of the members of a community (can be a full community or ad hoc) sitting in a circle and passing an object (either a talking stick, feather, drum, or an object the community creates together) to indicate who is able to talk freely. Interrupting is very rude and not allowed as it indicates a lack of respect not only for the person speaking but for the greater community as well. Circles hold a powerful pedagogical meaning for many (but not all) indigenous communities that represent a multitude.

Therefore, participation in community is highly prized, and many indigenous scholars have cited participatory action research (PAR) as a distinctly indigenous method for research and education. Shawn Wilson is keen to note, however, that PAR conducted by non-indigenous researchers or educators (etic research) runs the risk of furthering a colonial agenda if conducted haphazardly.[54] Many indigenous scholars have rightly called for more research agendas and educational programs conducted and founded by indigenous people (emic research), who are more likely to structure research and educational experiences that better follow indigenous ideologies.

Sovereignty and Stewardship

A challenging element of indigenous pedagogy for many Western educators, particularly for White Euro-American educators, is the notion of sovereignty and its usual concomitant rejection of national governments.[55] Sovereignty for indigenous American populations refers to land governance and the ability of indigenous peoples to self-determine. Looking at the American Indian Movement specifically, indigenous protesters sought to redress racially motivated murders in border towns, land theft, and the United States government's failure to honor past treaties and their interference in tribal affairs. Protests in 1968 and 1972, in Alcatraz (California) and Wounded Knee (South Dakota), respectively, brought to the forefront during the civil rights movement the truth that there can be no democracy for indigenous peoples within colonial governments occupying stolen land.* Since then, indigenous peoples and scholars have attempted to redress this false democracy in governance and education in small increments through self-determination, with varying degrees of success.

Summary

I started this chapter with an acknowledgment of my mostly outside (etic) but slightly inside (emic) perspective on this topic, which was followed by the traditional land acknowledgment in order to introduce indigenous values. I continued with a summary of those values interwoven with pedagogy and specifically dance pedagogy. Though the perspective is largely North American, many perspectives apply to indigenous people regardless of location. My "voice" was both personal and scholarly because the impetus for this journey was entirely personal, and yet I felt a need to ground what I felt in scholarly and emic material.

Many values of indigenous life covered here which are central to performance and dance are the very values that colonialism tried to strip and mark as evil or inappropriate according to Western lifestyles. These values define that there has always been a holistic sense in indigenous pedagogy, making it actually closer to the true definition of dance education as the education of the whole person. As summarized earlier in the section on Relationality, these values were stripped from indigenous people when they were forced into Western schools and Western religions. Honoring indigenous values has a lot to offer both education and the arts that have traditionally been constructed in Western society.

---

*A teacher once gave the example of US democracy being like a burglar breaking into your apartment and then not-so-peacefully insisting that, as you are both here and hungry, the fairest thing is that you both have equal claim over the food in the fridge.

12

Dance as an Aspect of Everyday Living

Introduction

This chapter summarizes all the chapters of the book leading to a holistic definition of dance education based on research practices and philosophical perspectives. The discussion then advocates for future directions and possibilities for dance education as a central aspect of life, communication, and interpersonal engagement. It culminates in envisioning dance education as an essential element of a changing global world by bringing elements from each chapter into a comprehensive and holistic focus.

Maxine Greene wrote, "If we attend from our own centers, if we are present as living, perceiving beings, there is always, always more."[1] I often use this as a mantra when I am teaching because I want to immediately dismantle the sense of the teacher knowing everything. I think of myself as a facilitator who points to open doors and helps to guide people through them. It is the same as my aspirations for this text. I have opened doors for ideas and ways of looking at dance education. This text does not intend to provide answers, but to frame essential questions. In Greene's words, I have been writing this text to say that there is always more, more than we can ever know or experience, and yet we must open our beings to experience and be available for the "more" that there is.

Greene repeated this refrain later in a different essay in the same text: "As I view it, there are implications here for all kinds of learning, if we value the sense of personal agency and pursuit of possibility. And, indeed, that is what lies ahead for all of us: openings, adventures into meaning, the sense that there is always more."[2] Based on Greene's writings, I have constructed this text to be without prescriptive ideas or descriptions of how dance education should be constructed. In both Greene's and Dewey's writings, imagination is emphasized, so we can envision and move toward future possibilities.[3] My aim is to present the possibilities through a series of historical milestones in dance education, considering philosophical grounding, looking at today's educational contexts, and then leaving space for possibilities, rather than a final period. I will summarize the journey of this text.

Summary of Previous Chapters

The first section begins with a fresh look at dance in general and how dance is discussed. The purpose of this chapter is to look at dance and speak/write about dance from a perspective that is without categories or labels. This new outlook hopes to disrupt the hierarchical ordering of dance forms. In order to do so, language that has been used in the past is identified and discussed so that how dance is named and viewed can be considered.

This continues with the formal history of dance education and the manner in which it became recognized as a subject area in formal elementary, secondary, and tertiary education, predominantly in the Western world. That model has been replicated in other parts of the world or, in some instances, was spread through colonialism. In the Western world, the history of formal dance education resides largely in physical education, but this connection to physical education and growth does not encompass the history of dance in other settings, or in other parts of the world. Though formal dance education eventually separated from physical education, the lasting legacy of this separation remains centered around its purpose in formal settings: should it be for self-discovery or for professionalism?

The title of this book, *Dance Education: A Redefinition*, is the focus that continues as an underlying thread throughout this text. Dance education, as a term or profession, is often misunderstood. I continue by returning to the history and formalization of a profession, with research, publications, and academic and professional meetings or gatherings where people share their ideas. After this summary of the background, I turn to Maxine Greene's words. She drew frequently on the ideas of John Dewey and Paulo Freire and built upon them with her own ideas and eloquence. I bring more of her words into focus, again as an aspect of this redefinition: "There are those who say that the aesthetics of dance, for instance, confront the question of what it means to be human ... The focus is on process and practice; the skill in the making is embodied in the object. In addition, the dance provides occasions for the emergence of the integrated self."[4] "The emergence of the integrated self" is what this book imagines *is* the definition of dance education. The focus on "what it means to be human" allows dance educators to transcend teaching steps and promotes a well-rounded education for the whole child or person.

The first section of this book continues with a historical overview of pedagogy and the application of pedagogy in movement teaching and learning. The last section of the chapter on pedagogy develops the ideas of culturally responsive pedagogy and relates it to dance education. All concepts of pedagogy are theories and suggestions for applications; however, this discussion avoids finite descriptions of applications. It presents an awareness of the possibilities in pedagogy as well as the full spectrum of all the students who can participate.

The second section introduces a dance education research project that I conducted with three other colleagues who live in three different countries. This project is ongoing, but it is summarized here in order to highlight the perspective of those who have experienced dance in formal, non-formal, and informal settings. These terms, from UNESCO, are then articulated from the dance education perspective so that they are comprehended in a way that those who have experienced dance education in all three settings may not realize. The complexity of dance education is clarified once again through these three chapters covering formal, non-formal, and informal dance education. The chapter on formal dance education culminates with boxes that illuminate personal experience of the theoretical discussions. The section then has a final chapter that is a personal story of someone whose life is an interwoven history of dance education from formal, non-formal, and informal settings. This encompassing story began as boxed text but was then inserted as a stand-alone chapter because of its richness and how it beautifully interweaves so many of the concepts presented.

The last section continues in the spirit of opening up possibilities by examining dance education from contexts that have not often been fully explored, especially because they have been limited by colonialism. This last section culminates here, not as a closing, but as an opening in Maxine Greene's words. Now I will highlight some ideas about what this means to me, how I have seen it in action, and what I hope for the future.

From a philosophical perspective, LaMothe eloquently wrote:

> We must ask. What would it be like to live in a society where dancing—the act of creating and becoming patterns of sensation and response—were nurtured in every child, integral to every educational system, and expected of every competent adult? What if learning to cultivate a sensory awareness of ourselves as movement and participate consciously in the rhythms of bodily becoming were considered a fundamental human right? What if people grew up believing in the practice of dancing as necessary for their best becoming? What if this dance was taught as a resource for solving problems, reconciling conflicts, and building relationships? What if people learned to dance as a practice for clearing their minds, opening their hearts, and mending their bodily selves? What if people learned to dance as a means to personal, interpersonal, and social health—as a vital resource for moving in relation to one another so as to catalyze the next generation of new ideas? What would it be like if there were spaces and places to dance in houses and hospitals, in churches and office buildings, in airports and bus stations, beaches and parks? What would it be like

if people everywhere danced alone and with others, for themselves or for others, on the field or along the sidewalk, waiting for a plane or bus or bank machine, as a way to relax, recoup, or rev up? What if we fed ourselves a daily diet of inspiring movement patterns—putting ourselves in situations where we could move and be moved by the dancing of others? What would it be like to live in a society where people of all ages dance everywhere and anywhere for the pleasure of it, the health of it, the healing, pain-transforming power of it? What kind of humans would we be? How would we think and feel? What would we want? How would we relate to the earth in us and around us? What kind of worlds would we bring into reality? It is worth finding out.[5]

I feel LaMothe's passion and I can imagine this world. It is my goal to approach all these possibilities from the following concrete questions that I continually ponder. As a dance education community, I want us all to work together on these questions:

1. How do we guarantee the right to dance to everyone?
2. How can we present dance as a way to engage in nonverbal expression, as a fundamental value of being human?
3. How can we remove the hierarchy of dance forms so that racism, sexism, and class discrimination are no longer present in any dance?
4. How can we retain respect for the gifted and talented without shutting the door in the face of all who want to engage in dance?
5. How can we share the joy of dance and remove barriers to access?

For a start, I will offer some of my thoughts. In light of Maxine Greene's words, "there is always more," this book is only a beginning. In order to guarantee the right to dance, barriers to access must be removed. Those barriers have been depicted throughout this text in many different contexts. There are various barriers, including socioeconomic status, capability, body type, size, able-ness, race and religion, and, finally, the effects of colonialism. The beginning of overcoming barriers is acknowledging that they exist and that they present themselves differently depending upon the setting.

Returning to the concepts that were summarized in Chapters 1–3 will help to emphasize that dance is a fundamental value of being human. It is important, then, to present dance in all settings with an emphasis placed on historical context and artistic values within that setting. When dance is available for an audience in a formal performance setting, the summary of its history can help to educate those who have no experience. Audiences at any form of dance performance should be encouraged to know that both the audience and the creators/choreographers are making an aesthetic choice, and that we each have our own artistic voice. As performance is one of the ways that dance makes itself known to a wider variety of people, education and some engagement with the actual experience of moving and dancing should be the responsibility of all performers. With or without a performance, finding opportunities to create experiences with dance (as in the Dewey definition of experience articulated in Chapter 4) will present dance as a fundamental value.

Chapter 1 is about changing the way we view and talk about dance. This approach illuminates a path to remove the hierarchy of forms, so that any form, regardless of its background, focus, or country of origin, can be appreciated for its unique qualities. Someone who is new to that form will benefit from engaging with one who can provide an emic perspective or inside view. Simultaneously, when reflecting on culturally responsive teaching, the perspective of the person new to the form should also be considered. Bringing all of this together, with openness and void of value judgment, allows us as viewers and participants to be fully available to the experience.

All dance forms have beauty, and all dance forms have people who epitomize the pinnacle of excellence in that form. Those performers should be celebrated and lauded for their excellence. However, their talent or proficiency should not create barriers for those who want to experience and practice that form. This returns to the pedagogical discussion of developmental appropriateness and teaching for access. Good pedagogy, with responsiveness to the origin and meaning of a dance form, can offer a point of entry to all or part of the form, while allowing us to appreciate those who exemplify the form. Most importantly, we want to celebrate excellence in each unique dance form, without creating comparisons or universal values and applying them to another form. This allows us to appreciate gifted and talented performers and see excellence for its unique place in any dance form.

Skill

Education is essential for addressing these questions, and the key is to include the type of education that considers who the students or the participants are and gives them a voice in the educational process. Though not every mover will naturally excel, helping every mover and, by extension, dancer become skillful will allow all dancers to participate in the most authentic way. Skill has been mentioned throughout many of the previous chapters as something that can be measured, taught, and observed. However, the caution throughout all those instances is that skill should not become the end goal, but that skill serves something larger.

Skill opens up the possibility of freedom mentioned in Chapter 3 and allows the dancer to become a fully realized human being. Scott Kretchmar, a noted physical activity philosopher, stated that skill in movement provides the freedom to discover, explore, express, and invent.[6] The level of skill is not the goal; rather, the goal is to enable the mover to participate with these freedoms.

There are many levels of skill, and the highest level is not the only level. For those who want to participate in dance, providing skill offers a tangible entry way and removes another barrier to access. The important point is access rather than restriction, experience of dance for all, while valuing all levels of skill. Education again is key.

Dance for Wellbeing/Quality of Life

In this discussion, the student or dancer is at the center of dance education (rather than content), and, through a holistic perspective, the conversation returns to Chapter 3 and a definition of dance education. Two concepts that have recently been explored, from a holistic perspective, is dance for wellbeing and dance for quality of life. Some of the reasons for dance discussed in Chapter 1 might have touched upon these concepts, but they have taken on more prominence as a way to view an entire discipline, rather than types of dance.[7] As was emphasized in Chapter 1, no concepts are universal, and all must be contextually considered with the values of the culture in which they are considered. This is the same for wellbeing and quality of life.

Holistic education can be considered in dance to include the actual art form, creativity, "imagination, symbolism and metaphor," as well as nonverbal communication.[8] It can relate to many population descriptors such as ability or able-ness, age, body, gender, and culture of origin. Arts anthropologist Ellen Dissanayake explores definitions even further, proposing that art is a characteristic of human behavior, innate in all. She defines dance as one of the oldest human behaviors. She then states that dance is the foundation of all arts because of this holistic approach, leading to life, wellness, and wholeness.[9] As stated by Alma Hawkins in the 1950s, "Dance as education can serve as a satisfying outlet for expression and at the same time help the individual gain emotional release, develop personality, increase sensitiveness to environment, and develop skill in working creatively."[10] Though Hawkins was specifically addressing the purpose of dance in tertiary education, she spoke to the same issues addressed by all those speaking about dance, wellbeing, and quality of life. She continued this sentiment about quality of life by stating, "The ultimate purpose of education as I see it today is the fullest possible development of the individual."[11]

The comments by Hawkins and Dissanayake, made more than sixty years apart, have some relationship to the values presented in Chapter 11, those of indigenous peoples. Perhaps thinking about dance for wellbeing or quality of life is not new at all, but something that has been considered or assumed by many different people without such specific language. Considering this further, some elements of Western society, perpetuated through colonialism, have denied some of these fundamental values. These statements of dance for wellbeing and quality of life are merely a call to return to a holistic form of life. This is not meant to be an argument against development and progress, but rather a call to pause and recognize that there are values that already exist in this world that are worth considering and honoring.

Global Implications

Beyond research and publications about dance education and justifications for dance education, moving into the future entails dissemination, followed by a plan of action. UNESCO, a United Nations agency, has taken the lead in promoting and advocating arts education through the governmental work of the United Nations.[12] The Seoul Agenda mentioned in Chapter 6 provides clear grounding for standards in arts education in a global context and includes many guiding principles that go beyond the formal context in which it was originally presented in Chapter 6.[13] The three main goals of the Seoul Agenda are:

Goal 1: Ensure that arts education is accessible as a fundamental and sustainable component of a high-quality renewal of education
Goal 2: Assure that arts education activities and programs are of a high quality in conception and delivery
Goal 3: Apply arts education principles and practices to contribute to resolving the social and cultural challenges facing today's world.

These goals were written for all arts education disciplines and specifically address governments as a point of activism and demand for action. The response expected from governments is support for arts education in all its forms of delivery. It is then up to local participants to advocate for these principles in their own contexts. Some examples of the Seoul Agenda being put into action provide models of future directions dance education can take to begin to address the five questions posed earlier in this chapter. To date of this publication, there have been five declarations connected to a conference or meeting concerning arts education, each in a different part of the world. Each declaration was a reiteration of the Seoul Agenda with a call to action at the local level, supported by the government and local UNESCO entities. Two of these declarations are detailed here as they specifically address dance education.

Copenhagen Declaration

In Copenhagen in 2015, Dance and the Child International (daCi), a UNESCO-affiliated international organization held its thirteenth conference. At this event, the Copenhagen Declaration was signed by conference delegates and presented to the Danish UNESCO observatory at the end of the conference. This was in response to the Seoul Agenda and a move to progress forward with the above three goals. The main points of the Copenhagen Declaration were in the following calls:

2.1 Calls upon dance educators to explore ways in which they can empower and mobilize young people around the world to contribute to sustainable development;

2.2 Calls upon dance educators to support education that is based on principles of equity, inclusion and gender equality;

2.3 Calls upon dance educators to advocate for all learners to be taught by professional, competent, committed, and well supported teachers at all levels of education who are able to respond to diverse learning needs.[14]

These elements were agreed upon by all delegates at the conference and were presented with an action plan for all in attendance to take back to their localities and create programs and projects.

Adelaide Declaration

A similar declaration was created during the fourteenth daCi conference, held in conjunction with WDA Education and Training Network in 2018 in Adelaide, Australia.[15] The goals built upon the Copenhagen Declaration and then went a bit further:

2.1 Calls upon dance and other educators to respect dance traditions and diverse perspectives;

2.2 Calls upon dance and other educators to explore innovative and inclusive ways forward that address UNESCO's aims for quality dance teaching and learning using a 21st century social justice lens;

2.3 Calls upon dance and other educators to value and honour intergenerational learning and teaching in formal and informal contexts;

2.4 Calls upon dance and other educators to advocate for engagement with diverse communities and to engage in critical and empathetic perspectives;

2.5 Calls upon dance and other educators to explore ways in which they can listen to, empower and mobilize young people around the world to contribute to sustainable development;

2.6 Calls upon dance and other educators to work across boundaries with diverse disciplines, people, and beliefs for sustainable growth and development.[16]

In this version, the delegates, especially those under age 18, participated in workshops throughout the conference to shape the final declaration document, which was presented at Adelaide City Hall at the conclusion of the week-long event. These two declarations were created to give some practical direction to the conference delegates to promote action in their local communities. When speaking about applied research, charting these actions would be a good way to move such aspirational documents into practical reality. None of the declarations were made with any method of tracking what would occur once all the conference delegates departed and returned to their home environments.

Moving Forward

The world is such that we can never turn back and undo all that has already been done. Instead, we must be reflective and responsive and learn about what has been done that allows our communities to progress and what prevents us from moving forward. This is the very reason that this book began first with context and then with history, and history has returned throughout. It is only by looking backward and examining what has occurred in the past that we can learn from our strengths and weaknesses to move forward. As humans, we have progressed and we have made mistakes. We can pause, learn from these past events, and progress. So, progress itself is strong.

But also, as humans, we are always in the process of becoming, never having arrived. This philosophical concept returns the discussion to Scott Kretchmar, philosopher of movement. The human is not a machine, but rather a thinking, feeling, holistic being. This is beyond a description of mind and body (presented in Chapter 3) and returns to the concept of play (presented in Chapter 4). Kretchmar wrote of an intimate and deep relationship with play, meaning activities that are not organized around formal outcomes: "When this more intimate relationship has been achieved, we know that our quality of life—indeed our very identity—at least for now, has been tethered to this playground—whether it be theater, good novels, music, dance."[17] The outcome is not faster or better but, rather, quality of life. So many concepts presented throughout this book are brought together in this statement, a statement fitting for the summary of these discussions.

We can ask ourselves all these questions and seek answers in the lives that we construct, as we move within the contexts in which we live and throughout all the formal, non-formal, and informal settings of our growth and life. In some ways, our entire lives can fit an integrated description of formal, non-formal, and informal education. So, it is through these processes that we are always moving forward in becoming.

GLOSSARY

Certification This is a qualification to be a teacher.

Colonialism One group colonializes another, with domination.

Commercial Sometimes a synonym for a for-profit entity.

Culturally responsive teaching "The process of using familiar cultural information and processes to scaffold learning."[1]

Curriculum A delineation of content to be covered in the context of an education.

Dualisms "A theory that considers reality to consist of two irreducible elements." https://www.merriam-webster.com/dictionary/dualism

Emic Seeing something from an inside, experienced, anthropological perspective; intrinsic

Epistemology The nature of knowledge and belief.

Ethnorelativism An acquired ability to see many values and behaviors as cultural rather than universal. https://www.yourdictionary.com/ethnorelativism

Etic Seeing something from an outside, not experienced, anthropological perspective; extrinsic

Feedback "Information about reactions to a product, a person's performance of a task, etc. which is used as a basis for improvement." https://www.lexico.com/en/definition/feedback

For-profit A business venture to earn money for its owner or investors.

Formal field of learning Concerned with curriculum offerings in education and training institutions, "Formal learning takes place in education and training institutions, is recognised by relevant national authorities and leads to diplomas and qualifications. Formal learning is structured according to educational arrangements such as curricula, qualifications and teaching–learning requirements."[2]

Indigenous Native or occurring naturally in a location.

Informal learning "[L]earning that occurs in daily life, in the family, in the workplace, in communities and through activities of all individuals."[3] "In some cases, the term experiential learning is used to refer to informal learning that focuses on learning from experience."[4]

Marginalization Placing a person or group on the side, out of a central focus and consideration.

Multiculturalism Representing different cultures.

Native Americans Indigenous groups in the United States, formerly called American Indians

Non-formal learning "Non-formal learning that has been acquired in addition or alternatively to formal learning. In some cases, it is also structured according to educational and training arrangements, but more flexible. It usually takes place in community-based settings, the workplace and through the activities of civil society organisations."[5]

Non-profit An entity that is not for the purpose of earning money but rather directs its profits back into the entity, in order to promote a cause or shared purpose.

Pedagogy The actual study of teaching and methods.

PK-12 This is a US abbreviation that includes pre-kindergarten through Grade 12 education, or primary (elementary) and secondary education.

Primary education This includes the early years of compulsory education through Grade 6.

Progressive education "Progressive education, movement that took form in Europe and the United States during the late 19th century as a reaction to the alleged narrowness and formalism of traditional education. One of its main objectives was to educate the "whole child"—that is, to attend to physical and emotional, as well as intellectual, growth." https://www.britannica.com/topic/progressive-education

Secondary education The second six years of compulsory education.

Spectrum of teaching styles A unified theory of teaching and learning (originally for physical education) developed by Muska Mosston in 1964.

Standards Agreed upon ideas, concepts, and levels to achieve a certain education.

Tertiary education Any education that follows compulsory education, but frequently refers to university.

Tokenism "Actions that are the result of pretending to give advantage to those groups in society who are often treated unfairly, in order to give the appearance of fairness." https://dictionary.cambridge.org/us/dictionary/english/tokenism

NOTES

Introduction

1 Stanford Encyclopedia of Philosophy, https://plato.stanford.edu/entries/colonialism/, retrieved March 8, 2020.

2 john a. powell and Stephen Menendian, "The Problem of Othering: Towards Inclusiveness and Belonging," *Othering Belonging: Expanding the Circle of Human Concern*, Issue 1, June 29, 2017. http://www.otheringandbelonging.org/the-problem-of-othering/, retrieved March 8, 2020.

3 Maxine Greene, *Variations on a Blue Guitar* (New York: Teachers College Press, 2001), 16.

Chapter 1

1 Charlotte Svendler Nielsen and Susan R. Koff, "Exploring Identities in Dance," in *Proceedings from the 13th Congress of Dance and the Child International*, Copenhagen, Denmark, July 5–10, 2015, The Dance Halls, Department of Nutrition, Exercise and Sport, University of Copenhagen and the Danish National School of Performing Art, http://ausdance.org.au/publications/details/exploring-identities-in-dance.

2 Nyama McCarthy-Brown, "Decolonizing Dance Curriculum in Higher Education: One Credit at a Time," *Journal of Dance Education* 14, no. 4 (2014): 125–9.

3 Susan Leigh Foster, ed., *Worlding Dance* (New York: Palgrave Macmillan, 2009).

4 Ibid., 10.

5 Pegge Vissicaro, *Studying Dance Cultures Around the World: An Introduction to Multicultural Dance Education* (Dubuque: Kendall/Hunt Publishing Company, 2004), 3.

6 Thomas N. Headland, Kenneth L. Pike, and Marvin Harris, eds., *Emics and Etics: The Insider/Outsider Debate. Frontiers of Anthropology*, vol. 7 (Newbury Park: Sage, 1990).

7 Adrienne L. Kaeppler, "Ballet, Hula and 'Cats': Dancing as a Discourse on Globalization," *2006 World Dance Alliance Global Assembly Proceedings, Toronto, Canada*, ed. Karen Rose Cann (2006), 251–9. https://wda-americas.com/wp-content/uploads/2014/01/WDA-2006-Global-Proceedings.pdf

8   Jessica Sand Blonde, Dance as an Art Form, for New York University Dance Education Program.
9   Kerry Freedman, "About This Issue: The Social Reconstruction of Art Education," *Studies in Art Education* 35, no. 3 (Spring 1994): 131–4.
10 Vissicaro, *Studying Dance Cultures Around the World*.
11 Ibid.
12 Sam Gill, *Dancing, Culture, Religion* (Lantham: Lexington Books, 2012), 11.
13 Ann Dils and Ann Cooper Albright, Foreword to *Moving History/Dancing Cultures: A Dance History Reader*, eds. Ann Dils and Ann Cooper-Albright (Middletown: Wesleyan University Press, 2001), xvii.
14 Franziska Boas, "Dance in the Liberal Arts College Curriculum," *Impulse: Annual of Contemporary Dance 1953*, 28, accessed August 1, 2019, https://digital.library.temple.edu/digital/collection/p15037coll4/id/1514/rec/4.
15 Janet Adshead, *Study in Dance* (London: Dance Books, 1981), 4.
16 Karen E. Bond, "Dance and Quality of Life," in *Encyclopedia of Quality of Life and Well-Being Research*, ed. Alex C. Michalos (Dordrecht, the Netherlands: Springer, 2014), 1419.
17 Patricia Beaman, *World Dance Cultures: From Ritual to Spectacle* (New York: Routledge, 2018).
18 Curt Sachs, *World History of the Dance* (New York: W. W. Norton & Co., 1937), 3.
19 Though this quote has many attributes to offer this text, it is used with apprehension because of the word "primitive" which is disputed through this text as a racist and derogatory term.
20 Suzanne Langer, "Virtual Powers," in *What Is Dance?*, eds. Roger Copeland and Marshall Cohen (Oxford: Oxford University Press, 1983), 44.
21 Sachs, *World History of the Dance*, 6.
22 Kimerer L. LaMothe, *Why We Dance: A Philosophy of Bodily Becoming* (New York: Columbia University Press, 2015), 57.
23 Ibid., 105.
24 Maxine Sheets-Johnstone, *Primacy of Movement: Expanded second edition* (Amsterdam: John Banjamins Publishing, 2011).
25 Ibid., 438.
26 Antonio Damasio, *Descartes' Error: Emotion, Reason and the Human Brain* (New York: G.P. Putnam, 1994).
27 Sheets-Johnstone, *Primacy of Movement: Expanded second edition*.
28 Sachs, *World History of the Dance*.
29 Rhonda Grauer, Preface to *Dancing: The Pleasure, Power, and Art of Movement*, by Gerald Jonas (New York: Harry N. Abrams, 1992).
30 Adshead, *Study in Dance*.
31 LaMothe, *Why We Dance*, 183.

32 Ralph Buck, "Teaching Dance in the Curriculum," in *Handbook of Physical Education*, eds. David Kirk, Doune MacDonald, and Mary O'Sullivan (London: Sage, 2006), 701–19.

33 Graham McFee, *The Concept of Dance Education* (London: Routledge, 1994).

34 Anne Morrison, Lester-Irabinna Rigney, Robert Hattam, and Abigail Diplock, *Toward an Australian Culturally Responsive Pedagogy: A Narrative Review of the Literature* (Adelaide: University of South Australia, 2019).

35 LaMothe, *Why We Dance*, 187–8.

36 Bond, "Dance and Quality of Life."

37 Joann W. Keali'inohomoku, Foreword to *Studying Dance Cultures Around the World*, by Pegge Vissicaro (Dubuque: Kendall/Hunt Publishing Company, 2004), ix.

38 Savigliano, "Worlding Dance and Dancing Out There in the World," 173.

39 Joann W. Keali'inohomoku, "An Anthropologist Looks at Ballet as a Form of Ethnic Dance," in *Moving History/Dancing Cultures: A Dance History Reader*, eds. Ann Dils and Ann Cooper-Albright (Middletown: Wesleyan University Press, 2001).

40 Kaeppler, "Ballet, Hula and 'Cats.'"

41 Colonialization is a complex and large topic which cannot be expanded here. For a clear example of one indigenous dance culture, and its complex changes due to colonialization and politics, see all cited here plus:

Kathleen Foreman, "Dancing on the Endangered List: Aesthetics and Politics of Indigenous Dance in the Philippines," in *Moving History/Dancing Cultures: A Dance History Reader*, eds. Ann Dils and Ann Cooper-Albright (Middletown: Wesleyan University Press, 2001), 384–8.

42 Foster, ed., *Worlding Dance*.

43 Vissicaro, *Studying Dance Cultures Around the World*, 90.

44 Crystal U. Davis and Jesse Phillips-Fein, "Tendus and Tenancy: Black Dancers and the White Landscape of Dance Education," in *The Palgrave Handbook of Race and the Arts in Education*, eds. Amelia M. Kraehe, Ruben Gaztambide-Fernandez, and B. Stephen Carpenter, II (Champaign: Palgrave Macmillan, 2018).

45 Crystal U. Davis, "Laying New Ground: Uprooting White Privilege and Planting Seeds of Equity and Inclusivity," *Journal of Dance Education* 18, no. 3 (2018): 120–5.

46 Foster, ed., *Worlding Dance*.

47 Savigliano, "Worlding Dance and Dancing Out There in the World," 167.

48 Foster, ed., *Worlding Dance*, 2.

49 Ibid., 187.

50 Vissicaro, *Studying Dance Cultures Around the World*.

51 Rose Casement, "Differentiating between the Terms 'Multicultural' and 'Diversity': Broadening the Perspective," *Language Arts Journal of Michigan* 18, no. 1 (2002): 5–8.

52 Stanley Fish, "Boutique Multiculturalism, or Why Liberals Are Incapable of Thinking About Hate Speech," *Critical Inquiry* 23, no. 2 (Winter, 1997): 278–395.

53 Vissicaro, *Studying Dance Cultures Around the World*.

Chapter 2

1 Buck, "Teaching Dance in the Curriculum."

2 Education, Wikipedia, https://en.wikipedia.org/wiki/Education, retrieved February 17, 2020.

3 Earle F. Zeigler, "Past, Present and Future Development of Physical Education and Sport," in *The Academy Papers: Issues and Challenges: A Kaleidoscope of Change* (Washington, DC: The American Academy of Physical Education, 1979), 9–19.

4 YMCA, Wikipedia, https://en.wikipedia.org/wiki/YMCA, retrieved February 22, 2020.

5 Sarah Chapman, *Movement Education in the United States: Historical Development and Theoretical Bases* (Philadelphia: Movement Education Publications, 1974).

6 Ibid.

7 Thomas D. Wood and Rosalind F. Cassidy, *The New Physical Education* (New York: Macmillan and Company, 1934).

8 Ibid.

9 Chapman, *Movement Education in the United States*.

10 Mabel Lee, *A History of Physical Education and Sport in the U.S.A.* (New York: John Wiley & Sons, 1983), 133.

11 Susan Manning, "Modern Dance in the Third Reich, Redux," in *The Oxford Handbook of Dance and Politics*, eds. Rebekah J. Kowal, Gerald Siegmund, and Randy Martin (New York: Oxford University Press, 2017), 395–415.

12 Aileene S. Lockhart, "The President's Address: The Values That Guide Us," in *The Academy Papers: Reunification* (Reston: The American Academy of Physical Education, 1981), 7–10.

13 John Lucas, "The Academy Presidents: Physical Education Futurists 1926–1976," in *The Academy Papers: Beyond Research—Solutions to Human Problems* (Iowa City: The American Academy of Physical Education, 1976), 106–15.

14 For more detailed information about German and Swedish gymnastics systems see: Gertrud Pfister, "Cultural Confrontations: German *Turnen*, Swedish Gymnastics and English Sport – European Diversity in Physical Activities From a Historical Perspective," *Culture, Sport, Society* 6, no. 1 (2003): 61–91; Earle F. Zeigler, *History of Physical Education and Sport* (Englewood Cliffs: Prentice-Hall Inc., 1979). Additionally, for a more complete world view of the history of physical education, see: Deobold B. Van Dalen and Bruce L. Bennett,

A World History of Physical Education (Englewood Cliffs: Prentice-Hall Inc., 1971).

15 Richard Kraus, Sarah Chapman Hilsendager, and Brenda Dixon, *History of the Dance in Art and Education*, 3rd ed. (Englewood Cliffs: Prentice Hall Inc., 1991).
16 John Dewey, *Democracy and Education* (New York: Macmillan, 1916).
17 Chapman, *Movement Education in the United States.*
18 Patricia Vertinsky, "Schooling the Dance: From Dance Under the Swastika to Movement Education in the British School," *Journal of Sport History* 31, no. 3 (2004): 273–95.
19 Ibid.; Buck, "Teaching Dance in the Curriculum."
20 Peter C. McIntosh, *Physical Education in England Since 1800* (London: G Bell & Sons Ltd., 1968).
21 Ibid.
22 Lilian Karina and Marion Kant, *Hitler's Dancers: German Modern Dance and the Third Reich* (New York: Berghahn Books, 2004); Vertinsky, "Schooling the Dance," 273–95; Manning, "Modern Dance in the Third Reich, Redux."
23 Karina, *Hitler's Dancers*, 6.
24 Jeff Meiners, "So We Can Dance? In Pursuit of an Inclusive Dance Curriculum for the Primary School Years in Australia" (Ed.D. diss., University of South Australia, 2017).
25 Marvin H. Eyler, "What the Profession Was Once Like: Nineteenth Century Physical Education," in *The Academy Papers: Reunification* (Reston: The American Academy of Physical Education, 1981), 14–20.
26 Kraus, Hilsendager and Dixon, *History of the Dance in Art and Education*, 3rd ed. (Englewood Cliffs: Prentice Hall, 1991).
27 Zeigler, *History of Physical Education and Sport*; Van Dalen and Bennett, *A World History of Physical Education*; Lee, *A History of Physical Education and Sport in the U.S.A.*
28 Jane M. Bonbright, "Dance Education in 1999: Status, Challenges, and Recommendations," *Arts Education Policy Review* 101, no. 1 (1999): 33–9.
29 Susan Koff, "Meaning Making Through the Arts: Description of an Urban High School's Arts-Based Program" (Ed.D. diss., Temple University, 1995).
30 National Core Arts Standards, June 4, 2014, https://www.nationalartsstandards.org/
31 Buck, "Teaching Dance in the Curriculum."
32 Anne Schley Duggan, "The Place of Dance in the School Physical Education Program," *Journal of the American Association for Health, Physical Education, and Recreation* 22, no. 3 (1951): 26–9.
33 Thomas K. Hagood, *A History of Dance in American Higher Education* (Lewiston: The Edwin Mellon Press, 2000), 91.
34 Elizabeth McPherson, *The Contributions of Martha Hill to American Dance and Dance Education* (Lewiston: The Edwin Mellen Press, 2008), 28.

35 Martha Hill, "Implications for the Dance," *The Journal of Health and Physical Education* 13, no. 6 (1942): 347–8.
36 Thomas K. Hagood, *Legacy in Dance Education: Essays and Interviews on Values, Practices, and People – An Anthology* (Amherst: Cambria Press, 2008); Janice Ross, *Moving Lessons: Margaret H'Doubler and the Beginning of Dance in American Education* (Madison: The University of Wisconsin Press, 2000).
37 Ibid.; Hagood, *A History of Dance in American Higher Education*; John M. Wilson, Thomas K. Hagood, and Mary A. Brennan, *Margaret H'Doubler: The Legacy of America's Dance Education Pioneer* (Youngstown: Cambria Press, 2006).
38 Ross, *Moving Lessons*.
39 Dewey, *Democracy and Education*.
40 Wilson, Hagood, and Brennan, *Margaret H'Doubler: The Legacy of America's Dance Education Pioneer*, 15–35.
41 Ross, *Moving Lessons*.
42 Dewey, *Democracy and Education*; Hagood, *A History of Dance in American Higher Education*; Ibid.
43 Ross, *Moving Lessons*, 143.
44 Ibid.
45 Ibid., 204.
46 Ibid., 13.
47 McPherson, *The Contributions of Martha Hill to American Dance and Dance Education*.
48 Hagood, *A History of Dance in American Higher Education*, 135.
49 Ibid.
50 Ibid., 145; original emphasis.
51 Wilson, Hagood, and Brennan, *Margaret H'Doubler: The Legacy of America's Dance Education Pioneer*, 15–35.
52 Ross, *Moving Lessons*.
53 John M. Wilson, "Margaret H'Doubler's Mottos in Context," in *Margaret H'Doubler: The Legacy of America's Dance Education Pioneer*, eds. John M. Wilson, Thomas K. Hagood, and Mary A. Brennan (Youngstown: Cambria Press, 2006), 305–51.
54 Chapman, *Movement Education in the United States*.
55 Wilson, Hagood, and Brennan, *Margaret H'Doubler: The Legacy of America's Dance Education Pioneer*.
56 Hagood, *A History of Dance in American Higher Education*, 144.
57 Ibid.
58 Hagood, *Legacy in Dance Education*.
59 Ross, *Moving Lessons*.

60 Hagood, *Legacy in Dance Education*; Alma Hawkins, *Modern Dance in Higher Education* (New York: Teachers College Press, 1954).

61 Hagood, *Legacy in Dance Education*.

62 Hawkins, *Modern Dance in Higher Education*.

63 Phyllis Pier Valente, "The Dance in American Colleges," *The Journal of the American Association for Health, Physical Education and Recreation* 20, no. 5 (1949): 312–13, 349.

64 Duggan, "The Place of Dance in the School Physical Education Program," 44–5, 51, 60.

65 Ross, *Moving Lessons*; Hagood, *A History of Dance in American Higher Education*.

66 Hagood, *A History of Dance in American Higher Education*.

67 Hawkins, *Modern Dance in Higher Education*.

68 Ibid., 23.

Chapter 3

1 Buck, "Teaching Dance in the Curriculum," 703–19.

2 Hagood, *Legacy in Dance Education*.

3 Thomas K. Hagood and Luke C. Kahlich, eds., *Perspectives on Contemporary Dance History: Revisiting Impulse 1950–1970* (Amherst: Cambria Press, 2013).

4 Ibid.

5 Mary A. Brennan, "Impulse 1965," in *Perspectives on Contemporary Dance History: Revisiting Impulse 1950–1970*, ed. Hagood and Kahlich, 313–39; Thomas K. Hagood, "Impulse 1968," in *Perspectives on Contemporary Dance History: Revisiting Impulse 1950–1970*, eds. Hagood and Kahlich, 391–412.

6 Katja Kolcio, *Moving Pillars: Organizing Dance 1956–1978* (Middletown: Wesleyan University Press, 2010).

7 Eugene C. Howe, "What Business Has the Modern Dance in Physical Education?" *Journal of Health and Physical Education* 8, no. 3 (1937): 131–3, 187–8.

8 Kolcio, *Moving Pillars*.

9 Ibid.

10 Adshead, *Study of Dance*.

11 Ibid.

12 Ibid.

13 Hagood, *A History of Dance in American Higher Education*.

14 Judith B. Alter, "Why Dance Students Pursue Dance: Studies of Dance Students from 1953–1993," *Dance Research Journal* 29, no. 2 (Fall 1997): 70–89.

15 Hagood, *A History of Dance in American Higher Education*.

16 Keali'inohomoku, Foreword to *Studying Dance Cultures Around the World*, ix.

17 Sherril Dodds, ed., *The Bloomsbury Companion to Dance Studies* (London: Bloomsbury Academic, 2019).

18 Randy Martin, *Critical Moves: Dance Studies in Theory and Politics* (Durham: Duke University Press, 1998).

19 Edward C. Warburton, "Dance Pedagogy," in *The Bloomsbury Companion to Dance Studies,* ed. Sherril Dodds (London: Bloomsbury Academic, 2019), 81–110.

20 Jill Green, "Student Bodies: Dance Pedagogy and the Soma," in *International Handbook of Research in Arts Education*, ed. Liora Bresler (Dordrecht, The Netherlands: Springer, 2007), 1129.

21 Wilson, Hagood, and Brennan, eds., *Margaret H'Doubler: Legacy of America's Dance Pioneer.*

22 Mortimer J. Adler, *Reforming Education* (New York: Macmillan Publishing Co., 1988).

23 James Bowen, *A History of Western Education: Vol. 3 The Modern West, Europe and the New World* (New York: St. Martin's Press, 1981), 555.

24 Randall Everett Allsup, *Remixing the Classroom: Toward an Open Philosophy of Music Education* (Bloomington: Indiana University Press, 2016).

25 Bowen, *A History of Western Education: Vol. 3 The Modern West, Europe and the New World.*

26 Ibid., 409.

27 Dewey, *Democracy and Education*, 87; Henry A. Giroux, *Border Crossings: Cultural Workers and the Politics of Education* (New York: Routledge, 1992), 14; Maxine Greene, *The Dialectic of Freedom* (New York: Teachers College Press, 1988).

28 Maxine Greene, *Landscapes of Learning* (New York: Teachers College Press, 1978).

29 Bowen, *A History of Western Education: Vol. 3 The Modern West, Europe and the New World*, 421–2.

30 John Dewey, *Experience and Education* (New York: Collier Books, 1938).

31 Ross, *Moving Lessons.*

32 Bowen, *A History of Western Education: Vol. 3 The Modern West, Europe and the New World.*

33 Ibid.

34 Ibid.

35 Ibid., 552.

36 Dewey, *Experience and Education*, 87.

37 Maxine Greene, *Releasing the Imagination* (San Francisco: Jossey-Bass Publishers, 1995), 140.

38 Eeva Anttila, "Children as Agents in Dance: Implications of the Notion of Child Culture for Research and Practice in Dance Education," in *International*

      Handbook of Research in Arts Education, ed. Liora Bresler (Dordrecht, The Netherlands: Springer, 2007), 865–79.
39 Martin, *Critical Moves*.
40 Justin Skirry, "René Descartes (1596-1650)," *Internet Encyclopedia of Philosophy*, https://www.iep.utm.edu/descarte/.
41 Thomas D. Wood and Rosalind F. Cassidy, *The New Physical Education: A Program of Naturalized Activities for Education Toward Citizenship* (New York: The Macmillan Company, 1927).
42 R. Scott Kretchmar, "T.D. Wood: On Chairs and Education," *Journal of Physical Education Recreation and Dance* 66, no. 1 (1995): 13.
43 Antonio R. Damasio, "Descartes' Error Revisited," *Journal of the History of the Neurosciences* 10, no. 2 (2001): 192–4.
44 R. Scott Kretchmar, *Practical Philosophy of Sport and Physical Activity*, 2nd ed. (Champaign: Human Kinetics, 2005).
45 Howard Gardner, *Frames of Mind*, 3rd ed. (New York: Basic Books, 2011).
46 Kretchmar, *Practical Philosophy of Sport and Physical Activity*, 116.
47 Ibid., 122.
48 Wilson, Hagood, and Brennan, ed., *Margaret H'Doubler: Legacy of America's Dance Pioneer*; Janice Ross, personal communication, October 2018.
49 Keali'inohomoku, Foreword to *Studying Dance Cultures Around the World*, ix.
50 Ibid.
51 McCarthy-Brown, "Decolonizing Dance Curriculum in Higher Education," 125–9.
52 Ibid.
53 Susan Leigh Foster, "Dance and/as Competition in the Privately Owned US Studio," in *The Oxford Handbook of Dance and Politics*, eds. Rebekah J. Kowal, Gerald Siegmund, and Randy Martin (New York: Oxford University Press, 2017), 55–76.
54 Brenda Dixon Gottschild, "Racing in Place: A Meta-Memoir on Dance Politics and Practice," in *The Oxford Handbook of Dance and Politics*, eds. Rebekah J. Kowal, Gerald Siegmund, and Randy Martin (New York: Oxford University Press, 2017), 91.
55 Wilson, Hagood, and Brennan, ed., *Margaret H'Doubler: Legacy of America's Dance Pioneer*.
56 Susan Koff, "Toward a Definition of Dance Education," *Childhood Education* 77, no. 1 (2000), 31.

Chapter 4

1 Vissicaro, *Studying Dance Cultures Around the World*, 125.
2 Warburton, "Dance Pedagogy," 81.

3. Vissicaro, *Studying Dance Cultures Around the World*, 125.
4. Paulo Freire, *Pedagogy of the Oppressed* (New York: Seabury Press, 1968).
5. Maxine Sheets-Johnstone, "On Learning to Move Oneself," in *Margaret H'Doubler: Legacy of America's Dance Pioneer*, eds. John M. Wilson, Thomas K. Hagood, and Mary A. Brennan (Youngstown: Cambria Press, 2006), 267.
6. Warburton, "Dance Pedagogy."
7. Buck, "Teaching Dance in the Curriculum," 713.
8. Denis Charles Phillips and Jonas F. Soltis, *Perspectives on Learning*, 3rd ed. (New York: Teachers College Press, 1992).
9. Adler, *Reforming Education*, 190.
10. Bowen, *A History of Western Education: Vol. 3 The Modern West, Europe and the New World*.
11. Adler, *Reforming Education*.
12. Bowen, *A History of Western Education: Vol. 3 The Modern West, Europe and the New World*.
13. Phillips and Soltis, *Perspectives on Learning*.
14. Paulo Freire, *Pedagogy of the Oppressed*, 30th anniversary ed. (New York: Continuum, 2006).
15. Bowen, *A History of Western Education: Vol. 3 The Modern West, Europe and the New World*.
16. Shapiro, *Dance, Power, and Difference*.
17. John Dewey, *How We Think* (Boston: D.C. Heath & Company, 1933), 292.
18. Jerome S. Bruner, Alison Jolly, and Kathy Sylva, eds., *Play—Its Role in Development and Evolution* (New York: Basic Books, 1976).
19. Ibid.
20. Dewey, *How We Think*, 287.
21. L. S. Vygotsky, "Play and Its Role in the Mental Development of the Child," in *Play—Its Role in Development and Evolution*, eds. Jerome S. Bruner, Alison Jolly, and Kathy Sylva (New York: Basic Books, 1976), 537–54.
22. Ibid.
23. Eric H. Erikson, "Play and Actuality," in *Play—Its Role in Development and Evolution*, ed. Jerome S. Bruner, Alison Jolly, and Kathy Sylva (New York: Basic Books, 1976), 688–703.
24. Nancy Armstrong Melser, *Teaching Soft Skills in a Hard World: Skills for Beginning Teachers* (Blue Ridge Summit: Rowman & Littlefield Publishers, 2018).
25. J. Huizinga, "Play and Contest as Civilizing Functions," in *Play—Its Role in Development and Evolution*, eds. Jerome S. Bruner, Alison Jolly, and Kathy Sylva (New York: Basic Books, 1976), 688–703.
26. Eleanor Leacock, "At Play in African Villages," in *Play—Its Role in Development and Evolution*, eds. Jerome S. Bruner, Alison Jolly, and Kathy Sylva (New York: Basic Books, 1976), 466.

27 Muska Mosston and Sara Ashworth, *Teaching Physical Education: First Online Edition, 2008* (Pearson Education, 2008). https://www.spectrumofteachingstyles.org/pdfs/ebook/Teaching_Physical_Edu_1st_Online_old.pdf.
28 Michael Goldberger, "Effective Learning: Through a Spectrum of Teaching Styles," *Journal of Physical Education, Recreation & Dance* 55, no. 8 (1984): 19, 21.
29 Richard A. Magill and David Anderson, *Motor Learning and Control: Concepts and Applications*, 11th ed. (New York: McGraw-Hill, 2017).
30 Ibid.
31 Sheets-Johnstone, "On Learning to Move Oneself," 272.
32 Morrison, Rigney, Hattam, and Diplock, *Toward an Australian Culturally Responsive Pedagogy*, 24.
33 Ibid.
34 Gloria Ladson-Billings, "Toward a Theory of Culturally Relevant Pedagogy," *American Educational Research Journal* 32, no. 3 (1995): 465–91; Nyama McCarthy-Brown, *Dance Pedagogy for a Diverse World* (Jefferson: McFarland & Co. Publishers, 2017). Liz Melchior, "Culturally Responsive Dance Pedagogy in the Primary Classroom," *Research in Dance Education* 12, no. 2 (2011): 119–35.
35 Zaretta Hammond, *Culturally Responsive Teaching & the Brain* (Thousand Oaks: Corwin, 2015), 156.
36 Ibid., 18–20.
37 Vissicaro, *Studying Dance Cultures Around the World*, 125.
38 Jan Bolwell, "Into the Light: An Expanding Vision of Dance Education," in *Dance, Power, and Difference: Critical and Feminist Perspectives on Dance Education*, ed. Sherry Shapiro (Champaign: Human Kinetics, 1998); Alfdaniels Mabingo and Susan R. Koff, "Altering the Paradigm," in *Undisciplining Dance in Nine Movement and Eight Stumbles*, eds. Carol Brown and Alys Longley (Newcastle upon Tyne: Cambridge Scholars Publishing, 2018); Vissicaro, *Studying Dance Cultures Around the World*.
39 Nyama McCarthy-Brown, "Owners of Dance: How Dance Is Controlled and Whitewashed in the Teaching of Dance Forms," in *The Palgrave Handbook of Race and the Arts in Education*, eds. Amelia M. Kraehe, Ruben Gaztambide-Fernandez, and B. Stephen Carpenter, II (Cham: Palgrave Macmillan, 2018), 479.
40 Vissicaro, *Studying Dance Cultures Around the World*, 125.
41 Inez Rovegno and Madeleine Gregg, "Using Folk Dance and Geography to Teach Interdisciplinary, Multicultural Subject Matter: A School-Based Study," *Physical Education and Sport Pedagogy* 12, no. 3 (2007): 205–23.
42 Ladson-Billings, "Toward a Theory of Culturally Relevant Pedagogy," 483.
43 Isabel A. Marquez, "Dance Education in/and the Postmodern," in *Dance, Power, and Difference: Critical and Feminist Perspectives on Dance Education*, ed. Sherry Shapiro (Champaign: Human Kinetics, 1998).
44 Diedre Sklar, "Five Premises for a Culturally Sensitive Approach to Dance," in *Moving History/Dancing Cultures: A Dance History Reader*,

eds. A. Dils and A. Cooper-Albright (Middletown: Wesleyan University Press, 2001), 32.
45 Vissicaro, *Studying Dance Cultures Around the World*, 90.
46 Jerome S. Bruner, *The Culture of Education* (Cambridge: Harvard University Press, 1996), 3.
47 Ibid., 4; original emphasis.
48 Ibid., 20.

Chapter 5

1 Ann Soot and Ele Viskus, "Contemporary Approaches to Dance Pedagogy: The Challenges of the 21st Century," *Procedia Social and Behavioral Sciences* 112, no. 4 (2014): 290–9.
2 Fiona Bannon, "Dance: The Possibilities of a Discipline," *Research in Dance Education* 11, no. 1 (2010): 49–59; Anne Green Gilbert, "Dance Education in the 21st Century: A Global Perspective," *Journal of Physical Education, Recreation & Dance* 76, no. 5 (2005): 26–35; S. W. Stinson, "My Body/Myself: Lessons From Dance Education," in *Knowing Bodies, Moving Minds: Towards Embodied Teaching and Learning*, ed. Liora Bresler (London: Kluwer Academic, 2004); Doug Risner, "Dance Education Matters: Rebuilding Postsecondary Dance Education for Twenty-First Century Relevance and Resonance," *Arts Education Policy Review* 111, no. 4 (2010): 123–35; Eeva Anttila, Rose Martin, and Charlotte Nielsen Svendler, "Performing Difference In/Through Dance: The Significance of Dialogical, or Third Spaces in Creating Conditions for Learning and Living Together," *Thinking Skills and Creativity* 31 (2019): 209–16.
3 *ISCED Fields of Education and Training 2013 (ISCED-F 2013)*. PDF. Montreal: UNESCO Institute for Statistics, 2014. http://uis.unesco.org/sites/default/files/documents/isced-fields-of-education-and-training-2013-en.pdf
4 Susanne Keuchel, "Arts Education Development Index (AEDI). A Comparative International Empirical Research Approach in Arts Education by Numbers," in *International Yearbook for Research in Arts Education 2*, eds. Larry O'Farrell, Shifra Schonmann, and Ernst Wagner (Münster: Waxmann Verlag, 2014), 42–51.
5 Norma Gonzáles, Luis C. Moll, and Cathy Amanti, eds., *Funds of Knowledge: Theorizing Practices in Households, Communities and Classrooms* (Mahwah: Lawrence Erlbaum Associates, 2005).
6 Max van Manen, "Phenomenology of Practice," *Phenomenology & Practice* 1, no. 1 (2007): 93.
7 Shapiro, ed., *Dance, Power, and Difference*.
8 Becky Dyer, "Merging Traditional Technique Vocabularies with Democratic Teaching Perspectives in Dance Education: A Consideration of Aesthetic Values and Their Sociopolitical Contexts," *The Journal of Aesthetic Education* 43, no. 4 (2009): 113.

9   Liz Melchior, "Making Connections: Culturally Responsive Pedagogy and Dance in the Classroom," in *Intersecting Cultures in Music and Dance Education*, ed. Linda Ashley and David Lines, Vol. 19 of *Landscapes: The Arts, Aesthetics, and Education* (Champaign: Springer, 2016); Risner and Stinson, "Moving Social Justice," 1–26.

10 *International Arts Education Standards: A Survey of Standards, Practices, and Expectations in Thirteen Countries and Regions*. PDF (New York: The College Board, 2013). https://www.nationalartsstandards.org/sites/default/files/College%20Board%20Research%20-%20International%20Standards_0.pdf

11 Nyama McCarthy-Brown, "The Need for Culturally Relevant Dance Education," *Journal of Dance Education* 9, no. 4 (2009): 120–5; Julie Kerr-Berry, "Dance Educator as Dancer and Artist," *Journal of Dance Education* 7, no. 1 (2011): 5–6; Risner and Stinson, "Moving Social Justice," 1–26.

12 *International Arts Education Standards: A Survey of Standards, Practices, and Expectations in Thirteen Countries and Regions*, 4.

13 Ibid.

Chapter 6

1   Keuchel, "Arts Education Development Index (AEDI) A Comparative International Empirical Research Approach in Arts Education," 43.

2   Beaman, *World Dance Cultures*.

3   Ibid.; Dorothy B. Barrere, Mary Kawena Pukui, and Marion Kelly, *Hula Historical Perspectives* (Honolulu: Bernice Pauahi Bishop Museum, 1980).

4   Davis, "Laying New Ground," 120–5.

5   Walter Doyle, "Curriculum and Pedagogy," in *Handbook for Research on Curriculum*, ed. Phillip W. Jackson (New York: Macmillan Publishing Co., 1992), 486–516.

6   "International Standard Classification of Education (ISCED)," *UNESCO*, last modified 2019, http://uis.unesco.org/en/topic/international-standard-classification-education-isced.

7   Susan R. Koff, "Applied Dance Curriculum: A Global Perspective," in *Dance Education Around the World: Perspectives on Dance, Young People and Change*, eds. Charlotte Svendler Nielsen and Stephanie Burridge (London: Routledge, 2015); Susan R. Koff, Charlotte Svendler Nielsen, Cornelia Baumgart, and Ivančica Janković, "Curriculum in Motion—Special Event," in *Dance, Young People and Change: Proceedings of the daCi and WDA Global Dance Summit*, eds. Susan W. Stinson, Charlotte Svendler Nielsen, and Shu-Ying Liu (Taipei National University of the Arts, Taiwan, July 14–20, 2012). http://www.ausdance.org/ [Accessed on January 1, 2019] ISBN 978-1-875255-19-1; Barbara Snook, "Dance in New Zealand Primary Schools: Moving Forward Toward a Realization of UNESCO's Aims for the Arts," in *Dance, Young People and Change: Proceedings of the daCi and WDA Global Dance Summit*, eds. Susan W. Stinson, Charlotte Svendler Nielsen, and Shu-Ying Liu

(Taipei National University of the Arts, Taiwan, July 14–20, 2012). http://www.ausdance.org/ [Accessed on January 1, 2019] ISBN 978-1-875255-19-1.

8   2010. "Seoul Agenda: Goals for the Development of Arts Education," in *UNESCO's Second World Conference on Arts Education* (Seoul, Republic of Korea, May 25–28, 2010), 2. Retrieved from http://www.unesco.org/new/en/culture/themes/creativity/arts-education/

9   Koff, "Meaning Making Through the Arts."

10 Ibid.

11 Buck, "Teaching Dance in the Curriculum."

12 Ibid.; Susan W. Stinson, *Embodied Curriculum Theory and Research in Arts Education: A Dance Scholar's Search for Meaning* (Dordrecht: Springer, 2016).

13 Paulo Freire, *Education, The Practice of Freedom* (London: Writers and Readers Publishing Cooperative, 1976); Freire, *Pedagogy of the Oppressed*, 30th anniversary ed.

14 AATE, MENC, NAEA, and NDA, *National Standards for Arts Education: What Every Young American Should Be Able to Do in the Arts* (Reston: Rowman & Littlefield Education, 1994); "Dance, Media Arts, Music, Theatre and Visual Arts," *National Core Arts Standards*, last modified June 4, 2014, https://www.nationalartsstandards.org/.

15 Meiners, "So We Can Dance?," 87.

16 Snook, "Dance in New Zealand Primary Schools."

17 Meiners, "So We Can Dance?"

18 Doyle, "Curriculum and Pedagogy," 486–516; Donald Blumenfeld-Jones and Sheaun-Yann Liang, "Dance Curriculum Research," in *International Handbook of Research in Arts Education*, ed. Liora Bresler (Dordrecht: Springer, 2007), 245–60; Elliot W. Eisner, *The Educational Imagination: On the Design and Evaluation of School Programs*, 2nd ed. (New York: Macmillan Publishing Co., 1985); Liora Bresler, "Imitative, Complementary, and Expansive: Three Roles of Visual Arts Curricula," *Studies in Art Education: A Journal of Issues and Research* 35, no. 2 (1994): 90–104.

19 David J. Flinders, Nel Noddings, and Stephen J. Thornton, "The Null Curriculum: Its Theoretical Basis and Practical Implications," *Curriculum Inquiry* 16, no. 1 (1986): 33–42.

20 Buck, "Teaching Dance in the Curriculum," 701–19.

21 Ibid.

22 Bolwell, "Into the Light: An Expanding Vision of Dance Education," 75–95.

23 Doyle, "Curriculum and Pedagogy," 486–516; Bresler, "Imitative, Complementary, and Expansive: Three Roles of Visual Arts Curricula," 90–104.

24 Doyle, "Curriculum and Pedagogy," 507.

25 Bresler, "Imitative, Complementary, and Expansive: Three Roles of Visual Arts Curricula," 90.

26 Blumenfeld-Jones and Liang, "Dance Curriculum Research," 245–60.

27 Flinders, Noddings, and Thornton, "The Null Curriculum: Its Theoretical Basis and Practical Implications," 35.
28 Blumenfeld-Jones and Liang, "Dance Curriculum Research," 245–60; Bolwell, "Into the Light: An Expanding Vision of Dance Education," 75–95.
29 Blumenfeld-Jones and Liang, "Dance Curriculum Research," 246.
30 Stinson, *Embodied Curriculum Theory and Research in Arts Education*.
31 Eisner, *The Educational Imagination*, 107.
32 Edward C. Warburton, "Toward Trust: Recalibrating Accreditation Practices for Postsecondary Arts Education," *Arts Education Policy Review* 119, no. 1 (2018): 37–41.

Chapter 7

1 Beaman, *World Dance Cultures*.
2 Susanne Keuchel, "Arts Education Development Index (AEDI) A Comparative International Empirical Research Approach in Arts Education," 43.
3 "Learning Portal: Planning Education for Improved Learning Outcomes," UNESCO, https://learningportal.iiep.unesco.org/en/glossary/non-formal-education
4 Jayne Stevens, "Pedagogies of Dance Teaching and Dance Leading," in *The Oxford Handbook of Dance and Wellbeing*, eds. Vicky Karkou, Sue Oliver, and Sophia Lycouris (New York: Oxford University Press, 2017.)
5 Beaman, *World Dance Cultures*.
6 Ibid.
7 Julie Malnig, "Athena Meets Venus: Visions of Women in Social Dance in the Teens and Early 1920s," *Dance Research Journal* 31, no. 2 (1999): 34–62; Linda J. Tomko, *Dancing Class: Gender, Ethnicity, and Social Divides in American Dance, 1890–1920* (Bloomington: Indiana University Press, 1999).
8 Foster, "Dance and/as Competition in the Privately Owned US Studio."
9 Ibid.
10 Pirkko Markula, "The Intersections of Dance and Sport," *Sociology of Sport Journal* 35, no. 2 (2018): 159–67.
11 Foster, "Dance and/as Competition in the Privately Owned US Studio."
12 Ibid.
13 Karen Schupp, "Dance Competition Culture and Commercial Dance," *Journal of Dance Education* 19, no. 2 (2019): 59.
14 Ibid., 58–67.
15 Ralph Buck and Jeff J. Meiners, "Contextualizing Dance Education Globally and Locally," in *The Palgrave Handbook of Global Arts Education*, eds. Georgina Barton and Margaret Baguley (New York: Macmillan, 2017), 35–53.
16 Foster, "Dance and/as Competition in the Privately Owned US Studio," 64.

17 Eve Tuck, "Neoliberalism as Nihilism? A Commentary on Educational Accountability, Teacher Education, and School Reform," *Journal for Critical Education Policy Studies* 11, no. 2 (2013): 324–47.
18 Foster, "Dance and/as Competition in the Privately Owned US Studio," 62.
19 Malnig, "Athena Meets Venus," 34–62.
20 Lilah Ramzi, "Inside Wendy Whelan's Triumphant Return to the New York City Ballet," *Vogue*, July 16, 2019.
21 Karin Von Nieuwkirk, "Changing Images and Shifting Identities: Female Performers in Egypt" in *Moving History/Dancing Cultures: A Dance History Reader*, eds. Ann Dils and Ann Cooper-Albright (Middletown: Wesleyan University Press, 2001), 136–43.
22 Green, "Student Bodies: Dance Pedagogy and the Soma," 1119–32.
23 Angela Russell, George Schaefer, and Erin Reilly, "Sexualization of Prepubescent Girls in Dance Competitions: Innocent Fun or 'Sexploitation'?" *Strategies* 31, no. 5 (2018): 3–7.
24 Dawn Clark, "Considering the Issue of Sexploitation of Young Women in Dance K-12 Perspectives in Dance Education," *Journal of Dance Education* 4, no. 1 (2004): 17–22.
25 Buck and Meiners, "Contextualizing Dance Education Globally and Locally," 35–53.
26 Ibid., 42.
27 Schupp, "Dance Competition Culture and Commercial Dance," 66.
28 Buck and Meiners, "Contextualizing Dance Education Globally and Locally," 36.
29 Foster, "Dance and/as Competition in the Privately Owned US Studio," 58.
30 Tomko, *Dancing Class*.

Chapter 8

1 Keuchel, "Arts Education Development Index (AEDI). A Comparative International Empirical Research Approach in Arts Education," 43.
2 "UNESCO Guidelines for the Recognition, Validation and Accreditation of the Outcomes of Non-formal and Informal Learning," UNESCO Institute for Lifelong Learning, last modified 2012, https://unesdoc.unesco.org/ark:/48223/pf0000216360.
3 "2017 Global Summit," *World Dance Alliance-Americas*, https://www.wda-americas.net/conference-festivals/2017-global-summit/.
4 "Recognition of Non-formal and Informal Learning—Home," Organisation for Economic Co-operation and Development, last modified 2019, http://www.oecd.org/education/skills-beyond-school/recognitionofnon-formalandinformallearning-home.htm
5 Vissicaro, *Studying Dance Cultures Around the World*, 128.

6   Minette Mans, "Framing Informality," in *International Handbook of Research in Arts Education,* ed. Liora Bresler (Dordrecht: Springer, 2007), 779.

7   Ibid., 779–82; Gunilla Lindqvist, "The Relationship between Play and Dance," *Research in Dance Education* 2, no. 1 (2001): 41–52; Judith Lynne Hanna, "Children's Own Dance, Play and Protest—An Untapped Resource for Education," *Proceedings of the International Conference of Dance and the Child International* (Stockholm: Dance and the Child International, 1982), 51–73.

8   Lev Vygotsky, *Mind in Society: The Development of Higher Psychological Processes* (Cambridge: Harvard University Press, 1980).

9   Dianne Smith, "How Play Influences Children's Development at Home and School," *Journal of Physical Education, Recreation & Dance* 66, no. 8 (1995): 19–23.

10 Melser, *Teaching Soft Skills in a Hard World.*

11 Barbara Ehrenreich, *Dancing in the Streets: A History of Collective Joy* (New York: Picador, 2006).

12 "Recognition of Non-Formal and Informal Learning – Home," Organisation for Economic Co-operation and Development.

13 Ojeya Cruz Banks, "Critical Postcolonial Dance Recovery and Pedagogy: An International Literature Review," *Pedagogy, Culture & Society* 17, no. 3 (2009): 355–67.

14 Susanne Keuchel, "Arts Education by Numbers. Cartography and Quantitative Measurement of Arts Education in Germany," in *International Yearbook for Research in Arts Education*, eds. Eckart Liebau, Ernst Wagner, and Max Wyman (Münster: Waxmann, 2013), 129–37.

15 Martin, *Critical Moves*, 188.

16 David Walsh, "'Saturday Night Fever': An Ethnography of Disco Dancing," in *Dance, Gender and Culture*, ed. Helen Thomas (New York: St. Martin's Press, 1993), 114.

17 Mabingo and Koff, "Altering the Paradigm," 58–82.

18 "UNESCO Guidelines for the Recognition, Validation and Accreditation of the Outcomes of Non-formal and Informal Learning," UNESCO Institute for Lifelong Learning.

Chapter 10

1   Catherine Beauchamp and Lynn Thomas, "Understanding Teacher Identity: An Overview of Issues in the Literature and Implications for Teacher Education," *Cambridge Journal of Education* 39, no. 2 (2009): 182.

2   Lori-Anne Dolloff, "Imagining Ourselves as Teachers: The Development of Teacher Identity in Music Teacher Education," *Music Education Research* 1, no. 2 (1991): 193.

3   Milton J. Bennett, "Towards Ethnorelativism: A Developmental Model of Intercultural Sensitivity," *Education for the Intercultural Experience* 2 (1993): 21–71.

4   Monica Miller Marsh, *The Social Fashioning of Teaching Identities* (New York: Peter Lang, 2003).
5   Bennett, "Towards Ethnorelativism," 21–71.
6   Jack Mezirow, *Transformative Dimensions of Adult Learning* (San Francisco: Jossey-Bass, 1991).
7   Ibid., 87.
8   Judith N. Martin and Thomas K. Nakayama, "Reconsidering Intercultural (Communication) Competence in the Workplace: A Dialectical Approach," *Language and Intercultural Communication* 15, no. 1 (2015): 13–28.
9   Edward C. Warburton, "Beyond Steps: The Need for Pedagogical Knowledge in Dance," *Journal of Dance Education* 8, no. 1 (2008): 7–12.
10 Ibid., 10.
11 Carey E. Andrzejewski, "Toward a Model of Holistic Dance Teacher Education," *Journal of Dance Education* 9, no. 1 (2009): 17–26.
12 Ibid., 21.
13 Bennett, "Towards Ethnorelativism," 21–71.
14 Bruno Leutwyler, Danijela S. Petrovic, and Carola Mantel, "Constructivist Foundations of Intercultural Education: Implications for Research and Teacher Training," in *International Perspectives on Education: BCES Conference Book*, vol. 10, eds. Nikolay Popov, Charl Wolhuter, Bruno Leutwyler, Gillian Hilton, James Ogunleye, and Patrícia Albergaria Almeida (Sofia: Bulgarian Comparative Education Society, 2012), 11–118.
15 Carol R. Rodgers and Katherine H. Scott, "The Development of the Personal Self and Professional Identity in Learning to Teach," in *Handbook of Research in Teacher Education: Enduring Questions and Changing Contexts*, eds. Marilyn Cochran-Smith, Sharon Feiman-Nemser, and D. John McIntyre, 3rd ed. (New York: Routledge, 2008), 739.
16 Mezirow, *Transformative Dimensions of Adult Learning*, 7.
17 Ibid., 167.
18 Ibid.
19 F. Michael Connelly and D. Jean Clandinin, eds., *Shaping a Professional Identity: Stories of Educational Practice* (London: The Althouse Press, 1999); Anna Sfard and Anna Prusak, "Telling Identities: In Search of an Analytic Tool for Investigating Learning as a Culturally Shaped Activity," *Educational Research* 34, no. 4 (2005): 14–22.
20 Therese Riley and Penelope Hawe, "Researching Practice: The Methodological Case for Narrative Inquiry," *Health Education Research* 20, no. 2 (2005): 226–36.
21 Gerhard Kubik, "Neo-Traditional Popular Music in East Africa Since 1945," *Popular Music* 1 (1981): 83:104; Sylvia Nannyonga-Tamusuza, "Baakisimba Music, Dance and Gender of the Baganda People of Uganda" (Unpublished PhD diss., University of Pittsburgh, 2001); Nicholas Ssempijia, "Ethnomusicological Study of Compositional Techniques in the Roman Catholic Church of the Metropolitan of Kampala" (Unpublished Master's thesis, Makerere University, 2006).

22 Abdu Basajabaka Kawalya Kasozi, *The Crisis of Secondary School Education in Uganda, 1960–1970* (Kampala: Longman, 1979).

23 Judith Lynne Hanna, "African Dance: The Continuity of Change," *Yearbook of the International Folk Music Council* 5 (1973): 165–74.

24 Kasozi, *The Crisis of Secondary School Education in Uganda, 1960–1970*; Jean Ngoya Kidula, "Making and Managing Music in African Christian Life," in *Music in the Life of the African Church*, eds. Roberta Rose King, Jean Ngoya Kidula, James R. Krabill, and Thomas Oduro (Waco: Baylor University Press, 2008), 101–16.

25 Molefi Kete Asante, *The Afrocentric Idea* (Philadelphia: Temple University Press, 1987); Molefi Kete Asante, *Afrocentricity* (Trenton: Africa World Press, 1988); Molefi Kete Asante, *Kemet, Afrocentricity and Knowledge* (Trenton: Africa World Press, 1990); Molefi Kete Asante, "The Afrocentric Idea in Education," *The Journal of Negro Education* 60, no. 2 (1991): 170–80; Molefi Kete Asante, *Afrocentricity: The Theory of Social Change* (Chicago: African American Images, 2003).

26 George J. Sefa Dei, "African Development: The Relevance and Implications of 'Indigenousness,'" in *Indigenous Knowledges in Global Contexts: Multiple Readings of Our World*, eds. George J. Sefa Dei, Dorothy Goldin Rosenberg, and Budd L. Hall (Toronto: University of Toronto, 2000), 70–86.

27 *Anti-Defamation League*, https://www.adl.org/.

28 Sachs, *World History of the Dance*.

29 Giroux, *Border Crossings*; Peter McLaren, *Critical Pedagogy and Predatory Culture: Oppositional Politics in a Postmodern Era* (New York: Routledge, 1995); Freire, *Pedagogy of the Oppressed*; Brenda Dixon Gottschild, "Stripping the Emperor: The Africanist Presence in American Concert Dance," in *Looking Out: Perspectives on Dance and Criticism in Multicultural World*, eds. Elizabeth Zimmer, Lewis Segal, and David Gere (New York: Schirmer, 1995), 95–121; Brenda Dixon Gottschild, *Digging the Africanist Presence in American Performance: Dance and Other Contexts* (Westport: Greenwood Press, 1996); Brenda Dixon Gottschild, *The Black Dancing Body: A Geography from Coon to Cool* (New York: Palgrave Macmillan, 2003); Brenda Dixon Gottschild, "By George! Oh Balanchine," *Discourse in Dance* 3, no. 1 (2005): 73–9.

30 Thomas K. Nakayama and Judith N. Martin, eds., *Whiteness: The Communication of Social Identity* (Thousand Oaks: Sage Publications, 1998).

31 Daniel P. Liston and Kenneth M. Zeichner, *Reflective Teaching: An Introduction* (Mahwah: Lawrence Erlbaum Associates Inc., 1996).

Chapter 11

1 Karen Gayton Swisher, "Why Indian People Should Be the Ones to Write about Indian Education," *American Indian Quarterly* 20, no. 1 (1996): 83–90; The First Nations Information Governance Centre. Ownership, Control, Access and Possession (OCAP™): The Path to First Nations Information

Governance. May 2014. (Ottawa: The First Nations Information Governance Centre, May 2014).

2   Jacqueline Shea Murphy, *The People Have Never Stopped Dancing* (Minneapolis: University of Minnesota Press, 2007).

3   Bessie Evans and May G. Evans, *Native American Dance Steps* (Mineola: Dover Publications, Inc., 2003); Reginald Laubin and Gladys Laubin, *Indian Dances of North America* (Norman: University of Oklahoma, 1976); Jill Drayson Sweet, *Dances of the Tewa Pueblo Indians: Expressions of New Life* (Santa Fe: School of American Research Press, 1985).

4   Murphy, *The People Have Never Stopped Dancing*.

5   Sandy Grande, *Red Pedagogy* (New York: Rowman & Littlefield Publishers, Inc., 2004); Michael G. Doxtater, "Indigenous Knowledge in the Decolonial Era," *American Indian Quarterly* 28, no. 3 and 4 (2004): 618–33; Vine Deloria Jr., *Custer Died for Your Sins: An Indian Manifesto* (New York: Macmillan, 1969).

6   Waziyatawin Angela Wilson, "Introduction: Indigenous Knowledge Recovery Is Indigenous Empowerment," *American Indian Quarterly* 28, no. 3 and 4 (2004): 265–366.

7   Alysse Kennedy, "Dancing to the Beat of Their Own Drum: Incorporating Art, Dance and Music as Culturally Relevant Pedagogy for Indigenous Students" (Unpublished Master's thesis, University of Toronto, 2016), 22–3.

8   Marie Battiste, Lynne Bell, and L. M. Findlay, "Decolonizing Education in Canadian Universities: An Interdisciplinary, International, Indigenous Research Project," *Canadian Journal of Native Education* 26, no. 2 (2002): 90–1; Waziyatawin Angela Wilson, "Introduction: Indigenous Knowledge Recovery Is Indigenous Empowerment," *American Indian Quarterly* 28, no. 3 and 4 (2004): 365–6.

9   Ministry of Education, *Strengthening Our Learning Journey: Third Progress Report on the Implementation of the Ontario First Nation, Métis, and Inuit Education Policy Framework* (Ontario: Queen's Printer for Ontario, 2018), PDF e-book.

10 Kelly Fayard, "Native American Dance History and Powwow Styles," in *Dance Pedagogy for a Diverse World*, ed. Nyama McCarthy-Brown (Jefferson: McFarland & Co. Publishers, 2017), 154–68; Ministry of Education, *Ontario, First Nation, Métis, Inuit Education Policy Framework* (Ontario: Queen's Printer for Ontario, 2007), PDF e-book; Kennedy, "Dancing to the Beat of Their Own Drum."

11 Battiste, Bell, and Findlay, "Decolonizing Education in Canadian Universities," 87.

12 Landson-Billings, "Towards a Theory of Culturally Relevant Pedagogy," 465–91.

13 Shawn Wilson, *Research Is Ceremony: Indigenous Research Methods* (Halifax and Winnipeg: Fernwood Publishing, 2008), 28.

14 Grande, *Red Pedagogy*, 28.

15 Gregory Cajete, *Look to the Mountains: An Ecology of Indigenous Education* (Durango: Kivaki Press, 1994); Peter McLaren, *Life in Schools: An*

Introduction to Critical Pedagogy in the Foundations of Education, 4th ed. (Boston: Allyn & Bacon, 2002).
16 Wilson, *Research Is Ceremony*, 15.
17 Wilson, "Introduction: Indigenous Knowledge Recovery Is Indigenous Empowerment," 361.
18 Fayard, "Native American Dance History and Powwow Styles," 160.
19 Battiste, Bell, and Findlay, "Decolonizing Education in Canadian Universities," 83.
20 Ann Axtmann, "Performative Power in Native America: Powwow Dancing," *Dance Research Journal* 33, no. 1 (2001): 11–12.
21 Battiste, Bell, and Findlay, "Decolonizing Education in Canadian Universities," 92.
22 Fayard, "Native American Dance History and Powwow Styles," 157.
23 Wilson, "Introduction: Indigenous Knowledge Recovery Is Indigenous Empowerment," 618–19.
24 Ibid.
25 Wilson, *Research Is Ceremony*, 69.
26 Murphy, *The People Have Never Stopped Dancing*; Diane Morris Bernstein and Don Contreras, *We Dance Because We Can* (Marietta: Longstreet Press, Inc., 1996).
27 Axtmann, "Performative Power in Native America: Powwow Dancing," 14.
28 Siobhan Burke, "Round (and Hoop, and Eagle and Deer) Dancing on First Avenue," *The New York Times* (2019): 2.
29 Karen Swisher and Donna Deyhle, "Styles of Learning and Learning of Styles: Educational Conflicts for American Indian/Alaskan Native Youth," *Journal of Multilingual and Multicultural Development* 8, no. 4 (1987): 345–60.
30 Battiste, Bell, and Findlay, "Decolonizing Education in Canadian Universities."
31 Marliese Kimmerle and Paulette Côté-Laurence, *Teaching Dance Skills: A Motor Learning and Developmental Approach* (Andover: J. Michael Ryan Publishing, Inc., 2003); Muska Mosston, *Teaching: From Command to Discovery* (Belmont: Wadsworth Publishing Company, Inc., 1973).
32 Wilson, *Research Is Ceremony*, 80.
33 Swisher and Deyhle, "Styles of Learning and Learning of Styles," 347.
34 Koff, "Toward a Definition of Dance Education," 27–31.
35 Wilson, *Research Is Ceremony*, 84–92.
36 Ibid., 97.
37 Kimmerle and Côté-Laurence, *Teaching Dance Skills*.
38 Wilson, *Research Is Ceremony*, 80.
39 Karen Swisher, "Cooperative Learning and the Education of American Indian/Alaskan Native Students: A Review of Literature and Suggestions for Implementation," *Journal of American Indian Education* 29, no. 2 (1990): 36–43.

40 Swisher and Deyhle, "Styles of Learning and Learning of Styles," 345–60; Ibid., 36–4.
41 Swisher and Deyhle, "Styles of Learning and Learning of Styles," 353.
42 Ibid.; Wilson, *Research Is Ceremony*.
43 Gerald Mohatt and Frederick V. Erickson, "Cultural Differences in Teaching Styles in Odawa School: A Sociolinguistic Approach," in *Culture and the Bilingual Classroom*, eds. Henry T. Trueba, Grace Pung Guthrie, and Kathryn Hu-Pei Au (Rowley: Newbury House Publishers, Inc., 1981), 105–19.
44 Murray L. Wax, Rosalie H. Wax, and Robert V. Dumont Jr., "Formal Education in an American Indian Community," *Social Problems* 11 (1964): 95–6.
45 Keali'inohomoku, "An Anthropologist Looks at Ballet as a Form of Ethnic Dance."
46 Battiste, Bell, and Findlay, "Decolonizing Education in Canadian Universities," 91.
47 Kennedy, "Dancing to the Beat of Their Own Drum," 31; Lorenzo Cherubini, *Aboriginal Student Engagement and Achievement: Educational Practices and Cultural Sustainability*, 1st ed. (Vancouver: University of British Columbia Press, 2014).
48 Wilson, *Research Is Ceremony*; Melanie MacLean and Linda Wason-Ellam, *When Aboriginal and Métis Teachers Use Storytelling as an Instructional Practice* (A Grant Report to the Aboriginal Education Research Network, Saskatchewan Learning: Research Area, Cultural Affirmation and School Climate, 2006); Kennedy, "Dancing to the Beat of Their Own Drum"; Burke, "Round (and Hoop, and Eagle and Deer) Dancing on First Avenue"; Murphy, *The People Have Never Stopped Dancing*.
49 Kennedy, "Dancing to the Beat of Their Own Drum," 35; Grande, *Red Pedagogy*; Wilson, *Research Is Ceremony*.
50 Wilson, "Introduction: Indigenous Knowledge Recovery Is Indigenous Empowerment," 369.
51 Wilson, *Research Is Ceremony*; Grande, *Red Pedagogy*; Murphy, *The People Have Never Stopped Dancing*.
52 Bernstein and Contreras, *We Dance Because We Can*.
53 Kennedy, "Dancing to the Beat of Their Own Drum," 27.
54 Wilson, *Research Is Ceremony*, 16–17.
55 Doxtater, "Indigenous Knowledge in the Decolonial Era," 618–33.

Chapter 12

1 Greene, *Variations on a Blue Guitar*, 16.
2 Ibid., 56.
3 Ibid.; Greene, *Releasing the Imagination*; Dewey, *How We Think*.

4 Greene, *Releasing the Imagination*, 131.
5 LaMothe, *Why We Dance*, 207–8.
6 R. Scott Kretchmar, *Why Useless Play Is so Useful in Educational Settings* (Unpublished Manuscript).
7 Vicky Karkou, Sue Oliver, and Sophia Lycouris, eds., *The Oxford Handbook of Dance and Wellbeing* (New York: Oxford University Press, 2017); Karen Bond, ed., *Dance and the Quality of Life* (Cham: Springer, 2019).
8 Karkou, Oliver, and Lycouris, eds., *The Oxford Handbook of Dance and Wellbeing*.
9 Ellen Dissanayake, "Coda," in *Dance and the Quality of Life*, ed. Karen Bond (Cham: Springer, 2019), 549–54.
10 Hawkins, *Modern Dance in Higher Education*, 84.
11 Ibid, 38.
12 "Home," UNESCO, last modified 2019, https://en.unesco.org/.
13 2010. "Seoul Agenda: Goals for the Development of Arts Education," in *UNESCO's Second World Conference on Arts Education*.
14 "Home," daCi, last modified 2019, https://daci.international/en/.
15 "2017 Global Summit," *World Dance Alliance-Americas*.
16 "Home," daCi.
17 Kretchmar, *Why Useless Play Is so Useful in Educational Settings*.

Glossary

1 Zaretta Hammond, *Culturally Responsive Teaching the Brain* (Thousand Oaks: Corwin, 2015), 156.
2 Susanne Keuchel, "Arts Education Development Index (AEDI) A Comparative International Empirical Research Approach in Arts Education," in *International Yearbook for Research in Arts Education, Vol 2*, eds. Larry O'Farrell, Shifra Schonmann, and Ernst Wagner. (Münster: Waxmann, 2014), 43.
3 Keuchel, "Arts Education Development Index (AEDI)," 43.
4 "UNESCO Guidelines for the Recognition, Validation and Accreditation of the Outcomes of Non-formal and Informal Learning," *UNESCO Institute for Lifelong Learning,* last modified 2012, https://unesdoc.unesco.org/ark:/48223/pf0000216360.
5 Keuchel, "Arts Education Development Index (AEDI)," 43.

BIBLIOGRAPHY

"2017 Global Summit," World Dance Alliance—Americas, https://www.wda-americas.net/conference-festivals/2017-global-summit/.
AATE, MENC, NAEA, and NDA, *National Standards for Arts Education: What Every Young American Should Be Able to Do in the Arts* (Reston: Rowman & Littlefield Education, 1994).
Mortimer J. Adler, *Reforming Education* (New York: Macmillan Publishing Co., 1988).
Janet Adshead, *Study in Dance* (London: Dance Books Ltd., 1981).
Randall Everett Allsup, *Remixing the Classroom: Toward an Open Philosophy of Music Education* (Bloomington: Indiana University Press, 2016).
Judith B. Alter, "Why Dance Students Pursue Dance: Studies of Dance Students from 1953–1993," *Dance Research Journal* 29, no. 2 (Fall 1997): 70–89.
Carey E. Andrzejewski, "Toward a Model of Holistic Dance Teacher Education," *Journal of Dance Education* 9, no. 1 (2009): 17–26.
Anti-Defamation League, https://www.adl.org/.
Eeva Anttila, "Children as Agents in Dance: Implications of the Notion of Child Culture for Research and Practice in Dance Education," in *International Handbook of Research in Arts Education*, ed. Liora Bresler (Dordrecht, The Netherlands: Springer, 2007), 865–79.
Eeva Anttila, Rose Martin, and Charlotte Nielsen Svendler, "Performing Difference In/Through Dance: The Significance of Dialogical, or Third Spaces in Creating Conditions for Learning and Living Together," *Thinking Skills and Creativity* 31 (2019): 209–16.
Molefi Kete Asante, *The Afrocentric Idea* (Philadelphia: Temple University Press, 1987).
Molefi Kete Asante, *Afrocentricity* (Trenton: Africa World Press, 1988).
Molefi Kete Asante, *Kemet, Afrocentricity and Knowledge* (Trenton: Africa World Press, 1990).
Molefi Kete Asante, "The Afrocentric Idea in Education," *The Journal of Negro Education* 60, no. 2 (1991): 170–80.
Molefi Kete Asante, *Afrocentricity: The Theory of Social Change* (Chicago: African American Images, 2003).
Ann Axtmann, "Performative Power in Native America: Powwow Dancing," *Dance Research Journal* 33, no. 1 (2001): 7–22.
Ojeya Cruz Banks, "Critical Postcolonial Dance Recovery and Pedagogy: An International Literature Review," *Pedagogy, Culture & Society* 17, no. 3 (2009): 355–67.
Fiona Bannon, "Dance: The Possibilities of a Discipline," *Research in Dance Education* 11, no. 1 (2010): 49–59.
Dorothy B. Barrere, Mary Kawena Pukui, and Marion Kelly, *Hula Historical Perspectives* (Honolulu: Bernice Pauahi Bishop Museum, 1980).

Marie Battiste, Lynne Bell, and L. M. Findlay, "Decolonizing Education in Canadian Universities: An Interdisciplinary, International, Indigenous Research Project," *Canadian Journal of Native Education* 26, no. 2 (2002): 82–95.
Patricia Beaman, *World Dance Cultures: From Ritual to Spectacle* (New York: Routledge, 2018).
Catherine Beauchamp and Lynn Thomas, "Understanding Teacher Identity: An Overview of Issues in the Literature and Implications for Teacher Education," *Cambridge Journal of Education* 39, no. 2 (2009): 182.
Milton J. Bennett, "Towards Ethnorelativism: A Developmental Model of Intercultural Sensitivity," *Education for the Intercultural Experience* 2 (1993): 21–71.
Diane Morris Bernstein and Don Contreras, *We Dance Because We Can* (Marietta: Longstreet Press, Inc., 1996).
Jessica Sand Blonde, Dance as an Art Form, for New York University Dance Education Program.
Donald Blumenfeld-Jones and Sheaun-Yann Liang, "Dance Curriculum Research," in *International Handbook of Research in Arts Education*, ed. Liora Bresler (Dordrecht: Springer, 2007), 245–60.
Franziska Boas, "Dance in the Liberal Arts College Curriculum," *Impulse: Annual of Contemporary Dance 1953*, 28, accessed August 1, 2019, https://digital.library.temple.edu/digital/collection/p15037coll4/id/1514/rec/4.
Jan Bolwell, "Into the Light: An Expanding Vision of Dance Education," in *Dance, Power, and Difference: Critical and Feminist Perspectives on Dance Education*, ed. Sherry Shapiro (Champaign: Human Kinetics, 1998).
Jane M. Bonbright, "Dance Education in 1999: Status, Challenges, and Recommendations," *Arts Education Policy Review* 101, no. 1 (1999): 33–9.
Karen Bond, ed., *Dance and the Quality of Life* (Cham: Springer, 2019).
Karen E. Bond, "Dance and Quality of Life," in *Encyclopedia of Quality of Life and Well-Being Research*, ed. Alex C. Michalos (Dordrecht, The Netherlands: Springer, 2014).
James Bowen, *A History of Western Education: Vol. 3. The Modern West, Europe and the New World* (New York: St. Martin's Press, 1981).
Mary A. Brennan, "Impulse 1965," in *Perspectives on Contemporary Dance History: Revisiting Impulse 1950–1970*, eds. Thomas K. Hagood and Luke C. Kahlich (Amherst: Cambria Press, 2013), 313–39.
Liora Bresler, "Imitative, Complementary, and Expansive: Three Roles of Visual Arts Curricula," *Studies in Art Education: A Journal of Issues and Research* 35, no. 2 (1994): 90–104.
Jerome S. Bruner, *The Culture of Education* (Cambridge: Harvard University Press, 1996).
Jerome S. Bruner, Alison Jolly, and Kathy Sylva, eds., *Play—Its Role in Development and Evolution* (New York: Basic Books, 1976).
Ralph Buck, "Teaching Dance in the Curriculum," in *Handbook of Physical Education*, eds. David Kirk, Doune MacDonald, and Mary O'Sullivan (London: Sage, 2006), 701–19.
Ralph Buck and Jeff J. Meiners, "Contextualizing Dance Education Globally and Locally," in *The Palgrave Handbook of Global Arts Education*, eds. Georgina Barton and Margaret Baguley (New York: Macmillan, 2017), 35–53.

Siobhan Burke, "Round (and Hoop, and Eagle and Deer) Dancing on First Avenue," *The New York Times* (2019): 2, January 29, 2019.

Gregory Cajete, *Look to the Mountains: An Ecology of Indigenous Education* (Durango: Kivaki Press, 1994).

Rose Casement, "Differentiating Between the Terms 'Multicultural' and 'Diversity': Broadening the Perspective," *Language Arts Journal of Michigan* 18, no. 1 (2002): 5–8.

Sarah Chapman, *Movement Education in the United States: Historical Development and Theoretical Bases* (Philadelphia: Movement Education Publications, 1974).

Lorenzo Cherubini, *Aboriginal Student Engagement and Achievement: Educational Practices and Cultural Sustainability*, 1st ed. (Vancouver: University of British Columbia Press, 2014).

Dawn Clark, "Considering the Issue of Sexploitation of Young Women in Dance K-12 Perspectives in Dance Education," *Journal of Dance Education* 4, no. 1 (2004): 17–22.

F. Michael Connelly and D. Jean Clandinin, eds., *Shaping a Professional Identity: Stories of Educational Practice* (London: The Althouse Press, 1999).

daCi, last modified 2019, https://daci.international/en/.

Antonio Damasio, *Descartes' Error: Emotion, Reason and the Human Brain* (New York: G.P. Putnam, 1994).

Antonio R. Damasio, "Descartes' Error Revisited," *Journal of the History of the Neurosciences* 10, no. 2 (2001): 192–4.

"Dance, Media Arts, Music, Theatre and Visual Arts," *National Core Arts Standards*, last modified June 4, 2014, https://www.nationalartsstandards.org/

Crystal U. Davis, "Laying New Ground: Uprooting White Privilege and Planting Seeds of Equity and Inclusivity," *Journal of Dance Education* 18, no. 3 (2018): 120–5.

Crystal U. Davis and Jesse Phillips-Fein, "Tendus and Tenancy: Black Dancers and the White Landscape of Dance Education," in *The Palgrave Handbook of Race and the Arts in Education*, eds. Amelia M. Kraehe, Ruben Gaztambide-Fernandez, and B. Stephen Carpenter, II (Cham: Palgrave Macmillan, 2018).

George J. Sefa Dei, "African Development: The Relevance and Implications of 'Indigenousness,'" in *Indigenous Knowledges in Global Contexts: Multiple Readings of our World*, eds. George J. Sefa Dei, Dorothy Goldin Rosenberg, and Budd L. Hall (Toronto: University of Toronto, 2000), 70–86.

Vine Deloria Jr., *Custer Died for Your Sins: An Indian Manifesto* (New York: Macmillan, 1969).

John Dewey, *Democracy and Education* (New York: Macmillan, 1916).

John Dewey, *How We Think* (Boston: D.C. Heath and Company, 1933).

Ann Dils and Ann Cooper Albright, Forward to *Moving History/Dancing Cultures: A Dance History Reader*, eds. Ann Dils and Ann Cooper-Albright (Middletown: Wesleyan University Press, 2001), xvii.

Ellen Dissanayake, "Coda," in *Dance and the Quality of Life*, ed. Karen Bond (Cham: Springer, 2019), 549–54.

Sherril Dodds, ed., *The Bloomsbury Companion to Dance Studies* (London: Bloomsbury Academic, 2019).

Lori-Anne Dolloff, "Imagining Ourselves as Teachers: The Development of Teacher Identity in Music Teacher Education," *Music Education Research* 1, no. 2 (1991): 193.
Michael G. Doxtater, "Indigenous Knowledge in the Decolonial Era," *American Indian Quarterly* 28, no. 3–4 (2004): 618–33.
Walter Doyle, "Curriculum and Pedagogy," in *Handbook for Research on Curriculum*, ed. Phillip W. Jackson (New York: Macmillan Publishing Co., 1992), 486–516.
Anne Schley Duggan, "The Place of Dance in the School Physical Education Program," *Journal of the American Association for Health, Physical Education, and Recreation* 22, no. 3 (1951): 26–9.
Becky Dyer, "Merging Traditional Technique Vocabularies With Democratic Teaching Perspectives in Dance Education: A Consideration of Aesthetic Values and Their Sociopolitical Contexts," *The Journal of Aesthetic Education* 43, no. 4 (2009): 113.
https://en.wikipedia.org/wiki/Education, retrieved February 17, 2020.
Elliot W. Eisner, *The Educational Imagination: On the Design and Evaluation of School Programs*, 2nd ed. (New York: Macmillan Publishing Co., 1985).
Barbara Ehrenreich, *Dancing in the Streets: A History of Collective Joy* (New York: Picador, 2006).
Eric H. Erikson, "Play and Actuality," in *Play—Its Role in Development and Evolution*, eds. Jerome S. Bruner, Alison Jolly, and Kathy Sylva (New York: Basic Books, 1976), 688–703.
Bessie Evans and May G. Evans, *Native American Dance Steps* (Mineola: Dover Publications, Inc., 2003).
Marvin H. Eyler, "What the Profession Was Once Like: Nineteenth Century Physical Education," in *The Academy Papers: Reunification* (Reston: The American Academy of Physical Education, 1981), 14–20.
The First Nations Information Governance Centre. Ownership, Control, Access and Possession (OCAP™): The Path to First Nations Information Governance. May 2014 (Ottawa: The First Nations Information Governance Centre, May 2014).
Stanley Fish, "Boutique Multiculturalism, or Why Liberals Are Incapable of Thinking About Hate Speech," *Critical Inquiry* 23, no. 2 (Winter, 1997): 278–395.
David J. Flinders, Nel Noddings, and Stephen J. Thornton, "The Null Curriculum: Its Theoretical Basis and Practical Implications," *Curriculum Inquiry* 16, no. 1 (1986): 33–42.
Susan Leigh Foster, "Dance and/as Competition in the Privately Owned US Studio," in *The Oxford Handbook of Dance and Politics*, eds. Rebekah J. Kowal, Gerald Siegmund, and Randy Martin (New York: Oxford University Press, 2017): 53–76.
Susan Leigh Foster, ed., *Worlding Dance* (New York: Palgrave Macmillan, 2009).
Kerry Freedman, "About This Issue: The Social Reconstruction of Art Education," *Studies in Art Education* 35, no. 3 (Spring 1994): 131–4.
Paulo Freire, *Education, The Practice of Freedom* (London: Writers and Readers Publishing Cooperative, 1976).
Paulo Freire, *Pedagogy of the Oppressed*, 30th anniversary ed. (New York: Continuum, 2006).
Howard Gardner, *Frames of Mind*, 3rd ed. (New York: Basic Books, 2011).

Anne Green Gilbert, "Dance Education in the 21st Century: A Global Perspective," *Journal of Physical Education, Recreation & Dance* 76, no. 5 (2005): 26–35.

Sam Gill, *Dancing, Culture, Religion* (Lantham: Lexington Books, 2012).

Henry A. Giroux, *Border Crossings: Cultural Workers and the Politics of Education* (New York: Routledge, 1992).

Michael Goldberger, "Effective Learning: Through a Spectrum of Teaching Styles," *Journal of Physical Education, Recreation & Dance* 55, no. 8 (1984): 19, 21.

Norma Gonzáles, Luis C. Moll, and Cathy Amanti, eds., *Funds of Knowledge: Theorizing Practices in Households, Communities and Classrooms* (Mahwah: Lawrence Erlbaum Associates, 2005).

Brenda Dixon Gottschild, *Digging the Africanist Presence in American Performance: Dance and Other Contexts* (Westport: Greenwood Press, 1996).

Brenda Dixon Gottschild, *The Black Dancing Body: A Geography from Coon to Cool* (New York: Palgrave Macmillan, 2003).

Brenda Dixon Gottschild, "By George! Oh Balanchine," *Discourse in Dance* 3, no. 1 (2005): 73–9.

Brenda Dixon Gottschild, "Racing in Place: A Meta-Memoir on Dance Politics and Practice," in *The Oxford Handbook of Dance and Politics*, eds. Rebekah J. Kowal, Gerald Siegmund, and Randy Martin (New York: Oxford University Press, 2017), 77–97.

Brenda Dixon Gottschild, "Stripping the Emperor: The Africanist Presence in American Concert Dance," in *Looking Out: Perspectives on Dance and Criticism in Multicultural World*, eds. Elizabeth Zimmer, Lewis Segal, and David Gere (New York: Schirmer, 1995), 95–121.

Sandy Grande, *Red Pedagogy* (New York: Rowman & Littlefield Publishers, Inc., 2004).

Rhonda Grauer, Preface to *Dancing: The Pleasure, Power, and Art of Movement*, by Gerald Jonas (New York: Harry N. Abrams Inc., 1992).

Jill Green, "Student Bodies: Dance Pedagogy and the Soma," in *International Handbook of Research in Arts Education*, ed. Liora Bresler (Dordrecht, The Netherlands: Springer, 2007), 1129.

Maxine Greene, *Landscapes of Learning* (New York: Teachers College Press, 1978).

Maxine Greene, *The Dialectic of Freedom* (New York: Teachers College Press, 1988).

Maxine Greene, *Releasing the Imagination* (San Francisco: Jossey-Bass Publishers, 1995).

Maxine Greene, *Variations on a Blue Guitar* (New York: Teachers College Press, 2001).

Thomas K. Hagood, *A History of Dance in American Higher Education* (Lewiston: The Edwin Mellon Press, 2000).

Thomas K. Hagood, *Legacy in Dance Education: Essays and Interviews on Values, Practices, and People—An Anthology* (Amherst: Cambria Press, 2008).

Thomas K. Hagood, "Impulse 1968," in *Perspectives on Contemporary Dance History: Revisiting Impulse 1950–1970*, eds. Thomas K. Hagood and Luke C. Kahlich (Amherst: Cambria Press, 2013), 391–412.

Thomas K. Hagood and Luke C. Kahlich, ed., *Perspectives on Contemporary Dance History: Revisiting Impulse 1950–1970* (Amherst: Cambria Press, 2013).

Zaretta Hammond, *Culturally Responsive Teaching & the Brain* (Thousand Oaks: Corwin, 2015), 156.

Judith Lynne Hanna, "African Dance: The Continuity of Change," *Yearbook of the International Folk Music Council* 5 (1973): 165–74.

Judith Lynne Hanna, "Children's Own Dance, Play and Protest—An Untapped Resource for Education." *Proceedings of the International Conference of Dance and the Child International* (Stockholm: Dance and the Child International, 1982), 51–73.

Alma Hawkins, *Modern Dance in Higher Education* (New York: Teachers College Press, 1954).

Thomas N. Headland, Kenneth L. Pike, and Marvin Harris, eds., *Emics and Etics: The Insider/Outsider Debate Frontiers of Anthropology*, vol. 7 (Newbury Park: Sage Publications, 1990).

Martha Hill, "Implications for the Dance," *The Journal of Health and Physical Education* 13, no. 6 (1942): 347–8.

Eugene C. Howe, "What Business Has the Modern Dance in Physical Education?" *Journal of Health and Physical Education* 8, no. 3 (1937): 131–3, 187–8.

Johan Huizinga, "Play and Contest as Civilizing Functions," in *Play—Its Role in Development and Evolution*, eds. Jerome S. Bruner, Alison Jolly, and Kathy Sylva (New York: Basic Books, 1976), 688–703.

Delia P. Hussey, "Dance Education," *Journal of Health, Physical Education and Recreation* (1954): 44–5, 60, 51.

International Arts Education Standards: A Survey of Standards, Practices, and Expectations in Thirteen Countries and Regions. PDF. New York: The College Board, 2013. https://www.nationalartsstandards.org/sites/default/files/College%20Board%20Research%20-%20International%20Standards_0.pdf.

"International Standard Classification of Education (ISCED)," UNESCO, last modified 2019, http://uis.unesco.org/en/topic/international-standard-classification-education-isced.

ISCED Fields of Education and Training 2013 (ISCED-F 2013. PDF. Montreal: UNESCO Institute for Statistics, 2014. http://uis.unesco.org/sites/default/files/documents/isced-fields-of-education-and-training-2013-en.pdf.

Adrienne L. Kaeppler, "Ballet, Hula and 'Cats': Dancing as a Discourse on Globalization." *2006 World Dance Alliance Global Assembly Proceedings, Toronto, Canada*, ed. Karen Rose Cann, 2006, 251–259. https://wda-americas.com/wp-content/uploads/2014/01/WDA-2006-Global-Proceedings.pdf.

Vicky Karkou, Sue Oliver, and Sophia Lycouris, eds., *The Oxford Handbook of Dance and Wellbeing* (New York: Oxford University Press, 2017).

Lillian Karina and Marion Kant, *Hitler's Dancers: German Modern Dance and the Third Reich* (New York: Berghahn Books, 2004).

Abdu Basajabaka Kawalya Kasozi, *The Crisis of Secondary School Education in Uganda, 1960–1970* (Kampala: Longman, 1979).

Joann W. Keali'inohomoku, "An Anthropologist Looks at Ballet as a Form of Ethnic Dance," in *Moving History/Dancing Cultures: A Dance History Reader*, eds. Ann Dils and Ann Cooper-Albright (Middletown: Wesleyan University Press, 2001), 33–43.

Alysse Kennedy, "Dancing to the Beat of Their Own Drum: Incorporating Art, Dance and Music as Culturally Relevant Pedagogy for Indigenous Students" (Unpublished Master's thesis, University of Toronto, 2016).

Julie Kerr-Berry, "Dance Educator as Dancer and Artist," *Journal of Dance Education* 7, no. 1 (2011): 5–6.

Susanne Keuchel, "Arts Education by Numbers. Cartography and Quantitative Measurement of Arts Education in Germany," in *International Yearbook for Research in Arts Education*, eds. Eckart Liebau, Ernst Wagner, and Max Wyman (Münster: Waxmann, 2013), 129–37.

Susanne Keuchel, "Arts Education Development Index (AEDI). A Comparative International Empirical Research Approach in Arts Education by Numbers," in *International Yearbook for Research in Arts Education 2*, eds. Larry O'Farrell, Shifra Schonmann, and Ernst Wagner (Münster: Waxmann Verlag, 2014), 42–51.

Jean Ngoya Kidula, "Making and Managing Music in African Christian Life," in *Music in the Life of the African Church*, eds. Roberta Rose King, Jean Ngoya Kidula, James R. Krabill, and Thomas Oduro (Waco: Baylor University Press, 2008), 101–16.

Marliese Kimmerle and Paulette Côté-Laurence, *Teaching Dance Skills: A Motor Learning and Developmental Approach* (Andover: J. Michael Ryan Publishing, Inc., 2003).

Susan Koff, "Meaning Making Through the Arts: Description of an Urban High School's Arts-Based Program" (Ed.D. diss., Temple University, 1995).

Susan Koff, "Toward a Definition of Dance Education," *Childhood Education* 77, no. 1 (2000): 31.

Susan R. Koff, "Applied Dance Curriculum: A Global Perspective," in *Dance Education Around the World: Perspectives on Dance, Young People and Change*, eds. Charlotte Svendler Nielsen and Stephanie Burridge (London: Routledge, 2015).

Susan R. Koff, Charlotte Svendler Nielsen, Cornelia Baumgart, and Ivančica Janković. 2013. "Curriculum in Motion – Special Event," in *Dance, Young People and Change*: *Proceedings of the daCi and WDA Global Dance Summit*, eds. Susan W. Stinson, Charlotte Svendler Nielsen, and Shu-Ying Liu (Taipei National University of the Arts, Taiwan, July 14–20, 2012), http://www.ausdance.org/ [Accessed on January 1, 2019] ISBN 978-1-875255-19-1.

Katja Kolcio, *Moving Pillars: Organizing Dance 1956–1978* (Middletown: Wesleyan University Press, 2010).

Richard Kraus, Sarah Chapman Hilsendager, and Brenda Dixon, *History of the Dance in Art and Education*, 3rd ed. (Englewood Cliffs: Prentice Hall Inc., 1991).

R. Scott Kretchmar, "T.D. Wood: On Chairs and Education," *Journal of Physical Education Recreation and Dance* 66, no. 1 (1995): 12–15.

R. Scott Kretchmar, *Practical Philosophy of Sport and Physical Activity*, 2nd ed. (Champaign: Human Kinetics, 2005).

R. Scott Kretchmar, *Why Useless Play Is so Useful in Educational Settings* (Unpublished Manuscript).

Gerhard Kubik, "Neo-Traditional Popular Music in East Africa Since 1945," *Popular Music* 1 (1981): 83, 104.

Gloria Ladson-Billings, "Toward a Theory of Culturally Relevant Pedagogy," *American Educational Research Journal* 32, no. 3 (1995): 465–91.

Suzanne Langer, "Virtual Powers," in *What Is Dance?*, eds. Roger Copeland and Marshall Cohen (Oxford: Oxford University Press, 1983), 44.

Reginald Laubin and Gladys Laubin, *Indian Dances of North America* (Norman: University of Oklahoma, 1976).

Eleanor Leacock, "At Play in African Villages," in *Play—Its Role in Development and Evolution*, eds. Jerome S. Bruner, Alison Jolly, and Kathy Sylva (New York: Basic Books, 1976), 466.

Mabel Lee, *A History of Physical Education and Sport in the U.S.A.* (New York: John Wiley & Sons, 1983).

"Learning Portal: Planning Education for Improved Learning Outcomes," UNESCO, https://learningportal.iiep.unesco.org/en/glossary/non-formal-edu cation.

Bruno Leutwyler, Danijela S. Petrovic, and Carola Mantel, "Constructivist Foundations of Intercultural Education: Implications for Research and Teacher Training," in *International Perspectives on Education: BCES Conference Book*, vol. 10, eds. Nikolay Popov, Charl Wolhuter, Bruno Leutwyler, Gillian Hilton, James Ogunleye, and Patrícia Albergaria Almeida (Sofia: Bulgarian Comparative Education Society, 2012), 11–118.

Gunilla Lindqvist, "The Relationship Between Play and Dance," *Research in Dance Education* 2, no. 1 (2001): 41–52.

Daniel P. Liston and Kenneth M. Zeichner, *Reflective Teaching: An Introduction* (Mahwah: Lawrence Erlbaum Associates Inc., 1996).

Aileene S. Lockhart, "The President's Address: The Values that Guide Us," in The Academy Papers: *Reunification* (Reston: The American Academy of Physical Education, 1981), 7–10.

John Lucas, "The Academy Presidents: Physical Education Futurists 1926–1976," in The Academy Papers: *Beyond Research—Solutions to Human Problems* (Iowa City: The American Academy of Physical Education, 1976), 106–15.

Alfdaniels Mabingo and Susan R. Koff, "Altering the Paradigm," in *Undisciplining Dance in Nine Movement and Eight Stumbles*, eds. Carol Brown and Alys Longley (Newcastle upon Tyne: Cambridge Scholars Publishing, 2018).

Melanie MacLean and Linda Wason-Ellam, *When Aboriginal and Métis Teachers Use Storytelling as an Instructional Practice* (A Grant Report to the Aboriginal Education Research Network, Saskatchewan Learning: Research Area, Cultural Affirmation and School Climate, 2006).

Richard A. Magill and David Anderson, *Motor Learning and Control: Concepts and Applications*, 11th ed. (New York: McGraw-Hill, 2017).

Julie Malnig, "Athena Meets Venus: Visions of Women in Social Dance in the Teens and Early 1920s," *Dance Research Journal* 31, no. 2 (1999): 34–62.

Susan Manning, "Modern Dance in the Third Reich, Redux," in *The Oxford Handbook of Dance and Politics*, eds. Rebekah J. Kowal, Gerald Siegmund, and Randy Martin (New York: Oxford University Press, 2017), 395–415.

Minette Mans, "Framing Informality," in *International Handbook of Research in Arts Education*, ed. Liora Bresler (Dordrecht: Springer, 2007), 779–82.

Pirkko Markula, "The Intersections of Dance and Sport," *Sociology of Sport Journal* 35, no. 2 (2018): 159–67.

Isabel A. Marquez, "Dance Education in/and the Postmodern," in *Dance, Power, and Difference: Critical and Feminist Perspectives on Dance Education*, ed. Sherry Shapiro (Champaign: Human Kinetics, 1998).

Monica Miller Marsh, *The Social Fashioning of Teaching Identities* (New York: Peter Lang, 2003).

Randy Martin, *Critical Moves* (Durham: Duke University Press, 1998).
Judith N. Martin and Thomas K. Nakayama, "Reconsidering Intercultural (Communication) Competence in the Workplace: A Dialectical Approach," *Language and Intercultural Communication* 15, no. 1 (2015): 13–28.
Nyama McCarthy-Brown, "The Need for Culturally Relevant Dance Education," *Journal of Dance Education* 9, no. 4 (2009): 120–5.
Nyama McCarthy-Brown, "Decolonizing Dance Curriculum in Higher Education: One Credit at a Time," *Journal of Dance Education* 14, no. 4 (2014): 125–9.
Nyama McCarthy-Brown, *Dance Pedagogy for a Diverse World* (Jefferson: McFarland & Co. Publishers, 2017).
Nyama McCarthy-Brown, "Owners of Dance: How Dance Is Controlled and Whitewashed in the Teaching of Dance Forms," in *The Palgrave Handbook of Race and the Arts in Education*, eds. Amelia M. Kraehe, Ruben Gaztambide-Fernandez, and B. Stephen Carpenter, II (Cham: Palgrave Macmillan, 2018), 479.
Graham McFee, *The Concept of Dance Education* (London: Routledge, 1994).
Peter C. McIntosh, *Physical Education in England since 1800* (London: G. Bell & Sons Ltd., 1968).
Peter McLaren, *Critical Pedagogy and Predatory Culture: Oppositional Politics in a Postmodern Era* (New York: Routledge, 1995).
Peter McLaren, *Life in Schools: An Introduction to Critical Pedagogy in the Foundations of Education*, 4th ed. (Boston: Allyn & Bacon, 2002).
Elizabeth McPherson, *The Contributions of Martha Hill to American Dance and Dance Education* (Lewiston: The Edwin Mellen Press, 2008).
Jeff Meiners, "So We Can Dance? In Pursuit of an Inclusive Dance Curriculum for the Primary School Years in Australia" (Ed.D., diss., University of South Australia, 2017).
Liz Melchior, "Culturally Responsive Dance Pedagogy in the Primary Classroom," *Research in Dance Education* 12, no. 2 (2011): 119–135.
Liz Melchior, "Making Connections: Culturally Responsive Pedagogy and Dance in the Classroom," in *Intersecting Cultures in Music and Dance Education*, eds. Linda Ashley and David Lines, Vol. 19 of *Landscapes: The Arts, Aesthetics, and Education* (Champaign: Springer, 2016).
Nancy Armstrong Melser, *Teaching Soft Skills in a Hard World: Skills for Beginning Teachers* (Blue Ridge Summit: Rowman & Littlefield Publishers, 2018).
Jack Mezirow, *Transformative Dimensions of Adult Learning* (San Francisco: Jossey-Bass, 1991).
Ministry of Education, *Ontario, First Nation, Métis, Inuit Education Policy Framework* (Ontario: Queen's Printer for Ontario, 2007), PDF e-book.
Ministry of Education, *Strengthening Our Learning Journey: Third Progress Report on the Implementation of the Ontario First Nation, Métis, and Inuit Education Policy Framework* (Ontario: Queen's Printer for Ontario, 2018), PDF e-book.
Gerald Mohatt and Frederick V. Erickson, "Cultural Differences in Teaching Styles in Odawa School: A Sociolinguistic Approach," in *Culture and the Bilingual Classroom*, eds. Henry T. Trueba, Grace Pung Guthrie, and Kathryn Hu-Pei Au (Rowley: Newbury House Publishers, Inc., 1981), 105–19.

Anne Morrison, Lester-Irabinna Rigney, Robert Hattam, and Abigail Diplock, *Toward an Australian Culturally Responsive Pedagogy: A Narrative Review of the Literature* (Adelaide: University of South Australia, 2019).

Muska Mosston, *Teaching: From Command to Discovery* (Belmont: Wadsworth Publishing Company, Inc., 1973).

Jacqueline Shea Murphy, *The People Have Never Stopped Dancing* (Minneapolis: University of Minnesota Press, 2007).

Thomas K. Nakayama and Judith N. Martin, eds., *Whiteness: The Communication of Social Identity* (Thousand Oaks: Sage Publications, 1998).

Sylvia Nannyonga-Tamusuza, "Baakisimba Music, Dance and Gender of the Baganda People of Uganda" (Unpublished PhD diss., University of Pittsburgh, 2001).

National Core Arts Standards, June 4, 2014, https://www.nationalartsstandards.org/.

Karin Von Nieuwkirk, "Changing Images and Shifting Identities: Female Performers in Egypt," in *Moving History/Dancing Cultures: A Dance History Reader*, eds. Ann Dils and Ann Cooper-Albright (Middletown: Wesleyan University Press, 2001), 136–43.

Gertrud Pfister, "Cultural Confrontations: German *Turnen*, Swedish Gymnastics and English Sport – European Diversity in Physical Activities from a Historical Perspective," *Culture, Sport, Society* 6, no. 1 (2003): 61–91.

Denis Charles Phillips and Jonas F. Soltis, *Perspectives on Learning*, 3rd ed. (New York, Teachers College Press, 1992).

john a. powell and Stephen Menendian, "The Problem of Othering: Towards Inclusiveness and Belonging," *Othering & Belonging: Expanding the Circle of Human Concern*, Issue 1, June 29, 2017, http://www.otheringandbelonging.org/the-problem-of-othering/, retrieved March 8, 2020.

Lilah Ramzi, "Inside Wendy Whelan's Triumphant Return to the New York City Ballet," *Vogue*, July 16, 2019.

"Recognition of Non-formal and Informal Learning—Home," *Organisation for Economic Co- operation and Development*, last modified 2019, http://www.oecd.org/education/skills-beyond-school/recognitionofnon-formalandinformallearning-home.htm.

Therese Riley and Penelope Hawe, "Researching Practice: The Methodological Case for Narrative Inquiry," *Health Education Research* 20, no. 2 (2005): 226–36.

Doug Risner, "Dance Education Matters: Rebuilding Postsecondary Dance Education for Twenty-First Century Relevance and Resonance," *Arts Education Policy Review*, 111, no. 4 (2010): 123–35.

Doug Risner and Susan W. Stinson, "Moving Social Justice: Challenges, Fears, and Possibilities in Dance Education," *International Journal of Education & the Arts* 8, no. 6 (2010): 1–26.

Carol R. Rodgers and Katherine H. Scott, "The Development of the Personal Self and Professional Identity in Learning to Teach," in *Handbook of Research on Teacher Education: Enduring Questions and Changing Contexts*, 3rd ed., eds. Marilyn Cochran-Smith, Sharon Feiman-Nemser and D. John McIntyre, (New York: Routledge, 2008), 739.

Janice Ross, *Moving Lessons: Margaret H'Doubler and the Beginning of Dance in American Education* (Madison: The University of Wisconsin Press, 2000).

Inez Rovegno and Madeleine Gregg, "Using Folk Dance and Geography to Teach Interdisciplinary, Multicultural Subject Matter: A School-Based Study," *Physical Education and Sport Pedagogy* 12, no. 3 (2007): 205–23.

Angela Russell, George Schaefer, and Erin Reilly, "Sexualization of Prepubescent Girls in Dance Competitions: Innocent Fun or 'Sexploitation'?" *Strategies* 31, no. 5 (2018): 3–7.

Curt Sachs, *World History of the Dance* (New York: W. W. Norton & Co., 1937).

Marta Elena Savigliano, "Worlding Dance and Dancing Out There in the World," in *Worlding Dance*, ed. Susan Leigh Foster (New York: Palgrave Macmillan, 2009), 173.

Karen Schupp, "Dance Competition Culture and Commercial Dance," *Journal of Dance Education* 19, no. 2 (2019): 59.

"Seoul Agenda: Goals for the Development of Arts Education," in *UNESCO's Second World Conference on Arts Education* (Seoul, Republic of Korea, May 25–28, 2010). Retrieved from http://www.unesco.org/new/en/culture/themes/creativity/arts-education/.

Anna Sfard and Anna Prusak, "Telling Identities: In Search of an Analytic Tool for Investigating Learning as a Culturally Shaped Activity," *Educational Research* 34, no. 4 (2005): 14–22.

Sherry Shapiro, ed., *Dance, Power, and Difference: Critical and Feminist Perspectives on Dance Education* (Champaign: Human Kinetics, 1998).

Maxine Sheets-Johnstone, *Primacy of Movement: Expanded second edition* (Amsterdam: John Banjamins Publishing Company, 2011).

Justin Skirry, "René Descartes (1596–1650)," *Internet Encyclopedia of Philosophy*, https://www.iep.utm.edu/descarte/.

Diedre Sklar, "Five Premises for a Culturally Sensitive Approach to Dance," in *Moving History/Dancing Cultures: A Dance History Reader*, eds. A. Dils and A. Cooper-Albright (Middletown: Wesleyan University Press, 2001), 32.

Dianne Smith, "How Play Influences Children's Development at Home and School," *Journal of Physical Education, Recreation & Dance* 66, no. 8 (1995): 19–23.

Barbara Snook. "Dance in New Zealand Primary Schools: Moving Forward Toward a Realization of UNESCO's Aims for the Arts," in *Dance, Young People and Change: Proceedings of the daCi and WDA Global Dance Summit*, eds. Susan W. Stinson, Charlotte Svendler Nielsen, and Shu-Ying Liu (Taipei National University of the Arts, Taiwan, July 14–20, 2012), http://www.ausdance.org/ [Accessed on January 1, 2019]. ISBN 978-1-875255-19-1.

Ann Soot and Ele Viskus, "Contemporary Approaches to Dance Pedagogy—The Challenges of the 21st Century," *Procedia Social and Behavioral Sciences* 112, no. 4 (2014): 290–9.

Nicholas Ssempijia, "Ethnomusicological Study of Compositional Techniques in the Roman Catholic Church of the Metropolitan of Kampala" (Unpublished Master's thesis, Makerere University, 2006).

Jayne Stevens, "Pedagogies of Dance Teaching and Dance Leading," in *The Oxford Handbook of Dance and Wellbeing*, eds. Vicky Karkou, Sue Oliver, and Sophia Lycouris (New York: Oxford University Press, 2017.)

Susan W. Stinson, "My Body/Myself: Lessons from Dance Education," in *Knowing Bodies, Moving Minds: Towards Embodied Teaching and Learning*, ed. Liora Bresler (London: Kluwer Academic, 2004).

Susan W. Stinson, *Embodied Curriculum Theory and Research in Arts Education: A Dance Scholar's Search for Meaning* (Dordrecht: Springer, 2016).

Charlotte Svendler Nielsen and Susan R. Koff. "Exploring Identities in Dance," in *Proceedings from the 13th Congress of Dance and the Child International*, Copenhagen Denmark, July 5–10, 2015, The Dance Halls, Department of Nutrition, Exercise and Sport, University of Copenhagen and the Danish National School of Performing Art, http://ausdance.org.au/publications/details/exploring-identities-in-dance.

Jill Drayson Sweet, *Dances of the Tewa Pueblo Indians: Expressions of New Life* (Santa Fe: School of American Research Press, 1985).

Karen Gayton Swisher, "Why Indian People Should Be the Ones to Write about Indian Education," *American Indian Quarterly* 20, no. 1 (1996): 83–90.

Karen Swisher, "Cooperative Learning and the Education of American Indian/Alaskan Native Students: A Review of Literature and Suggestions for Implementation," *Journal of American Indian Education* 29, no. 2 (1990): 36–43.

Karen Swisher and Donna Deyhle, "Styles of Learning and Learning of Styles: Educational Conflicts for American Indian/Alaskan Native Youth," *Journal of Multilingual and Multicultural Development* 8, no. 4 (1987): 345–60.

Linda J. Tomko, *Dancing Class: Gender, Ethnicity, and Social Divides in American Dance, 1890–1920* (Bloomington: Indiana University Press, 1999).

Eve Tuck, "Neoliberalism as Nihilism? A Commentary on Educational Accountability, Teacher Education, and School Reform," *Journal for Critical Education Policy Studies* 11, no. 2 (2013): 324–47.

UNESCO, last modified 2019, https://en.unesco.org/.

"UNESCO Guidelines for the Recognition, Validation and Accreditation of the Outcomes of Non-formal and Informal Learning," *UNESCO Institute for Lifelong Learning*, last modified 2012, https://unesdoc.unesco.org/ark:/48223/pf0000216360.

Phyllis Pier Valente, "The Dance in American Colleges," *The Journal of the American Association for Health, Physical Education and Recreation* 20, no. 5 (1949): 312–13, 349.

Deobold B. Van Dalen and Bruce L. Bennett, *A World History of Physical Education* (Englewood Cliffs: Prentice-Hall Inc., 1971).

Max van Manen, "Phenomenology of Practice," *Phenomenology & Practice* 1, no. 1 (2007): 93.

Patricia Vertinsky, "Schooling the Dance: From Dance under the Swastika to Movement Education in the British School," *Journal of Sport History* 31, no. 3 (2004): 273–95.

Pegge Vissicaro, *Studying Dance Cultures Around the World: An Introduction to Multicultural Dance Education* (Dubuque: Kendall/Hunt Publishing Company, 2004).

Karin Von Nieuwkirk, "Changing Images and Shifting Identities: Female Performers in Egypt," in *Moving History/Dancing Cultures: A Dance History Reader*, eds. Ann Dils and Ann Cooper-Albright (Middletown: Wesleyan University Press, 2001), 136–43.

Lev S. Vygotsky, "Play and Its Role in the Mental Development of the Child," in *Play—Its Role in Development and Evolution*, eds. Jerome S. Bruner, Alison Jolly, and Kathy Sylva (New York: Basic Books, 1976), 537–54.

Lev Vygotsky, *Mind in Society: The Development of Higher Psychological Processes* (Cambridge: Harvard University Press, 1980).
David Walsh, "'Saturday Night Fever': An Ethnography of Disco Dancing," in *Dance, Gender and Culture*, ed. Helen Thomas (New York: St. Martin's Press, 1993), 114.
Edward C. Warburton, "Beyond Steps: The Need for Pedagogical Knowledge in Dance," *Journal of Dance Education* 8, no. 1 (2008): 7–12.
Edward C. Warburton, "Toward Trust: Recalibrating Accreditation Practices for Postsecondary Arts Education," *Arts Education Policy Review* 119, no. 1 (2018): 37–41.
Edward C. Warburton, "Dance Pedagogy," in *The Bloomsbury Companion to Dance Studies*, ed. Sherril Dodds (London: Bloomsbury Academic, 2019), 81–110.
Murray L. Wax, Rosalie H. Wax, and Robert V. Dumont Jr., "Formal Education in an American Indian Community," *Social Problems* 11 (1964): 95–6.
John M. Wilson, Thomas K. Hagood, and Mary A. Brennan, *Margaret H'Doubler: The Legacy of America's Dance Education Pioneer* (Youngstown: Cambria Press, 2006).
Waziyatawin Angela Wilson, "Introduction: Indigenous Knowledge Recovery Is Indigenous Empowerment," *American Indian Quarterly* 28, no. 3–4 (2004): 359–72.
Shawn Wilson, *Research Is Ceremony: Indigenous Research Methods* (Halifax & Winnipeg: Fernwood Publishing, 2008).
Thomas D. Wood and Rosalind F. Cassidy, *The New Physical Education: A Program of Naturalized Activities for Education Toward Citizenship* (New York: The Macmillan Company, 1927).
https://en.wikipedia.org/wiki/YMCA, retrieved February 22, 2020.
Thomas D. Wood and Rosalind F. Cassidy, *The New Physical Education* (New York: Macmillan and Company, 1934).
Earle F. Zeigler, *History of Physical Education and Sport* (Englewood Cliffs: Prentice-Hall Inc., 1979).
Earle F. Zeigler, "Past, Present and Future Development of Physical Education and Sport," in The Academy Papers: *Issues and Challenges: A Kaleidoscope of Change* (Washington, DC: The American Academy of Physical Education, 1979), 9–19.

INDEX

advocacy
   Adelaide Declaration   155–6
   Copenhagen Declaration   154–5
   Seoul Agenda   81, 154–5
Ailey, Alvin, *see* modern dance pioneers, Ailey, Alvin
Anttila, Eeva   42–3

Bennington College   26, 27, 28, 30
Blake, Shirlene   88
boutique multiculturalism, *see* multiculturalism, boutique multiculturalism
Bruner, Jerome   50–1, 58–9
Buck, Ralph   83, 87–8, 98

certification   23, 35–6, 80–2
Colby, Gertrude   20, 25
colonialism
   application in dance   78–9
   definition   ix
   hierarchy of forms   44–6
   questions of language or naming   11–14
   Uganda   125–7, 130–2
commercial
   the body   97–8
   dance competitions/conventions   94–5
   dance studios/private study   93–4
   Dancing With The Stars   94
   definition   95
   politics   95–7
   socio-cultural impact   98–9
   So You Think You Can Dance   94–5
concert dance   36–7, 44, 46, 116
conferences
   2012 Dance and the Child International & World Dance Alliance (daCi/WDA)   65

2012 World Alliance for Arts Education Global Summit   65
2013 World Summit on Arts Education, Polylogue 11   65
2015 Dance and the Child International (daCi)   154
2017 World Dance Alliance Americas   101
2018 Dance and the Child International & World Dance Alliance   155
Dance as Discipline Conference   34
Developmental Conference on Dance   34
"cultural dance"   12–13
culturally responsive teaching, *see* pedagogy, culturally responsive teaching
curriculum   29–30, 44–5, 72–5, 82–6, 92, 107
   hidden curriculum   84–6, 111
   null curriculum   84–6, 115

Damasio, Antonio   43
Delsarte, François   22
Denishawn, *see* modern dance pioneers, Denishawn
Dewey, John   19–20, 40–1, 46, 51
   experience   25, 41, 50, 152
   progressive education   20, 25, 38–9, 46
diversity   11, 14, 45, 58, 59, 137
dualism   41, 43
Duncan, Isadora, *see* modern dance pioneers, Duncan, Isadora

emic   14–15
enculturation   4

INDEX

epistemology 134, 136, 138, 141
"ethnic dance" 12–13, 26
ethnorelativism 122–5
etic 15
Eurocentric 13, 99–100, 127, 132, 136–9

feedback, *see* pedagogy, feedback
feminist theory 50
folk dance 18, 24, 26, 44, 71, 81, 113–16
for-profit 90, 92, 99
formal field of learning 3, 16, 65, 77–81, 112–13
Freire, Paulo 50, 82, 136

Graham, Martha, *see* modern dance pioneers, Graham, Martha
Greene, Maxine 40–1, 148–9, 151
Gulick, Luther 17–18, 51
gymnastics systems 17–20, 22, 44

Hawkins, Alma 28–30, 33–4, 153
H'Doubler, Margaret 24–8, 38, 44–6
hegemony 22, 96
Hetherington, Clark 17–18
hidden curriculum, *see* curriculum, hidden curriculum
hierarchy of forms, *see* colonialism, hierarchy of forms
Hill, Martha 24, 26–8, 36
Holm, Hanya, *see* modern dance pioneers, Holm, Hanya
Horton, Lester, *see* modern dance pioneers, Horton, Lester
Hula 78–9, 110–11
Humphrey, Doris, *see* modern dance pioneers, Humphrey, Doris

Impulse 34–5
indigenous
    aboriginal 11, 103, 144
    ancestral knowledge 144
    communal identity 145–6
    education 135–8
    language 144–5
    learning methodologies 141–2
    Maori 11, 103, 135
    Native Americans 103, 127–9, 131
    principles influencing pedagogy 142–4
    sovereignty and stewardship 146–7
    teacher-learner relationship 140–1
    Uganda 125–7, 130–2
    values of ceremony 138–40
informal learning 63, 65, 69, 71–2, 75, 101–7, 109–13

Jaques-Dalcroze, Émile 20, 22

Keali'inohomoku, Joann 12, 36–7, 44, 136
Kretchmar, Scott 43–4, 152, 156

Limón, José, *see* modern dance pioneers, Limón, José

marginalized 11–14, 55, 103–5
Martin, Randy 37, 43, 95–6
mind/body holism 7, 25, 41–4, 68, 72, 156
modern dance pioneers
    Ailey, Alvin 135
    Denishawn 24
    Duncan, Isadora 18, 24, 97
    Graham, Martha 24, 30, 44, 116, 127, 131, 135
    Holm, Hanya 24, 30
    Horton, Lester 135
    Humphrey, Doris 24, 30, 44, 116
    Limón, José 116
    St. Denis, Ruth 24, 93, 135
    Shawn, Ted 24, 93, 135
    Weidman, Charles 24, 30, 116
    Wigman, Mary 21, 24
more knowledgeable other (MKO), *see* Vygotsky, Lev, more knowledgeable other (MKO)
multiculturalism 9, 11, 14, 44, 57, 132
    boutique multiculturalism 14–15

Native Americans, *see* indigenous, Native Americans
natural dance 18
nomenclature 12–13
non-Eurocentric 13
non-formal learning 33, 42, 65, 89–93, 107, 110–16

non-profit 82, 90, 92, 107
non-Western 3, 12, 32, 44–6, 56, 59, 78, 85
null curriculum, *see* curriculum, null curriculum

organizations
    American Alliance for Health, Physical Education, Recreation, and Dance (AAHPERD) 28
    American Alliance for Health and Physical Education (AAHPE) 28
    American Alliance for Health and Physical Education and Recreation (AHPER) 33
    American College Dance Festival Association (ACDFA) 34
    American Dance Guild (ADG) 34
    American Dance Therapy Association (ADTA) 34
    Congress on Research in Dance (CORD) 34, 37
    Dance and the Child International (daCi) 34, 65, 73, 154–5
    Dance Critics Association 34
    Dance Division 33
    Dance Masters of America 90, 93
    Dance Studies Association 37
    International Society of Teachers of Dance 91
    Jump Dance Convention 94
    Music Educators National Conference (MENC) 23
    National Association of Schools of Dance (NASD) 83
    National Dance Association (NDA) 34
    National Dance Education Organization (NDEO) 28
    National Dance Teachers Association of America 90
    National Section on Dancing 33–4
    One Dance UK 91
    Organization for Economic Cooperation and Development (OECD) 102–4
    Society of Dance History Scholars (SDHS) 34, 37
    United Nations Educational, Scientific, and Cultural Organization (UNESCO) 62–3, 65, 81, 98, 105, 150, 154–5
    World Alliance for Arts Education (WAAE) 65
    World Dance Alliance (WDA) 65, 73, 155
    World Dance Sport Federation 91
    Youth America Grand Prix (YAGP) 94
    Young Men's Christian Association (YMCA) 17
"othering" 12, 109

pedagogy
    agency, reflection, and transformation 122–4
    culturally responsive teaching 55–8
    definition 47–8
    Dewey 40
    feedback 53–4
    history 48–51
    indigenous 136–8
    motor learning 52–3
    Pedagogy of the Oppressed 50
    Spectrum of Teaching Styles 52
    theories and theorists 48–51
physical education 16–19, 22–4, 29–31, 38–9
PK-12 79–83
play 17–18, 51, 102–3, 105, 156
pluralism 11, 14
primary (or elementary) education 23, 30–1, 79
"primitive dance" 6, 12–13, 126–7, 131
professional Western concert dance companies
    Bolshoi Ballet Academy 94
    Martha Graham School 33
    Paris Opera Ballet School 33, 78, 94, 97
    Royal Academy of Dance 92
    Royal Ballet School 94
    Teatro alla Scala Academy 94
progressive education, *see* Dewey, John, progressive education

St. Denis, Ruth, *see* modern dance pioneers, St. Denis, Ruth

secondary education   23, 30–1, 79, 88
Shawn, Ted, *see* modern dance pioneers, Shawn, Ted
Spectrum of Teaching Styles, *see* pedagogy, Spectrum of Teaching Styles
standards   23, 35, 81–4, 91, 93
   Discipline Based Arts Education (DBAE)   82
   International Arts Education Standards   72–3, 75
   National Coalition for Core Arts Standards   73
   National Core Arts Standards   23, 82
   National Standards for Arts Education   82
   National Standards for the Arts   23

Teachers College, Columbia University   17, 20, 25
tertiary (or higher) education   23–4, 30, 34–5, 37, 79–80, 87–8
Title IX   23
tokenism   9

University of California at Los Angeles (UCLA)   13, 28, 29, 34, 45

Vissicaro, Pegge   12–13, 47, 56, 58
von Laban, Rudolf   19–22, 37–8, 54, 64
Vygotsky, Lev   50–1, 102
   more knowledgeable other (MKO)   50, 57
   zone of proximal development (ZPD)   50–1, 57

Weidman, Charles, *see* modern dance pioneers, Weidman, Charles
Western forms   3, 12–13, 26, 44–6, 56–7, 78–9, 130–1, 141
wide-awakeness   40, 46
Wigman, Mary, *see* modern dance pioneers, Wigman, Mary
Wisconsin, University of   24–7, 40, 80
Wood, Thomas   17–18, 43, 51
"world dance"   12–13

zone of proximal development (ZPD), *see* Vygotsky, Lev, zone of proximal development (ZPD)

www.ingramcontent.com/pod-product-compliance
Lightning Source LLC
Chambersburg PA
CBHW050139240426
43673CB00043B/1729